# EARLY BLIGHT DISEASE OF TOMATO

glasshouse screening, 129-130
inoculums production, 128
introduction, 122-124
laboratory assays, 130-131
mapping resistance genes, 137-138
pathogen, 124
screening methods, 128
sources of resistance, 131-132
toxin assays, 131
toxin production, 125
variability among isolates, 125-127

**U**

United States, 32
Upadhyay, Priti, 68
UPGMA technique, 9

**V**

Vegetable Improducement Division, 152
Voorrips, Piet Stam Roeland E., 12
Voorrips, Roeland E., 122, 159
Vosman, B., 159

# EARLY BLIGHT DISEASE OF TOMATO

*Editor*

**Dr. Virendra Kumar**

*Plant Protection Officer (Plant Pathology)*
*Government of India*
*Ministry of Agriculture & Farmers Welfare*
*Department of Agriculture, Cooperation & Farmers Welfare*
*Directorate of Plant Protection, Quarantine & Storage*
*Regional Pesticides Testing Laboratory*
*Kanpur - 208 022, U.P. (INDIA)*

**DISCOVERY PUBLISHING HOUSE PVT. LTD.**
**INDIA**

*Published by:*

**Namit Wasan**

**DISCOVERY PUBLISHING HOUSE PVT. LTD.**

4383/4B, Ansari Road, Darya Ganj
New Delhi-110 002 (India)
*Phone* : +91-11-23279245, 43596064-65
*Fax* : +91-11-23253475
*E-mail* : discoverypublishinghouse@gmail.com
namitwasan9@gmail.com
sales@discoverypublishinggroup.com

*website*: www.discoverypublishinggroup.com

***First Edition:* 2017**

**ISBN: 978-93-5056-879-8**

**Early Blight Disease of Tomato**



*Printed at:*
Infinity Imaging Systems
Delhi

# Preface

Tomato (Lycopersicon esculentum Miller) is one of the most popular and widely grown vegetable in the world ranking second in importance after potato in many countries. The fruits are eaten raw or cooked. Tomato is the world's largest vegetable crop after potato and sweet potato, but it tops the list of canned vegetables. The total global area under tomato is 46.16 lakh ha and the global production is to the tune of 1279.93 lakh tonnes. Because of its wider adaptability, and versatility, tomato is grown throughout the world. The estimated world production of tomato is about 32.8 MT/HA from an area of about 4582480 ha. During the last decade China has increased its production about 110 per cent and became the largest producer with an estimated production of 19.5 MT/HA pursing USA to third place.

Early blight is the most destructive disease and hence receives considerable attention in breeding. For over 60 years, breeding for early blight resistance has been practiced, but the development of cultivars with high levels of resistance has been hampered by the lack of sources of strong resistance in the cultivated tomato and by the quantitative expression and polygenic inheritance of the resistance. In some accessions of wild species, high levels of early blight resistance have been found, but breeding lines still have unfavorable horticultural traits from the donor parent.

So, this book gives us great pleasure to present before our readers, researchers on "Early blight Disease of Tomato " against the early blight disease of tomato crop because it cover a great collections of researches on early blight disease of tomato. Due to this information, readers will be benefitted to find out the resistance source of tomato and management options to control of early blight disease of Tomato. We are highlighted especially the early blight disease which is caused by Alternaria solani i.e. a fungal disease because it is a very important and common disease of tomato, <90% yield loss have been recorded by this fungus. So this book also provides comprehensive knowledge especially on different resistance sources of tomato cultivars/ germplasm, experimental field applications, Current practices and trends in the field of early blight disease management in tomato. This book consists of various researches which were conducted across the world and latest information has been given in this book on early blight of tomato. It is also extremely important to develop skill the correct farming of tomato with early blight resistance cultivars/germplasm and other practices in the management of early blight disease of tomato. This book will be highly useful for extension agencies, farmers, researchers including students and other stakeholders.

Particularly thanks are due to all contributors and publisher also for their contribution and assistance. We hope this book will provide a multidisciplinary forum to explore emerging areas in the field of "Early blight Disease of Tomato".

**Virendra Kumar**

# Acknowledgments

Behind every success there is certainly an unseen power of Almighty GOD, but aim is the external condition of success which is attainable at perfection in everything by who preserve with the association for giving me this unique opportunity to express my heartfelt gratitude to all those who have given me help to make this success.

It feels privileged to complete this book with my Co-supervisor Dr. K.K. Pandey, Principal Scientist, (Plant Pathology) at Indian Institute of Vegetable Research (IIVR) Varanasi. I am highly indebted to him for his excellent guidance, valuable suggestions, constant encouragement, and support.

I am unable to find out the word to express acknowledge for Dr. P.K. Pandey, Ex. Principle Scientist, Head Crop Protection Division, IIVR Varanasi. He always encouraged, helped, and extended valuable suggestion during the preparation of this book in various ways, and finally brought me to this level of presentation.

I would like to express my gratefulness which I owe to Dr. K. K. Mishra, Scientist, Wheat Improvement Project, JNKV, Zonal Agriculture Research Station, Powerkheda, Hoshangabad, M.P., India , Dr. Prabhash Chand Singh, Farm Manager K.V.K. Bejwan Sant Ravidas Nagar, Bhadohi and Dr. R. C. Gupta, National Horticultural Research and Development Foundation (NHRDF) Chitegaonphata, Nasik Aurangabad Road, Post-Darnasangvi, Taluka-Niphad, Nasik, Maharashtra, India for their excellent guidance and valuable suggestions.

I deem it my dutiful privilege to grateful acknowledge to Dr. Major Singh, Principle Scientist Biotechnology, IIVR Varanasi for providing me necessary facilities for molecular work in present investigation of this book.

Most cordial thanks are also expressed to all our respected teachers Dr. R.P. Singh, Professor, Department of Botany, Udai Pratap Autonomous College, Varanasi, Dr. R. N. Kharwar, Professor in Department of Botany, Banaras Hindu University, Varanasi for their valuable assistance in complication of this book for their help, fruitful suggestions and generous advice.

I feel my duty to record the value of the great affection, and inspiration of my reverend parents for their constant encouragement, financial, and moral support throughout the study period. I am specially very much thankful to my uncles Shri Kailash Prasad, Shri Kamlesh Kumar, Shri Mangla Prasad, and younger brothers Devendra Kumar, Pravin Kumar, Abhishek Anand, Amit Kumar, shailesh kumar sister Lakshmi, Gunja, Monika and Pooja, and all family members for their co-operation, and every possible help at a time of need and for their blessings without which I could never have reached at this stage of my academic career.

I am also thankful to my mama Ji Dr. Vijai Kumar, Scientist F, Department of Atomic Energy, Atomic Mineral Directorate for Exploration, and Research, Jaipur for his proper encouragement and moral support.

I express my heartful thanks to S. K. Gupta, Assistant Director (Chemistry), Mrs. Aarti Saraswat , & Mr. Ajai Kumar, Plant Protection Officer (Chemistry), Mr. P.K. Vats, Mr. Ali Ahmed, Mr. Ratnesh Kumar Mall, Dr. Nirmal Kumar Katiyar APPO (Chem.) and Mr. S.M.H. Jafri, Mrs. Angoori Devi, Mr. Mahendra Kumar, Mr. Rajendra Prasad and Mr. Jai Singh of Regional Pesticides Testing Laboratory, Kanpur for their kind moral supports..

Special thanks also goes to our better half life partner Mrs. Nandini Devi and my son Abhinav Kumar whose love cannot be denied and also their constant support at each and every moments of life.

Last but not least, I specially acknowledge my sincere thanks to all contributors of this book and all who love, and care for me. we are indeed grateful to our respected and beloved parents, who inspired us at every step and gave us steadfast and unflinching moral support, encouragement and showered packet of selfless love at each and every moments, we would have not achieved this goal without their blessings and support and my heartful thanks goes to whose encouragement enabled me to achieve this lofty goal.

*"Act with knowledge, Knowledge is truth,*
*The path of action is the truth; the path of truth is action"*

कर्म करो तुम ज्ञान से, श्रेज्ठ ज्ञान है धर्म।
कर्मयोगी ही धर्म है, धर्मयोग ही कर्म।।

**Virendra Kumar**

# Contents

*Preface*

*Acknowledgments*

1. Cultural, Morphological, Pathogenic and Molecular Variability amongst Tomato Isolates of *Alternaria solani* in India ........ 1

   *Virendra Kumar, Sanchita Haldar, Koshlendra K. Pandey, Rana P. Singh, Achuit K. Singh and Prabhash C. Singh*

2. Assessment of Early Blight (*Alternaria solani* ) Resistance in Tomato using a Droplet Inoculation Method........ 12

   *Reni Chaerani, Remmelt Groenwold, Piet Stam, Roeland E, Voorrips*

3. Screening of Tomato Genotypes against Early Blight in Natural Epiphytotic Condition ........ 26

   *V. Kumar, R.C. Gupta, P.C. Singh, R.P. Singh and J. Singh*

4. Evaluation of Different Germplasms/Cultivars of Tomato against Early Blight (*Alternaria solani*) in Field Conditions and by Artificial Inoculation Method: A Review Article........ 32

   *Virendra Kumar, Faiza Naeem and Ajay Kumar*

5. Identification of Resistant Sources and Epidemiology of Early Blight (*Alternaria solani*) of Tomato (*Lycopersicum esculentum*) in Jammu and Kashmir........ 42

   *Sunita Rani, Ranbir Singh, Sachin Gupta, Siddarth Dubey and V.K. Razdan*

6. Study of Variability and Sporulation by Isolates of *Alternaria solani* of *Lycopersicon esculentum* (Mill.) ........ 53

   *Virendra Kumar, Koshlendra Kumar Pandey and Kaushlesh Kumar Mishra*

7. Source of Resistance against Early Blight (*Alternaria solani*) of Tomato (*Solanum lycopersicum*) ........ 68

   *Priti Upadhyay, Prabhash C. Singh, B. Sinha, M. Singh, Rajesh Kumar, K.K. Pandey and Mathura Rai*

8. Efficacy and Safety of Some Plant Extract against Tomato Early Blight Disease Caused by *Alternaria solani*........ 71

   *A.S. Derbalah, M.S. El-Mahrouk and A.B. El-Sayed*

9. Control of Tomato Early Blight Disease by Certain Aqueous Plant Extract ........ 83
*Nashwa M.A. Sallam*

10. Resistance of Two Tomato Species to Five Isolates of *Alternaria solani* ........ 92
*Ali Ayaz Khan*

11. Performance Assessment of Tomato Advanced Lines to Late Blight and Early Blight under Natural Epiphytotics ........ 97
*Nazrul Islam, Bimal Kumar Pramanik, Md. Atiqur and M. Ashrafuzzaman*

12. Characterization of Tomato Accessions for Resistance to Early Blight ........ 104
*Jose Fernando Jurca Grigolli, Mirian Maristela Kubota, Daniel Pedrosa Alves, Gabriel Belfort Rodrigues, Carine Rezende Cardoso, Derly Jose Henriques da Silva and Eduardo Seiti Gomide Mizubuti*

13. Morphological and Physiological Characterization of *Alternaria solani* Isolates from Tomato in Jordan Valley ........ 115
*Khalaf M. Alhussaen*

14. Tomato Early Blight (*Alternaria solani*): The Pathogen, Genetics and Breeding for Resistance ........ 122
*Reni Chaerani, Roeland E. Voorrips*

15. Management of Early Blight Disease of Tomato c.v. 'Kashi Amrit' through Fungicides, Bio-agents and Cultural Practices in India ........ 148
*Virendra Kumar, R.C. Gupta, P.C. Sinch, K.K. Pandey, Rajesh Kumar, A.B. Rai and Mathura Rai*

16. Identification of Resistant Sources Against Early Blight disease of tomato ........ 151
*Prabhash C. Singh, Rajesh Kumar, Major Singh, Ashutosh Rai, M.C. Singh and Mathura Rai*

17. QTL Identification for Early Blight Resistance (*Alternaria solani*) in a *Solanum lycopersicum* × *S. arcanum* cross ........ 159
*R. Chaerani, M. J. M. Smulders, C. G. van der Linden, B. Vosman, P. Stam, and R. E. Voorrips*

18. In Vitro Control of *Alternaria solani*, the Cause of Early Blight ........ 178
*Ashraf Saber Hawamdeh and Shabeer Ahamad*

*Index* ........ 183

**Early Blight Disease of Tomato**
***Edited by:*** **Virendra Kumar**
**ISBN: 978-93-5056-879-8**
***Edition:*** **2017**
***Published by:*** **Discovery Publishing House Pvt. Ltd., New Delhi (India)**

# Cultural, Morphological, Pathogenic and Molecular Variability Amongst Tomato Isolates of *Alternaria solani* in India

[1]Virendra Kumar, [2]Sanchita Haldar, [3]Koshlendra K. Pandey, [4]Rana P. Singh, [5]Achuit K. Singh, [6]Prabhash C. Singh

## ABSTRACT

Early blight (*Alternaria solani*) is an important disease causing severe damage in tomato. The eleven isolates of *A. solani* designated as So, Dh, Sh, Va-5, Ka, Ma, Hy, Ba-1, My, Va-3 and Mi were collected from different agroclimatic conditions and these isolates were characterized for cultural, morphological, pathogenic and molecular variations. The pigmentation varied from yellow, brown, black, brownish to greenish black in isolates of *A. solani* on potato dextrose agar medium. In general, radial growth of all isolates ranged between 14.9 mm and 32.2 mm on PDA and 24.3 mm to 53.7 mm on three selective media i.e., ASM, V-8 juice agar and V-8 juice agar (synthetic) on the fourth day. The fastest radial growth was recorded in the So isolate and slowest in the Ka isolate on PDA, while isolates Dh, Ba-1 and Va-3 were recorded to be faster in growth on ASM, V-8 juice agar and V-8 juice agar (synthetic) medium. The thickness of conidiogenous hyphae varied between 1.17 $\mu$ and 9.56 $\mu$, with maximum in the Va-5 and Ma isolates. Most of the isolates showed smooth mycelial growth with circular and irregular margin and without concentric zonation. Sporulation was not found in any of the isolates on four different nutrient media, whereas conidiogenous hyphal length was observed in V-8 juice agar medium only. Based on the pathogenicity, isolates of *A. solani* were rated as virulent or less virulent based on percentage disease incidence data. Molecular variability studies were also done to find out the best annealing temperature and eighty-six primers were screened to select for maximum polymorphism of DNA. The best annealing temperature was recorded between 32.5°C and 34.0°C for the pathogen, and most efficient amplification and polymorphism of DNA was found with random primer 5′-CGCGTTCCTG-3′.

**Keywords:** Pathogenic variability Conidiogenous hyphae Virulent and RAPD-PCR.

1 V. Kumar, S. Haldar, K.K. Pandey, A.K. Singh, P.C. Singh
Division of Crop Protection, Indian Institute of Vegetable Research, P.B. # 01, P.O. Jakhani (Shahanshapur)m, Varanasi-211305, UP, India

2 V. Kumar, Department of Botany, Government Raza Post Graduate College, Rampur 244901, UP, India
e-mail: v1580k@yahoo.co.in

3 R.P. Singh, Department of Botany, Udai Pratap Autonomos College, Varanasi-221002, UP, India

## Introduction

*Alternaria solani* (Ellis and Martin) Sorauer is an important pathogen causing early blight disease in tomato. It is very difficult to manage, due to its broad host range, extreme variability in pathogenic isolates and prolonged active phase of the disease cycle. The yield loss of tomato fruit was 78% recorded at 72% disease intensity of *A. solani* and each 1% increase reduced tomato yield by 1.36% (Dater and Mayee 1985). It is also one of the most common causes of seedling blight or damping off in tomato, causing dark lesions on the rootlets (Bose *et al.* 2002). One of the best-known economically important members of the genus is *A. solani,* the causal agent of early blight on tomato (Lycopersicon esculentum Mill.). The conidia are dark muriform, pale golden or olivaceous brown, smooth and usually 150–300 lm in length and 15–19 lm thick in the broadest part, with 9–11 transverse septa and 1–4 longitudinal or oblique septa; sometimes branched 2.5–5 lm thick tapering gradually (Ellis 1971). Morphological and pathogenic variability among isolates of *A. solani* has given rise to claims of the existence of races, although this remains unproven (Rotem 1966). Morris *et al.* (2000) and Weir *et al.* (1998) reported high level of genetic diversity among the 69 isolates of tomato black mould pathogen by RAPD analysis of genetic variation among isolates of *A. solani* of tomato and potato. The RAPD profiling of 55 isolates of *Alternaria* spp. belonging to 13 small-spored species and three large-spored were carried out using 12 arbitrary primers. The large-spored species viz. *A. solani, A. porri* and *A. lecunthemi* were differentiated from small-spored species by a genetic distance of 0.44 and from each other by the genetic distance of 0.25, indicating that RAPD analysis can be used to analyse the phylogenetic relationship of Alternaria spp (Wang and Zhang 2003). The concentration of 104 conidia/mL made it possible to distinguish resistant and susceptible genotypes of the tomato (Castro *et al.* 1999). Some researchers have defined races according to cultural characteristics of various dimensions of spores and virulence (Bonde 1929; Neergard 1945). The variability of *A. solani* studies under greenhouse conditions based on the inoculation by several isolates on 14 tomato genotypes, resulted in the finding that all isolates differed from each other (Castro *et al.* 2000). In the present investigation, the extent of cultural, molecular diversity and pathogenic variability were studied among eleven isolates of *A. solani* collected from different agroclimatic conditions in India.

## Materials and Methods

Isolation and purification of *A. solani* cultures was done from fresh infected leaf, stem and fruit of tomato collected from different agroclimatic zones of India and purified by the hyphal tip method. They were stored at 4°C on PDA slants for further study.

Cultural variability of different isolates of *A. solani*

The cultural character was recorded on day 9 of inoculation of all isolates of *A. solani.* Characters like pigmentation on medium, mycelial growth, zonation were recorded by direct observation of culture-grown petri plates and sporulation was recorded on four tested media by slides of 9-day-old cultures under the microscope. For this purpose eleven selected isolates of *A. solani* were taken, representing Solan (So),

Dharwad (Dh), Shillong (Sh), Varanasi (Va-5), Kanpur (Ka), Mahabaleshwar (Ma), Hyderabad (Hy), Bangalore (Ba-1), Mysore (My), Varanasi (Va-3) and Mirzapur (Mi). All these isolates were tested for their cultural and morphological variations on PDA. In another set of experiments, three selective media *i.e.,* ASM (Alternaria sporulation medium), freshly prepared V-8 juice agar and readymade available V-8 juice agar medium containing asparagine were taken for the study of radial growth and sporulation. For each isólate five Petri plates were poured with those media. After solidification of the agar 5 mm culture bits of each isolate were inoculated onto the above-mentioned three nutrient media. These inoculated petri plates were kept in BOD at 25 ± 1°C for growth. The data were recorded after 3 days from inoculation and radial growth was measured per day on day 4 on PDA and a single data were taken on day 4 after inoculation on the above three selective nutrient media.

Morphological variability of different isolates of *A. solani*.

Slides were prepared from culture of all isolates of *A. solani* separately in 9-day-old cultures of PDA and examined under the light microscope to record the width of the conidiogenous hyphae. The calibration was done with the help of ocular and stage micrometer.

### Molecular Characterization

Descriptions of the isolates used in this study appear above. All isolates are being maintained at the Indian Institute of Vegetable Research, Varanasi.

### Fungal DNA extraction

Fungi were grown in 50 mL of potato dextrose broth medium for 10 days at 25 ± 1 °C temperature in BOD. DNA was extracted by pure mycelial culture by slight modification of CTAB protocol (Manicom *et al.* 1987). Mycelium was harvested by filtration through quantitative filter paper and washed exhaustively with distilled water. For each fungal isolates 5 g of fresh mycelium was dried on sterile blotter paper and was ground in liquid $N_2$ to make a fine powder. This powder was taken in a centrifuge tube and 15 mL of 2× CTAB (DNA extraction buffer) was added in each tube separately. Extraction buffer contained (per l) 2 g CTAB 1 M Tris pH-8(10 mL), 5 M NaCl (28 mL), 0.5 MEDTA (4 mL) with sterile distilled water (57 mL) and 1 mL β-mercaptoethanol were used. This was incubated at 65 °C water bath for 30 min with intermittent shaking. The mixture was centrifuged at 13,000 rpm/min for 15 min at 4 °C to pellet the mycelium. Supernatant was taken in a fresh Oakridge tube and an equal volume of phenol:chlor oform:isoamylalcohol (25:24:1) was added with 2–3 min slow inversion. The mixture was again centrifuged at 13,000 rpm/min for 15 min at 4 °C. The aqueous supernatant was taken in a fresh tube and added 0.6 volume isopropanol and was incubated at –20 °C overnight. After incubation, it was again centrifuged at 13,000 rpm/min for 20 min at 4 °C temperature. The supernatant was discarded and pellet was washed with 70% ethanol. The pellet was dissolved in 500 µl of T.E. buffer and was used for PCR amplification.

### PCR Amplification

PCR was carried out in a final volume of 25 µl, containing 10 mM of oligonucleotide primer (1 µl) 20 mM of each of the four deoxynucleotide triphosphates (0.75 µl) 25 mM $MgCl_2$ (1.0 µl), 0.35 µl of Taq DNA polymerase (Genei) 10 × Assay buffer (2.5 µl) and 1.0 µl template DNA (60 ng/µl). Primers 5′-GGGCGCCTAG-3′, 5′-CACGGC-GAGT-3′, 5′-CGCGTTCCTG-3′ and 5′-AAGCCTCGTC-3′ were chosen after preliminary screening of eighty-six primers. The reaction mixture was overlaid with 10 11 of mineral oil and the tube was microfuged at 13,000 g for 10 s. Amplification was carried out in a gradient thermal cycler (MJ Research) with initial denaturation of 94 °C for 4.0 min and 40 cycles of 94 °C for 1 min, 34 °C for 2 min and 72 °C for 2 min.

### Electrophoresis

Twenty µ1 of PCR product were mixed with 6 µ1 of gel loading buffer (0.25% bromophenol blue, 0.25% xylene cyanol and 30% glycerol were dissolved in 1 × TAE buffer) and subjected to electrophoresis at 65 V for 3 h in 1.2% agarose gel, prepared in 1 × TAE buffer (40 mM Tris acetate 1 mM EDTA, pH 8.0). Ethidium bromide was added to the agarose gel at 6 µl/100 mL for staining. A ladder (lambda DNA/Eco RI + Hind III) was used as a size standard. DNA was visualized by trans-illuminator with u.v. light and photographed. For each fungal isolates, individual RAPD markers were scored for their presence (value = 1) or absence (value = 0).

### Statistical Analysis

RAPD scores were used for similarity analysis using Jaccord coefficient and clustering using UPGMA (Unweighted Pair Group Method of Arithmetic average). It was constructed using numerical taxomomy and multivariate analysis system software (Weir *et al.* 1998).

### Pathogenic Variability

In order to confirm the identification of the disease and its causal agent, the pathogenicity test was conducted under polyhouse conditions in pot experiments using three highly susceptible varieties of tomato i.e. KDTS-71, CO-3 and Punjab Chhuhara. Seedlings were raised in pots filled with sterilized soil. One-month-old plants were used for inoculation. 10-day-old cultures of *A. solani* were ground in 50 mL of sterilized distilled water in a sterilized pestle and mortar. It was filtered with sterilized muslin cloth in a clean test tube aseptically. The culture suspensions were prepared separately for different isolates of *A. solani* and the c.f.u. of culture suspension was determined on potato dextrose rose Bengal agar medium. For maintaining the humidity, a humidifier was set up in this chamber and the temperature was maintained for the development of symptoms. The percentage disease incidence was rated as suggested by Pandey *et al.* (2002). The data were taken three times at periodical intervals to see the disease progress of early blight. Symptoms expressed were studied and reisolated from the infected stem. The pathogenicity test as above was repeated twice to confirm the results.

## Results and Disscusion

### *Radial growth*

The maximum radius was recorded for So isolate (32.2 mm) on PDA whereas the Dh isolate (50.3 mm), Ba-1 (53.2 mm) and Va-3 (57.7 mm) on ASM, V-8 Juice agar and V-8 Juice agar (synthetic) respectively on day 4. Radial growth ranged from 14.9 mm to 57.7 mm of *A. solani* isolates on tested media at ±25 °C (Fig. 1.1). Growth of most of the isolates were not significantly different among three different selective media, while radial growth recorded on PDA was different significantly except isolate So. In genera, radial growth of most of the isolates were lower except isolate Va-5 as compared to other three media on day 4.

### *Pigmentation*

Isolates of *A. solani* were showing great variability in pigment production on PDA medium. Four isolates (So, Hy, My and Va-3) produced black, one of the isolates was yellow pigmented (Dh), isolate Ma produced greenish black while other isolates produced brownish black pigment on PDA after nine days of inoculation at ±25 °C. (Table 1.1).

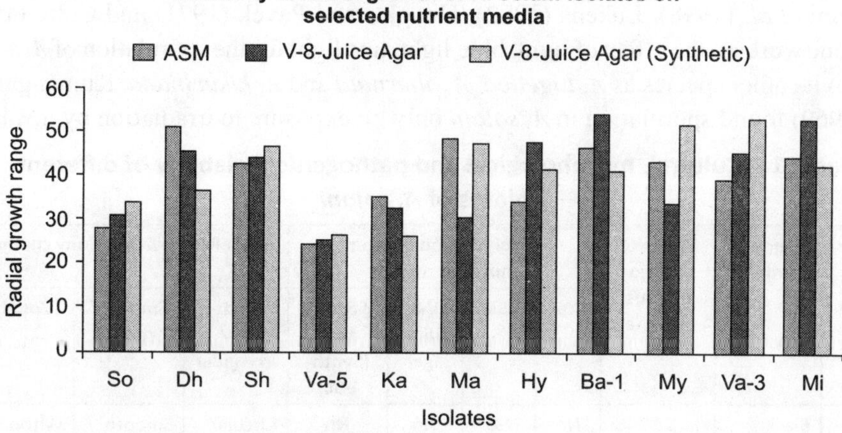


**Fig. 1.1 Variability in radial growth of *A. solani* isolates on selected nutrient media**

## Sporulation

Sporulation was not found in all isolates on four tested media on day 9 of observation under the microscope while conidiogenous hyphae (Chlamydospore like structure) were abundantly present on V-8 juice agar medium, whereas in the other three nutrient media conidiogenous hyphae were scanty. (Table 1.1)

## Mycelial Growth Pattern

Mycelial growth patterns were observed on PDA where So, Hy, Ba-1 and Mi grew with circular margin with smooth surfaced colony and Dh, Sh,Va-1, Ka, My and Va-3 isolates were growing with irregular margin (Table 1.1).

Some workers, Rath and Padhi (1973), Gupta and Nikharaj (1972), Prasad *et al.*, (1973), Stevenson and Pennypacker (1988), Sodlauskiene (2003) and Rodriguez and Santana (1991); number of isolate of *A. solani* on particular temperature for obseving the cultural characters and sporulation of *A. solani.* Gemawat and Ghosh (1979) observed the effect of pH, vitamins and growth regulators for sporulation of *A. solani.* The cultural characteristics (colour, growth, sporulation) also differ in various isolates, making it possible to find almost as many races as the number of isolates tested (Rotem 1966). These isolates exhibited significant variation for their cultural characters, pigmentation and growth rate per day. Few isolates grew very fast in the initial 4–5 days of observation and few were fast in the middle-age and rest grew fast at a later age. Therefore significant variation was recorded in the average radial growth per day after inoculation. As the isolates of *A. solani* were collected from different agroclimatic zones of the country, it might be possible that more infection or disease severity occurs after the initial infection and after a few days of field conditions according to the climatic conditions in which it was collected (Table 1.1). Sporulation was not observed in any of the isolates, only conidiogenous hyphae were formed on PDA. The cultural variability among different isolates of *A. solani* was not prominent on PDA. Some researcher such as Kumangai and Oda (1969), Kaoru and Mitsuo (1970), Prasad and Dutt (1974), Singh (1967), Fourtouni *et al.* (1998), Lukens (1962), Douglas and Pavek (1971) and Cotty (1987) have done work on the effect of light, blue light, u.v. light for the sporulation of *A. solani* and also its other species as *A. tagetica, A. alternata* and *A. kikuchiana*. Kumangai and Oda (1969) found sporulation in *A. solani* only on exposure to irradiation by u.v. light,

**Table 1.1 Cultural, morphological and pathogenic variability of different isolates of *A. solani***

| Isolates conidio-genous | Pigmen-tation | Width of conidio-genous hyphae (μ) | Sporulation on different nutrient media | | | | Mycelial growth/Colony character | | |
|---|---|---|---|---|---|---|---|---|---|
| | | | PDA | ASM | V-8 juice agar | V-8 juice agar (Synth-etic) | Circu-lar/ irre-gular | Smooth/ rough | Zonation |
| So | Black | 1.17 | No | No | No | No | Circular | Smooth | Without zonation |
| Dh | Yellow | 4.70 | No | No | No | No | Iregular | Rough | Without zonation |
| Sh | Brownish Black | 1.17 | No | No | No | No | Iregular | Smooth | Concentric zonation |
| Va-5 | Brown | 9.56 | No | No | No | No | Iregular | Smooth | Without zonation |
| Ka | Brownish Black | 4.70 | No | No | No | No | Iregular | Smooth | Concentric zonation |
| Ma | Greenish black | 9.56 | No | No | No | No | Circular | Smooth | Concentric zonation |
| Hy | Black | 4.70 | No | No | No | No | Circular | Smooth | Without zonation |

| | | | | | | | | | |
|---|---|---|---|---|---|---|---|---|---|
| Ba-1 | Brownish black | 1.17 | No | No | No | No | Circular | Smooth | Concentric zonation |
| My | Black | 4.70 | No | No | No | No | Iregular | Rough | Without zonation |
| Va-3 | Black | 2.70 | No | No | No | No | Iregular | Rough | Without zonation |
| Mi | Brownish black | 1.17 | No | No | No | No | Circular | Smooth | Without zonation |

followed by a period of darkness while Kaoru and Mitsuo (1970) reported that effect of continuous white fluorescent light (340 mμ and 365 mμ) exposed with short distance on culture plates of *A. solani* increased the spore production on three selective nutrient media *i.e.*, V-8 juice medium, pear leaf juice medium and dry apricot V-8 juice medium. We have also studied sporulation on V-8 juice medium but only conidiogenous hyphae were found on both PDA and V-8 juice medium. Therefore the present work is completely different from earlier workers. Our findings shows that sporulation was not found on PDA, Alternaria sporulation media, V-8 juice agar and V-8 juice agar (synthetic) without any light treatments.

## Pathogenicity

The pathogenicity test of *A. solani* isolates was conducted in polyhouse conditions using three highly susceptible varieties of tomato. Based on the observation and recorded data, six isolates (So, Dh, Va-5, Hy, Ba-1 and My) were found to be virulent, causing severe disease in all tested varieties. Other isolates were rated as less virulent and avirulent because these isolates were unable to cause symptoms of the disease in polyhouse experiments (Table 1.2), the percent disease incidence of virulent isolates ranged between 73.90 and 83.35% while other isolates was categorized under less virulent and avirulent the PDI was ranged between 0 and 42.07%.

Gorgan *et al.* (1975), Perez and Martinez (1995), Castro *et al.* (1999), Vloutoglou and Kalogerakis (2000) did a pathogenicity test with conidial suspensions. The present study is confined to test differential pathogenicity and infection potential by mycelial culture. Several problems were observed during the pathogenicity tests, as no consistent symptoms were observed. Therefore, an inoculation technique was developed first to test the pathogenicity with pure mycelial culture of *A. solani.* Optimum inoculation concentration was standardized in a pilot experiment from several level of colony forming unit (c.f.u.). Approximately 125 c.f.u./mL inoculum concentration from a 12-day-old culture was used to spray on healthy plants. CO-3 showed early and more severe infection than the other two varieties. These infected leaves were reisolated on PDA and similar colony of *A. solani* were obtained. This type of experiment for the pathogenic variability was reported by Castro *et al.* (2000). However he had taken a spore suspension of $1.25 \times 10^3$ conidia/mL. In present experiment only mycelial culture was used for inoculation, which indicates that mycelium is also capable of infecting the plant tissue in congenial conditions. Ba-1, Hy and My isolates were found to be highly virulent, as they infect all three-tomato varieties uniformly. The least infection potential was recorded by Ka, Ma, Va-3 and Mi isolates therefore it was considered as avirulent. Virulence and infection level was almost similar in case of isolates So, Dh, Sh and Va-5 isolates (Table 1.2). So in this study, pathogenic virulence by different isolates was clearly observed.

## Molecular Variability

Molecular studies were carried out to find variability in isolates of *A. solani* by RAPD-PCR. Four random primers (5′-GGGCGCCTAG-3′, 5′-CACGGAGT-3′, 5′-CGCGTTC CTG-3′ and 5′-AAGCCTCGTC-3′) were selected for the study based on preliminary

**Table 1.2 Pathogenic variability of *A. solani* against early blight of tomato under polyhouse conditions**

| Isolates | c.f.u./mL (approx) | Per cent disease incidence (PDI ) on three susceptible varieties | | | | | | | | | Virulency |
|---|---|---|---|---|---|---|---|---|---|---|---|
| | | CO-3 | | | KDTS-71 | | | Pb. Chhuhara | | | |
| | | Day 3 | Day 6 | Day 9 | Day 3 | Day 6 | Day 9 | Day 3 | Day 6 | Day 9 | |
| So | 125 | 49.00 | 61.00 | 94.00 | 44.00 | 60.00 | 81.00 | 38.00 | 54.33 | 83.00 | Virulent |
| Dh | 125 | 67.00 | 77.00 | 100.00 | 62.00 | 70.00 | 84.50 | 44.00 | 57.30 | 80.00 | Virulent |
| Sh | 125 | 54.00 | 70.00 | 80.00 | 48.00 | 72.00 | 88.00 | 40.00 | 55.00 | 82.00 | Virulent |
| Va-5 | 125 | 48.00 | 62.00 | 89.33 | 40.00 | 70.00 | 91.00 | 35.00 | 58.00 | 81.00 | Virulent |
| Ka | 125 | 6.33 | 10.00 | 20.00 | 8.33 | 15.00 | 28.33 | 6.00 | 12.00 | 15.00 | Avirulent |
| Ma | 125 | 11.00 | 25.00 | 33.33 | 7.00 | 15.00 | 25.00 | 8.33 | 16.00 | 25.00 | Avirulent |
| Hy | 125 | 44.00 | 64.00 | 88.00 | 57.10 | 66.00 | 89.33 | 53.33 | 50.00 | 78.00 | Virulent |
| Ba-1 | 125 | 60.00 | 70.00 | 98.00 | 57.66 | 76.00 | 80.00 | 56.00 | 74.00 | 84.00 | Virulent |
| My | 125 | 68.00 | 78.00 | 82.00 | 61.33 | 68.00 | 92.00 | 50.66 | 72.66 | 97.00 | Virulent |
| Va-3 | 125 | 20.2 | 35.00 | 40.00 | 10.00 | 20.00 | 38.00 | 10.00 | 30.00 | 41.00 | Avirulent |
| Mi | 125 | 8.00 | 25.00 | 36.00 | 10.00 | 35.00 | 41.33 | 25.00 | 33.33 | 42.07 | Avirulent |

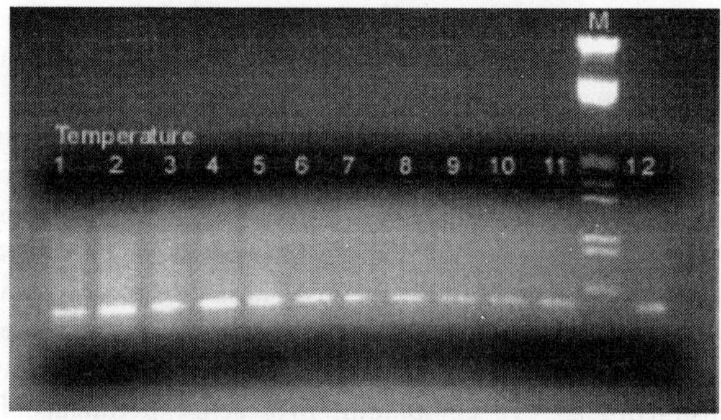


**Fig. 1.2 Standardization of different annealing temperatures. (1) 30 °C (2) 30.4 °C (3) 31.2 °C (4) 32.5 °C (5) 34.1 °C (6) 36.3 °C (7) 38.8 °C (8) 41.0 °C (9) 42.6 °C (10) 43.8 °C (11) 44.7 °C (12) 45.0 °C. M = molecular weight marker**

screening of 86 random primers because of their reproducible results of polymorphism between individuals. These primers were used to survey the genetic diversity within a collection of 11 isolates of *A. solani*. Of the eleven isolates from different localities, the isolates So, Va-5, Dh, Sh and Hy showed exactly the same RAPD profile with four primer tested. The same was true for Va-3 and Mi isolates. Ma, Ba-1 and Va-3 was found to be different as compared to the other tested isolates. There were no effect of place of isolation, rather two isolates from two different provinces (e.g., Ka from Uttar Pradesh and Ma from Maharashtra) were closer to each other. Isolates Ka and Ma was found to be genetically and pathogenically similar. These two isolates were not found virulent to all three susceptible tomato varieties. Also 12 different annealing temperatures were tested, ranging from 30 °C to 45 °C with primer 5′-GGGCGCCTAG-3′ and also 12 different temperature points were tested, the low temperature 32.5 °C and 34.1 °C was recorded as optimum annealing temperature and used for further subsequent PCR studies (Fig. 1.2).

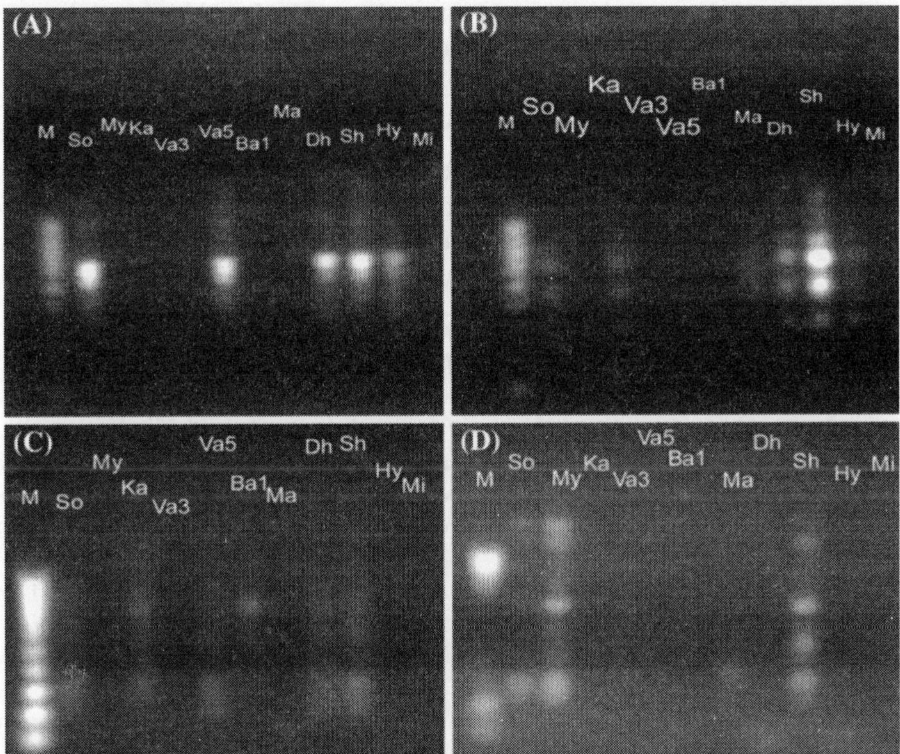


**Fig. 1.3 RAPD profile of *A. solani* isolates using random primers (A) 5′-CGCGTTCCTG-3′, (B) 5′-GGGCGCCTAG-3′ (C) 5′-CACGGCGAGT-3′ and (D) 5′-GAGTAAGCGG-3′, Eleven isolates i.e., So, My, Ka, Va-3, Va-5, Ba-1, Ma, Dh, Sh, Hy and Mi. M = Molecular weight marker**

The data was subjected to similarity analysis using Jaccord coefficient and clustering using UPGMA technique. The cluster analysis resulted in two main clusters at 30 percent similarity coefficient. Cluster 1 comprised So, Dh, Sh and Va-5 isolates of *A. solani.* In the present finding, RAPD analysis shows a close relation among So and Dh isolates with 80% similarity coefficient, while cultural characters indicates maximum similarity in So and Dh isolates and pathogenic similarity in Va-5 and Sh isolate. It is clear that even when similarity of isolates is observed at molecular level, variability exist in pathogenic and cultural characters.

RAPD analysis of *A. solani* isolates indicated that tomato isolates from India are hypervariable with distinct variation (Fig. 1.3). Genetic variability in *A. solani* from different parts of plants and different places of isolate collection have been studied using RAPD (Morris *et al.* 2000; Wang and Zhang 2003 and Weir *et al.* 1998) and AFLP (Perez and Martinez 2000). Weir *et al.* (1998) investigated the genetic variations among 35 isolates of *A. solani* and 30 isolates of *A. alternata.* One primer P-248 generated polymorphisms that could be used to distinguish between two fungal species. The present finding suggests that isolates from even the same lesions are genetically distinct, which further strengthens the variable nature of this pathogen. It should be noted, however that the groupings based on RAPD data could not be correlated to the ones based on morphology and pathogenicity in this study.

## Acknowledgements

Authors are very thankful to Dr. Mathura Rai, Director and Dr. P. K. Pandey, Head, Division of Crop Protection, Indian Institute of Vegetable Research (IIVR), Varanasi for their constant encouragement and providing the resources to carry out the research work.

## REFERENCES

Bonde R (1929) Physiological strains of *Alternaria solani.* Phytopa-thology 19:533–548

Bose TK, Kabir J, Maithy TK, Parthasarathy VA, Som MG (2002) Vegetable crops, vol 1, p 69, pp 1–154

Castro MEA, Chaves GM, Zambolim L, Cruz CD, Silva DJH (1999) Effect of inoculum concentration on the resistance of tomato to *Alternaria solani.* Fitopathologia Brasileira 24:463–465

Castro MEA, Zambolim L Chanes GM, Cruz CD, Matsuoka K (2000) Pathogenic variability of *Alternaria solani*, the causal agent of tomato early blight. Summa-Phytopathologica 26(1):24–28

Cotty JP (1987) Modulation of sporulation of *Alternaria tagetica* by carbon dioxide. Mycologia 74:508–513

Datar VV, Mayee CD (1985) Chemical management of early blight of tomato. J Maha Agri Univ 10(3):278–280

Douglas DR, Pavek JJ (1971) A efficient method of inducing sporulation of *Alternaria solani* in pure culture. Phytopathology 61:239

Ellis MB (1971) Dematiaceous hyphomycetes. Commonwealth Mycological Institute, Kew, England, pp 464–497

Fourtouni A, Menetas Y, Christias C (1998) Effect of UV-B radiation on growth, pigmentation and spore production in phytopatho-genic fungus *Alternaria solani.* Can J Bot 76:2093–2099

Gemawat PD, Gosh SK (1979) Studies on the physiology of growth of *Alternaria solani. India* J Mycol Plant Pathol 9(1):138–139

Gorgan RG , Kimble KA, Misaghi I (1975) A stem canker disease of tomato caused by *Alternaria alternata* f.sp. *lycopersici*. Phyto-pathology 65:880–886

Gupta DP, Nikhiraj NS (1972) Host relations in *Alternaria* blight of potato:germination of spore. J Bihar Bot Soc 1:22–26

Kuangai T, Oda Y (1969) Blue and near ultraviolet photo reaction in conidial development of the fungus, *Alternaria tomato*. Develop Growth Different 11:20–23

Kaoru O, Mitsuo N (1970) Effect of light on sporulation of *Alternaria kikuchina* TANAKA. Ann Phytopathol Soc Japan 36:11–16

Lukens RJ (1962) Photoinhibition of sporulation in *Alternaria solani.* Am J Bot 50:720–723

Manicom BQ, Bar-Joseph M, Rosner A, Vigodsky-Haas H, Kotze JM (1987) Potential applications of random DNA probes, and restriction fragment length polymorphisms in the taxonomy of Fusaria. Phytopathology 77:669–672

Morris PF, Connolly MS, St-Clair DA (2000) Genetic diversity of *Alternaria alternata* isolated from tomato in California assessed using RAPDs. Mycol Res 104:286–292

Neergarrd P (1945) Danish species of *Alternaria, and Stemphylium*. Oxford University Press, London

Pandey KK, Pandey PK, Satpathy S (2002) Integrated management of disease, and insects of tomato, chilli, and cole crops. Technical bulletin-9, 7 pp

Perez S, Martinez B (2000) Fungi associated with tomato early blight symptoms. Revista de Proteccion Vegetal 15:191–193

Perez S, Martinez B (1995) Selection, and characterization of *Alternaria solani.* Isolates of tomato. Revista de protection vegetal 10:163–167

Prasad B, Dutt BL, Nagaich BB (1973) Inducing sporulation in *Alternaria solani I.* Effect of water treatment. Mycopathol Mycol Appl 49:141–146

Prasad B, Dutt BL (1974) Inducing sporulation of *Alternaria solani* II. Effect of light. Mycopathol Mycol Appl 49:141–146

Rath GC, Padhi NN (1973) Sporulation of *Alternaria solani* in pure culture. Indian Phytopathol 26:495–501

Rodriquez ACM, Santana R (1991) Effect of new culture media, and temperature on the growth in vitro of *Alternaria solani*. Centro Agricola 18:86–88

Rotem J (1966) Variability in *Alternaria porri* f.sp. *solani*. Isr J Bot 15:47–57

Singh BM (1967) Inducing sporulaton of different strains of *Alternaria solani* II effect of ultra violet light. Mycopathologia 32:163–171

Sodlauskiene A, Rasinskiene A, Surviliene E (2003) Influence of environmental conditions upon the development of *Alternaria* genus fungi *in vitro*. Sodininkyste ir Darzininkyste 22:160–166 Stevenson RE, Pennypacker SP (1988) Effect of radiation, temper-ature, and moisture on conidial germination of Alternaria solani.

Phytopathology 78:926–930

Vloutoglou I, Kalogerakis SN (2000) Effect of inoculum concentra-tion, wetness duration, and plant age on development of early blight (*Alternaria solani*), and on shedding of leaves in tomato plant. Plant Pathol 49:339–345

Wang H, Zhang TY (2003) RAPD analysis on small spored *Alternaria* species. Mycosystema 22:35–41

Weir TL, Huff DR, Christ BJ, Romaine CP (1998) RAPD-PCR analysis of genetic variations among isolates of *Alternaria solani*, and *Alternaria alternata* from potato, and tomato. Mycologia 90:813–821

**Early Blight Disease of Tomato**
***Edited by:*** Virendra Kumar
**ISBN:** 978-93-5056-879-8
***Edition:*** 2017
***Published by:*** Discovery Publishing House Pvt. Ltd., New Delhi (India)

# Assessment of Early Blight (*Alternaria solani* ) Resistance in Tomato using a Droplet Inoculation Method

[1]Reni Chaerani, [2]Remmelt Groenworld,
[3]Piet Stam Roeland E. Voorrips

## ABSTRACT

A droplet inoculation method was used for evaluation of tomato resistance to early blight, a destructive fo-liar disease of tomato caused by *Alternaria solani* (Ellis and Martiŋ) Sorauer. In this test method, leaflets are inoculated with small droplets of a spore suspension in either water or a 0.1% agar solution. Early blight resistance was evaluated based on lesion size. The droplet method better discrimi-nated the level of resistance ($P < 0.001$) for a range of spore densities in comparison with the more commonly used spray inoculation method. Lesions generated by droplet inoculation at 7 days after inoculation ranged from small flecks to almost complete blight with an exponential-like distribution of lesion sizes. Significant correlations ($r = 0.52$, 0.58, and 0.63, $P < 0.001$) were observed across three glass-house tests of 54 accessions including wild species using the droplet method. The most resistant accessions included wild species: one accession of *Solanum arcanum*, three acces-sions of *Solanum peruvianum*, one accession of *Solanum neorickii*, and one of *Solanum chilense*. *Solanum pennellii* and *Solanum pimpinellifolium* accessions were susceptible, whereas Solanum habrochaites and Solanum lycopersicum accessions ranged from susceptible to moderately resistant. The droplet test method is simple to apply, offers a fine discrimination of early blight resistance levels, and allows objective evaluation.

**Keywords:** Early blight . *Altermaria solani* . Tomato . Resistance . Screening method

---

[1] Plant Research International, PO Box 16, Wageningen 6700 AA, The Netherlands
Tel. +31-317-47-7022; Fax +31-317-41-8094 e-mail: roeland.voorrips@wur.nl

[2] Laboratory of Plant Breeding, Department of Plant Sciences, Wageningen University, Wageningen, The Netherlands

[3] Indonesian Center for Agricultural Biotechnology and Genetic Resources Research and Development, Jln. Tentara Pelajar no. 3A, Bogor 16111, Indonesia.

## Introduction

Early blight of tomato, caused by *Alternaria solani* (Ellis and Martin) Sorauer, is a serious disease in warm and humid regions (Sherf and MacNab 1986) and in semiarid areas where frequent and prolonged night dew occurs (Rotem and Reichert 1964). Early blight (EB) reduces the photosynthetic area, and, in severe cases, can defoliate plants.

Cultivars highly resistant to EB are not known for cultivated tomato [*Solanum lycopersicum* (Peralta et al. 2005; formerly known as *Lycopersicon esculentum*)]. All breeding lines and released cultivars range in susceptibility from susceptible to moderately resistant (Vakalounakis 1983; Gardner 1988; Poysa and Tu 1996; Banerjee et al. 1998; Vloutoglou 1999; Gardner and Shoemaker 1999). Several wild species [*Solanum habrochaites* (syn. *Lycopersicon hirsutum*), *Solanum pimpinellifolium* (syn. *Lycopersicon pimpinellifolium*), *Solanum peruvianum* (syn. *Lycopersicon peruvianum*), and *Solanum chilense* (syn. *Lycopersicon chil-ense*)] have been identified as potential sources of resistance (Nash and Gardner 1988; Kalloo and Banerjee 1993; Poysa and Tu 1996; Foolad et al. 2000; Thirthamalappa and Lohithaswa 2000). Some of these, primarily *S. habrochaites* accession PI 126445, have been used to develop moderately resistant breeding lines (Gardner 1988; Gardner and Shoemaker 1999). Identification of additional sources of resistance could facilitate the development of resistant cultivars.

Field evaluations can identify sources of resistance, but the major drawbacks are the lengthy duration of the tests, uncontrollable environmental conditions necessary for in-fection, and the presence of other foliar pathogens (Locke 1948; Foolad et al. 2000; Pandey et al. 2003). Glasshouse tests using spray inoculation of a spore suspension on seed-lings are widely used since the establishment of efficient screening and spore inoculum production techniques by Barksdale (1969). The EB lesions resulting from spray in-oculation are scattered on the leaves so that the observer must estimate the combined area of all lesions on all leaflets as a percentage of the total leaf area. Disease estimates are rapid but rather subjective. Another disadvantage of the spray inoculation method is that the inoculum may not be uniformly distributed on the leaves. Furthermore, the meth-od is not sensitive enough to discriminate moderately resis-tant plants from those that are susceptible (Gardner 1990).

An alternative method to obtain more precise and reliable disease readings is offered by placing individual droplets of a fungal inoculum suspension on the leaflets. This method was first introduced by Locke (1948) to find sources of resistance to EB. Detached leaflets were inocu-lated with a mycelial suspension in a laboratory assay, and the disease reaction was evaluated using a diagram of a graded series of lesions with known diameters (Locke 1948, 1949). Henning and Alexander (1959) used the droplet method to investigate the existence of *A. solani* races by inoculating leaflets still attached to plants. Nash and Gardner (1988) applied the method, which they called point inoculation, on a whole plant assay and measured the EB lesion diameter. EB resistance of two parents and the F1s were tested in a glasshouse. Their results correlated well with field tests, but were based only on a few genotypes.

Large numbers of accessions have never been screened in the glasshouse using the droplet inoculation method. We describe here some improvements on the method and its application to identify potential EB resistance sources in a collection of tomato accessions.

## Materials and Methods

### Plant material and culture conditions

Tomato seeds were germinated on moistened filter paper in 90-mm-diameter petri dishes for 5–7 days in darkness at 19°C. Germinating seeds were planted in peat soil in boxes or plastic pots. Plants were grown in a glasshouse in Wageningen, The Netherlands, at day/night temperatures of 22°/20°C. Tomato accessions used in the screening ex-periments are listed in Table 3. They were propagated one generation before use; where possible, inbred lines were obtained by selfing, but in the case of *S. peruvianum*, half-sib families were harvested after intercrossing five plants per accession. In cases with clear morphological differences between the five plants of the original accession, two lines or two half-sib families were included in the screening experiments.

### Fungal culture and inoculum preparation

An *Alternaria solani* isolate obtained from infected tomato leaves in Sukabumi, West Java, Indonesia, was propagated on V8 juice agar in 90-mm-diameter petri dishes. The dish-es were incubated at 21°–22°C with a 12-h diurnal period of fluorescent light for 10–17 days. The cultures were in-duced to sporulate as described by Barksdale (1969). The number of spores in the suspension was counted in five 10-μl samples. The yield per plate was about $0.7–13.0 \times 10^5$ spores.

### Conditions during infection

For the first 40 h immediately after inoculation, plants were incubated on a glasshouse bench lined with a wet mat and covered with a transparent plastic tunnel. Periodic misting to maintain high humidity was supplied from a humidifier. After the initial incubation, each side of the tunnel was opened, and the humidifier was turned off for 8 h during the day to allow the plant surface to dry. Minimum light inten-sity in the plastic tunnel was approximately 14 $\mu$mol $m^{-2}$ $s^{-1}$; when necessary, daylight was supplemented with light from high-pressure sodium vapor lamps (17 $\mu$mol $m^{-2}$ $s^{-1}$) for 16 h $day^{-1}$. The temperature and relative humidity were re-corded with a thermohygrograph.

### Effect of spore concentration on early blight severity with two inoculation methods

One moderately resistant (FT94-978; 99-213) and one susceptible (HRC90.145) *S. lycopersicum* line were grown for 3 weeks on peat soil in boxes of 34 × 29.5 ×

4 cm. Two inoculation methods, the droplet and the standard spray inoculation methods, were compared. Spore density was varied (0, 1, 2, 4, 10, and 20 × $10^3$ ml$^{-1}$ water) to find the most discriminating level.

Plants inoculated using the droplet method were raised in boxes of 12 plants, with two rows of three plants of each genotype. A single drop (10 μl) of a spore suspension was placed on an interveinal space of the upper surface of three apical leaflets. The two first expanded leaves were used. The six spore concentrations were randomized over the six plants of each genotype in each box. The experiment was replicated over three boxes.

In the spray inoculation treatment, boxes contained four rows of four plants, with the two genotypes in alternating rows. Each pair of rows was sprayed with one spore con-centration until runoff. The experiment was replicated four times (24 boxes).

The boxes were covered with a transparent lid and placed in the tunnel with intermittent misting for 15 min at 45-min intervals. After the first 24 h, the lids were removed. The temperature during the day was 20°–27°C and during the night was 16°–24°C. The relative humidity ranged from 40% to 72% during the day and from 85% to 100% during the night. Symptom evaluations were done 7 days after in-oculation. Length and width of lesions after droplet inocula-tion were measured. EB severity on each leaf of the sprayed plants was recorded on a scale of 0 to 5, where 0 = no visible lesions on leaf; 1 = up to 10% leaf area affected; 2 = 11%– 25%; 3 = 26%–50%; 4 = 51%–75%; and 5 = more than 75% leaf area affected or leaf abscised (Vakalounakis 1983). Leaves that were not completely unfurled during the inocu-lation were not assessed. The disease scales were converted into percentage of EB index (PEBI) for each plant using the following formula (Pandey et al. 2003):

$$\text{PEBI} = \frac{\text{sum of all ratings}}{\text{no. of leaves sampled} \times \text{maximum disease scale}} \times 100$$

Resistance reaction of selected accessions with two inoculation methods in the glasshouse The repeatability of the droplet inoculation method in determining early blight resistance in a wider range of accessions was compared with the spray inoculation method. Nine accessions including wild species that were found to differ in mean EB lesion size in preliminary experiments were planted in pots and inoculated at 6 weeks after germination.

For spray inoculation, plants were sprayed with spores in water until runoff. For droplet inoculations, a single drop (10 μl) of 0.1% agar solution with $10^4$ spores ml$^{-1}$ was placed on an interveinal area of three apical leaflets of the four topmost expanded leaves. With agar, the droplets were more likely to adhere to the leaves. The spore concentra-tion of $10^4$ spores ml$^{-1}$ was selected based on the most opti-mal inoculum level found for the spray inoculation (see Results), was used for both inoculation methods. Two plants of each accession were tested in three replications for the droplet inoculation and four replications for the spray in-oculation. Noninoculated plants were used as controls for both inoculation methods. The plants were placed in a humidified tunnel directly after inoculation and received periodic misting for 45 s at 8-min intervals. Daytime temperatures ranged from 25° to 27°C and nighttime temperatures from 20° to 22°C. The relative humidity ranged from 59% to 69% during the day and was 98% during the night. Disease reactions were recorded at 7 days after inoculation using the procedure for the respective inoculation methods as previously described.

## Glasshouse screening of tomato accessions

### *Glasshouse screening 2001 (autumn)*

Forty-one accessions including wild species were tested (Table 3; GH I and GH II). For 11 accessions, two or three lines or half-sib families were tested because the original accession was not morphologically uniform. The plants were raised in boxes of 34 × 29.5 × 4 cm. Each box contained 12 plots of two plants of 12 different accessions, which were randomized in the boxes. The plants were inoculated using the droplet method at 3 weeks after sowing, when most of them had two fully expanded leaves. Boxes were closed with transparent lids for 24 h and placed in the tunnel. The misting period was 15 min $h^{-1}$. The length and the perpendicular width of lesions were recorded 7 days after inocula-tion. The experiment was replicated five times at weekly intervals; each replicate was treated as a block in the statistical analysis.

In the first two replicates, the three apical leaflets of the two basal leaves of two plants of each accession were inoculated with 2 × $10^4$ spores $ml^{-1}$ water. However, the basal leaves of some wild species, both with and without lesions were lost earlier (3 days after inoculation) than those of the cultivated tomato, possibly due to faster development and senescence. Early senescence and defoliation were accelerated by inoculation with the pathogen. On some susceptible accessions, lesions expanded rapidly and caused early de-velopment of blight. Because of these problems, the droplet inoculation procedures were modified in the subsequent replicates. These first two replicates were treated as a sepa-rate experiment, designated as "glasshouse test I" (GH I).

In the subsequent three replicates (GH II) the three apical leaflets of the four topmost leaves were inoculated to achieve a more uniform physiological age of leaves, and a lower inoculum density (4 × $10^3$ spores $ml^{-1}$ water) was used to prevent blight symptoms from developing too rapidly. Three replicates in time were performed. In the first replicate of GH II, some accessions were represented by less than two plants due to poor germination.

Temperatures ranged from 20° to 23°C during the day and from 17° to 19°C during the night. Relative humidity ranged from 43% to 64% during the day and from 97% to 100% during the night.

### *Glasshouse screening 2002 (summer)*

The same 41 accessions were retested together with 13 ad-ditional accessions in five replicated tests, performed at weekly intervals (Table 3; GH III). Plants were grown in 12-cm-diameter pots (one seedling per pot) to facilitate in-oculation and evaluation. Four weeks after sowing, plants were inoculated at the three apical leaflets of the four top-most expanded leaves with a single drop (10 μl) of 0.1% agar solution carrying $10^4$ spores $ml^{-1}$. Each replicate included one plant of each accession. Control plants, one plant of each species, which were inoculated with agar solu-tion without spores, were also included in the tests. Plants were placed in a tunnel and exposed to a fine mist for 45 s to 1 min at intervals of 6–8 min. Five replicate tests were performed during the season at 1-week intervals. The length and the perpendicular width of the lesions were measured at 7 days after inoculation. Day temperatures ranged from 22° to 27°C, night temperatures from 20° to 22°C. Relative humidity ranged from 40% to 66% during the day and from 91% to 93% during the night.

### Experimental design and statistical analyses

The elementary data consisted of lesion size (length × width) for the droplet inoculation, and PEBI per plant for the spray inoculation. Heterogeneity in the variances was observed in the data from both inoculation methods. Logarithmic and arcsine-square root transformation was applied before statistical analysis to the lesion size and PEBI data, respectively, to stabilize the variances.

**Table 2.1 Means of disease parameters after droplet inoculation (lesion size) and spray inoculation (percentage of early blight index, PEBI)**

| Spore density (× $10^3$ $ml^{-1}$) | Lesion size mean ($mm^2$)[a] | | *t* value | PEBI mean (%)[b] | | *t* value |
|---|---|---|---|---|---|---|
| | HRC90.145 | FT94-978; 99-213 | | HRC90.145 | FT94-978; 99-213 | |
| 1 | 29.92 | 10.50 | 2.16* | 18.12 | 14.68 | 1.63 |
| 2 | 86.50 | 16.60 | 4.38**** | 28.93 | 19.23 | 2.61* |
| 4 | 108.64 | 37.93 | 5.24**** | 44.88 | 27.64 | 2.53* |
| 10 | 135.83 | 53.09 | 4.16**** | 74.91 | 53.31 | 4.16**** |
| 20 | 213.80 | 80.91 | 6.18**** | 61.62 | 75.21 | 2.98*** |

*$P < 0.05$; ** $P < 0.01$; *** $P < 0.005$; **** $P < 0.001$

[a]Average of three replicates of 18 leaflets each (6 leaflets × 3 plants); values are back transformations of log (*x*)

[b]Average of four replicates of four plants each; values are back transformations of arcsine [√(*x*/100)].

Student's *t*-test was performed for the data from the spore concentration experiment to compare means. All other experimental data were analyzed by analysis of variance (ANOVA) as a randomized complete block design. Mean separations were done by means of least significant difference (LSD) tests ($P \leq 0.05$). GH II was analyzed using the unbalanced treatment structure procedure of ANOVA because of the unequal number of plants per block and

**Table 2 Mean early blight lesion size and percentage of early blight index (PEBI) of nine selected accessions**

| Species | Accessions | Lesion size ($mm^2$)[a] | PEBI[b] |
|---|---|---|---|
| *S. peruvianum* | PE44 | 1.19 a | 67.43 abc |
| *S. peruvianum* | PE33 | 6.67 b | 59.03 a |
| *S. lycopersicum* | HRC90.158 | 7.73 bc | 66.28 abc |
| *S. pimpinellifolium* | G1.1554 | 12.59 cd | 86.69 cd |
| *S. lycopersicum* | NC EBR-4 | 15.07 d | 62.43 ab |
| *S. habrochaites* | G1.1561 | 15.21 d | 84.98 bcd |
| *S. habrochaites* | 864086-2; PI272745 | 29.72 e | 97.71 d |
| *S. habrochaites* | PE36 | 40.18 e | 60.40 ab |
| *S. lycopersicum* | FT97-515; 99-214 | 45.92 e | 90.86 d |

[a] Length × width measured 7 days after inoculation. Each value is an average of three replicates of 24 leaflets (3 leaflets × 4 leaves × 2 plants); data are back transformations of log(*x*). Values within a column followed by the same letters are not significantly different at $P = 0.05$

[b] Based on individual leaf scores: 0 = no visible lesions on leaves; 1 = up to 10% leaf area affected; 2 = 11% – 25%; 3 = 26%–50%; 4 = 51% – 75%; and 5 = more than 75% leaf area affected or leaf shed. Each value is an average of four replicates of two plants; data are back transformation of arcsine [( *x*100) ]

per accession. All analyses were done using the GenStat 6 statistical package (Payne *et al.* 2002).

**Results**

The effect of spore concentration on EB severity under two inoculation methods

EB lesions resulting from both the droplet and spray inoculations appeared within 3 days after inoculation. Some droplet inoculations failed to yield substantial lesions; either small spots (≤ 1 mm in diameter) formed, or no symptoms developed. This was observed for both accessions. Symptomless inoculations were scored as missing values.

With both inoculation methods, FT94-978; 99-213 (moderately resistant) developed significantly smaller lesions or lower PEBI than HRC90.145 (susceptible) at all spore concentrations, except for PEBI at $20 \times 10^3$ $ml^{-1}$ (Table 2.1). At all concentrations, the droplet method better discriminated the resistance level than the spray method, as indicated by higher and more significant *t* values ($P < 0.001$). The most significant difference in PEBI between FT94-978; 99-213 and HRC90.145 was observed at a spore concentration of $10^4$ $ml^{-1}$, while the differences were highly significant at all concentrations above $10^3$ $ml^{-1}$ for the droplet inoculation method.

**Resistance reaction of selected accessions with two inoculation methods in glasshouse tests**

The comparison of the droplet and spray inoculations was expanded to a set of nine accessions representing four tomato species, which from preliminary experiments were known to represent large differences in EB resistance. The wild accessions occasionally developed spontaneous blisters or necroses under glasshouse conditions. When EB developed on *S. habrochaites* leaves with necroses, the lesions would expand rapidly and result in severe blight symptom, complicating the measurement of lesion size. Leaflets with blight symptoms so severe that lesion size could not be measured were scored as missing values.

The droplet method allowed a better separation of accessions than the spray inoculation method (Table 2.22) in accordance with the results of the

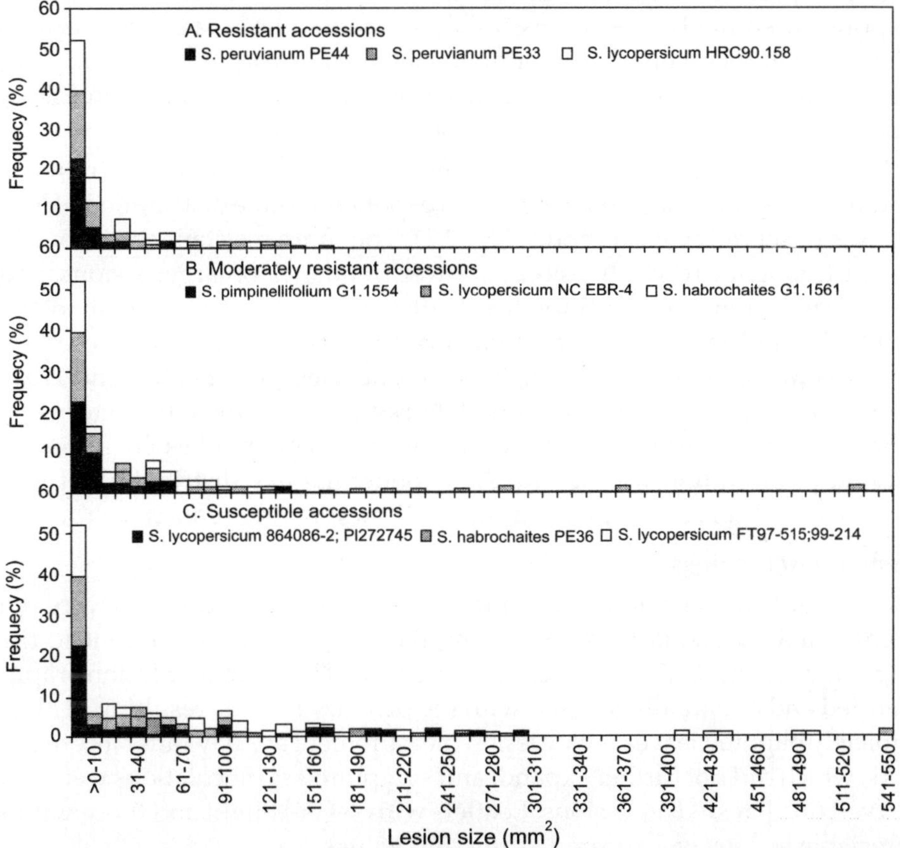


**Fig. 2.1 Frequency distribution of lesion sizes on droplet-inoculated plants in three groups of three accessions: A resistant, B moderately resistant, and C susceptible accessions**

spore concentration experiment. Accession reactions with the two inoculation methods were not significantly correlated ($r = 0.44$, $P > 0.2$). *S. habrochaites* PE36 had inconsistent results between the two inoculation methods: it was ranked as susceptible with the droplet method but resistant with the spray method. Occasional spontaneous necroses on this accession inoculated with the droplet method exacerbated EB lesions. Excluding this accession from the analysis increased the correlation considerably ($r = 0.66$).

EB lesions on petioles were observed on sprayed plants. Large, sunken lesions on petioles often caused loss of the leaf and thus raised the PEBI of accessions that had small leaf lesions when inoculated by the droplet method. The petiole lesions were generated randomly because the spray inoculation was not purposely directed to petioles.

### Lesion size distribution

Inoculations using the droplet method did not always develop into a noticeable lesion, irrespective of the level of resistance of a plant. We first assumed that the spores dried out before successfully penetrating the host tissue during the initial hours of incubation in the tunnel. However, incorporation of 0.1% agar solution into the spore suspension, which immobilized the droplets and slowed evaporation, did not influence the probability of lesion formation.

After grouping the nine accessions into three categories (resistant, moderately resistant, and susceptible), an exponential-like distribution of lesion sizes was observed in each group (Fig. 2.1). The more resistant accessions had a higher frequency of small lesions, a lower frequency of larger lesions, and a lower mean lesion size. Symptomless leaflets were observed with an average of 0.9%, 7%, and 18.2% for susceptible, intermediate, and resistant accessions, respec-tively; for flecks (d"1 $mm^2$), these frequencies were 2%, 9%, and 17%. In a microscopic evaluation of leaflets with flecks after staining with lactophenol–cotton blue, infection was evident by the presence of germ tube penetration, but my-celial proliferation was absent. An exponential-like distribution of lesion size was also observed for plants inoculated by spraying (data not shown).

### Glasshouse screenings

Lesions near leaf veins of the susceptible *S. lycopersicum* accessions were often accompanied by smaller lesions of angular shape without concentric rings along the vein and at the distal ends of the vein. These smaller lesions rapidly expanded and eventually merged with the primary lesions, resulting in almost completely blighted leaves before lesion measurement at 7 days after inoculation. Flecks, which did not further expand, and symptomless inoculations were again observed on all tested accessions. Leaflets with severe blight and those without appreciable lesions were scored as missing values.

The means of the lesion sizes from each glasshouse test were weighted with the reciprocals of the variances to obtain overall accession mean values. This adjustment was necessary since variances of the means among the three tests were unequal. After calculating the weighted average, we observed a continuous range of resistance levels, from highly susceptible (*S. pennellii* LA716, average lesion size 107.65 $mm^2$) to highly resistant (*S. arcanum* LA2157, 1.40 $mm^2$) (Table 3). However, no complete resistance was found. Among the glasshouse tests, significant correlations were observed ($P < 0.001$), with correlation coefficients of 0.58 (between GH I and II), 0.52 (GH I and III), and 0.63 (GH II and III). Most of the resistant accessions belonged to wild species (*S. arcanum, S. peruvianum, S. neorickii,* and *S. chilense*). However, both susceptible and moderately resistant *S. habrochaites* accessions were found, and other wild accessions belonging to *S. pimpinellifolium* and especially *S. pennellii* were susceptible. Among different lines of the previously reported moderately resistant accession HRC91.341 (Poysa and Tu 1996), there were significant differences in EB lesion sizes. One line of this accession was susceptible in GH II but resistant or moderately resistant in GH I and GH III, while the other line was resistant in all three tests. Lines derived from NC EBR-2 and NC EBR-3 also had a different reaction in GH II compared with GH I and GH III.

Single lesions resulting from the droplet inoculation permitted detailed observation of lesion phenotypes. Necrotic lesions on *S. neorickii* (syn. *L. parviflorum*), some accessions of *S. habrochaites* and *S. peruvianum,* and *S. lycopersicum* NC EBR-6 were surrounded by narrow chlorotic halos, whereas those on *S. pennellii, S. chilense,* and other accessions of *S. habrochaites* and *S. peruvianum* were not accompanied by chlorotic halos. *S. pimpinellifolium* and other *S. lycopersicum* genotypes had a range of intermediate to wide halos. The extent of the halos did not seem to correlate with the size of the necrotic lesions (data not shown).

## Discussion

The droplet inoculation method offers better discrimination among accessions than the spray method. This was observed in the spore concentration experiment and in the nine-accession experiment. Variance of lesion size increased with increasing means in both experiments. Distribution of lesion sizes seemed to be exponential, with many small lesions and few large ones. This trend was observed at all levels of resistance.

The discrepancy between the results of the droplet and spray methods can partly be explained by two factors. First, some wild species developed severe necroses in the glass-house experiment even without inoculation. After spray inoculation, these necroses were often indistinguishable from EB lesions, whereas after droplet inoculation they were simply recognized and treated as missing values. Second, spray inoculation may lead to random leaf shedding due to petiole lesions and therefore erratic, high symptom scores. The droplet method offers a possibility to test the effect of petiole lesions in a controlled way.

Across the three glasshouse screenings, significant correlations were observed. GH II and GH III yielded a better separation than GH I. Also the correlation between GH II and GH III was higher than that between GH I and the other two tests. This may be due to: (1) the lower number of observations in GH I, (2) the higher inoculum density in GH I, and (3) the difference in the selection of leaves between GH I and the other two tests. We used a lower inoculum concentration (40 to 200 spores per droplet) in the glasshouse screenings but observed overall larger lesion sizes than Nash and Gardner (1988) who applied more in-oculum (500 to 750 spores per droplet) on basal leaves. This indicates that our tests were performed in near-optimal conditions for infection and disease development. Another difference between our work and the study of Nash and Gardner (1988) was that they selected one lesion per plant to be measured, whereas we measured all inoculations without selection. As a result, we observed a large range of lesion types, from small lesions ($d^{-1}$ mm in diameter) to almost blighted leaflets and also symptomless leaflets within the same accession. Small lesions ($d^{-1}$ mm in diameter) occurred on all genotypes, but their frequency corresponded with the resistance level. This was indicated by a high correlation between lesion size and the percentage of small lesions, most notably in GH II and GH III where a lower spore concentration was applied: $r = -0.73$ (GH II, $P < 0.001$) and $r = -0.77$ (GH III, $P < 0.001$).

Variability in pathogenicity of *A. solani* isolates has been widely described (Bonde 1929; Henning and Alexander 1959; Rotem 1966), but no evidence has been presented for the existence of pathological races. The results of our study, in which we used a single highly pathogenic Indonesian isolate, can therefore be expected to be representative for other Indonesian isolates as well.

The droplet inoculation method is simple to apply and allows an objective evaluation of EB severity. The method has been used to evaluate EB resistance components (O'Leary and Shoemaker 1983). Single lesions created by the droplet method allow detailed observation of lesion phenotype such as differential formation of halos among genotypes. The importance of the chlorotic halo as an indi-cator of resistance has not been studied so far. Improvements of the method have been made by incorporating agar into the spore suspension and the use of upper leaves as opposed to the bottom leaves.

The considerable amount of time required to measure lesions may make this method less attractive for large-scale screenings, but this problem can be circumvented by determining the percentage of small lesions. The described advantages of the droplet inoculation method make this the method of choice where a fine discrimination of resistance level and accurate quantitative data are required, for example, in quantitative trait locus studies of resistance or in assessing breeding material during advanced backcross programs.

**Table 2.3 Early blight lesion sizes of *Lycopersicon* accessions in glasshouse tests**

| Species | Accessions | Source[a] | GH I[b,c] | GH II[d] | GH III[e] | Weighted average[f] |
|---|---|---|---|---|---|---|
| *Solanum arcanum* | LA2157 | 1 | NT | NT | 1.40 a | 1.40 |
| *S. peruvianum* | PE44 | 4 | NT | NT | 1.46 ab | 1.46 |
| *S. peruvianum* | PI 390665 | 4 | NT | NT | 4.07 c–h | 4.07 |
| *S. peruvianum* | PE33 | 4 | 11.38 a | 1.54 a | 3.30 c–f | 6.23 |

| | | | | | | |
|---|---|---|---|---|---|---|
| *S. neorickii* | G1.1601 | 2 | NT | NT | 6.68 g–m | 6.68 |
| *S. chilense* | G1.1556 | 2 | NT | NT | 6.68 g–m | 6.68 |
| *S. lycopersicum* | NC EBR-6 | 3 | 16.90 ab | 2.59 a–d | 5.02 d–k | 9.56 |
| *S. lycopersicum* | NC EBR-6 | 3 | 17.10 ab | 4.56 a–i | 2.61 bc | 10.49 |
| *S. lycopersicum* | HRC86.320 | 4 | 24.27 a–d | 1.57 a | 4.32 c–l | 10.61 |
| *S. lycopersicum* | cv. Santacruz | 6 | NT | NT | 11.67 m–p | 11.67 |
| *S. habrochaites* | LA2650 | 4 | 18.58 ab | 3.60 a–g | 16.79 p–u | 12.24 |
| *S. lycopersicum* | HRC90.159 | 4 | 25.82 a–d | 2.92 a–e | 3.16 c–f | 12.56 |
| *S. lycopersicum* | HRC86.320 | 4 | 32.36 a–e | 2.06 ab | 2.93 cd | 13.29 |
| *S. habrochaites* | PE36 | 4 | 31.48 a–e | 2.34 a–c | 10.45 m–p | 15.00 |
| *S. peruvianum* | PI390665 | 4 | 16.94 ab | 11.00 f–k | 16.52 p–u | 15.19 |
| *S. lycopersicum* | HRC90.159 | 4 | 30.55 a–e | 3.90 a–i | 4.84 d–j | 15.65 |
| *S. lycopersicum* | HRC91.341 | 4 | 30.97 a–e | 4.62 a–j | 4.56 c–l | 16.40 |
| *S. lycopersicum* | NC EBR-1 | 3 | 28.91 a–e | 4.73 a–j | 10.69 m–p | 16.94 |
| *S. lycopersicum* | NC EBR-3 | 3 | 22.49 a–d | 9.59 e–k | 7.59 i–n | 16.97 |
| *S. lycopersicum* | HRC90.190 | 4 | 32.58 a–e | 4.98 a–j | 4.82 d–j | 17.36 |
| *S. peruvianum* | PI270435 | 4 | NT | NT | 17.50 p–u | 17.50 |
| *S. lycopersicum* | cv. Sufan n.1 | 6 | NT | NT | 17.54 p–u | 17.54 |
| *S. habrochaites* | LA1777 | 2 | NT | NT | 17.54 p–u | 17.54 |
| *S. lycopersicum* | NC EBR-2 | 3 | 21.43 a–c | 15.10 jk | 10.40 l–p | 18.46 |
| *S. lycopersicum* | NC EBR-5 | 3 | 42.46 b–e | 3.10 a–f | 5.73 f–l | 18.67 |
| *S. lycopersicum* | HRC86.329 | 4 | 36.39 a–e | 3.71 a–h | 12.94 n–r | 18.88 |
| *S. lycopersicum* | HRC86.329 | 4 | 32.66 a–e | 5.16 a–j | 14.16 o–s | 19.23 |
| *S. lycopersicum* | HRC90.157 | 4 | 30.76 a–e | 8.24 c–k | 3.83 c–g | 19.28 |
| *S. lycopersicum* | HRC86.321 | 4 | 41.88 b–e | 4.00 a–i | 5.33 e–k | 19.60 |
| *S. lycopersicum* | HRC90.159 | 4 | 39.08 a–e | 5.93 b–k | 3.12 c–e | 19.72 |
| *S. lycopersicum* | NC EBR-3 | 3 | 33.50 a–e | 6.04 b–k | NT | 20.34 |
| *S. lycopersicum* | HRC90.157 | 4 | 41.40 b–e | 4.33 a–i | 8.36 j–o | 20.60 |
| *S. lycopersicum* | FT94-978; 99-213 | 5 | 39.72 a–e | 4.60 a–j | 9.73 l–p | 20.62 |
| *S. lycopersicum* | NC EBR-4 | 3 | 36.90 a–e | 6.50 b–k | 15.63 p–t | 22.50 |
| *S. lycopersicum* | FT94-968; 99-212 | 5 | 33.11 a–e | 10.80 f–k | 11.35 m–p | 22.86 |
| *S. habrochaites* | G1.1561 | 2 | 42.95 b–e | 6.67 b–k | 7.62 i–n | 23.33 |
| *S. lycopersicum* | HRC91.341 | 4 | 34.28 a–e | 12.80 g–k | 7.76 i–n | 23.63 |
| *S. lycopersicum* | FT97-515; 99-214 | 5 | 40.18 b–e | 6.38 b–k | 17.50 p–u | 23.69 |

| *S. lycopersicum* | FT94-978; 99-213 | 5 | 42.07 b–e | 7.80 c–k | 9.04 k–p | 24.27 |
|---|---|---|---|---|---|---|
| *S. lycopersicum* | cv. Allround | 1 | NT | NT | 24.32 s–u | 24.32 |
| *S. pimpinellifolium* | G1.1554 | 1 | 47.53 b–e | 8.59 d–k | 6.75 g–m | 24.70 |
| *S. lycopersicum* | HRC90.158 | 4 | 49.66 b–e | 7.24 b–k | 4.60 c–j | 25.13 |
| *S. lycopersicum* | NC EBR-2 | 3 | 39.36 a–e | 13.20 h–k | 10.21 l–p | 26.73 |
| *S. lycopersicum* | PI79532 | 6 | NT | NT | 26.98 t–v | 26.98 |
| *S. lycopersicum* | FT94-968; 99-212 | 4 | 48.19 b–e | 9.57 e–k | 9.77 l–p | 28.15 |
| *S. lycopersicum* | cv. Vogliotti | 6 | NT | NT | 29.17 uv | 29.17 |
| *S. lycopersicum* | HRC89.302 | 4 | 44.26 b–e | 12.20 g–k | 21.04 q–u | 30.15 |
| *S. lycopersicum* | 864084-2; PI 273048 | 5 | 68.39 c–e | 12.10 g–k | 7.05 h–m | 36.63 |
| *S. lycopersicum* | HRC89.302 | 4 | 53.33 b–e | 16.40 jk | 21.09 r–u | 36.74 |
| *S. lycopersicum* | cv. Money-maker | 1 | 75.34 de | 12.40 g–k | 17.62 p–u | 42.52 |
| *S. lycopersicum* | HRC86.327 | 4 | 72.11 c–e | 13.70 l–k | 45.08 v | 45.88 |
| *S. lycopersicum* | HRC90.145 | 4 | 71.45 c–e | 20.50 k | 28.84 uv | 48.49 |
| *S. lycopersicum* | 864086-2; PI 272745 | 5 | 94.84 e | 18.80 k | 45.08 v | 59.49 |
| *S. pennellii* | LA716 | 1 | NT | NT | 107.65 w | 107.65 |

Lesion sizes are given in units of mm$^2$ (length × width) measured 7 days after inoculation. Data are back transformations of log(*x*) NT, Not tested

[a] 1, Plant Research International, Wageningen, The Netherlands; 2, Dr. P. Lindhout, Laboratory of Plant Breeding, Wageningen University, The Netherlands; 3, Dr. R.G. Gardner, North Carolina Agricultural Research Institute, North Carolina State University, Raleigh, North Carolina, USA; 4, Dr. V. Poysa, Agriculture and Agri-Food Canada, Harrow Research Center, Harrow, Ontario, Canada; 5, Prof. M. Mutschler, Department of Plant Breeding, Cornell University, Ithaca, New York, USA; 6, Nunhems Zaden BV, Haelen, the Netherlands

[b] Values followed by the same letters within a column are not significantly different at $P = 0.05$

[c] Inoculated with 2 × 10$^4$ spores ml$^{-1}$ water. Each value is the average of two replicates of 12 leaflets (3 leaflets × 2 leaves × 2 plants)

[d] Inoculated with 4 × 10$^3$ spores ml$^{-1}$ water. Each value is the average of three replicates of 12 or 24 leaflets (3 leaflets × 4 leaves × 1 plants or 3 leaflets × 4 leaves × 2 plants)

[e] Inoculated with 10$^4$ spores ml$^{-1}$ in 0.1% agar. Each value is an average of five replicates of 12 leaflets (3 leaflets × 4 leaves × 1 plant)

[f] $(Y_i s_i^2)/(1\ s_i^2)$.

## Acknowledgments

We thank Dr. Suhardi (Indonesian Ornamental Plants Research Institute, IOPRI) and Dr. E. Sofiari (Indonesian Vegetables Research Institute, IVEGRI) for providing the *Alternaria solani* isolate, and D. Geurtsen and A. Hermsen for their assistance in the glasshouse. Financial support was provided by the Royal Nether-lands Academy of Arts and Sciences in the framework of the Scientific Programme Indonesia–Netherlands.

## REFERENCES

Banerjee MK, Chhabra ML, Saini PS (1998) Responses of tomato cultivars to Alternaria blight. Test Agrochem Cult 19:50–51

Barksdale TH (1969) Resistance of tomato seedlings to early blight. Phytopathology 59:443–446

Bonde R (1929) Physiological strains of *Alternaria solani*. Phytopathology 19:533–548

Foolad MR, Ntahimpera N, Christ BJ, Lin GY (2000) Comparison of field, greenhouse, and detached-leaflet evaluations of tomato germ plasm for early blight resistance. Plant Dis 84:967–972

Gardner RG (1988) NC EBR-1 and NC EBR-2 early blight resistant tomato breeding lines. HortScience 23:779–781

Gardner RG (1990) Greenhouse disease screen facilitates breeding resistance to tomato early blight. HortScience 25:222–223

Gardner RG, Shoemaker PB (1999) "Mountain Supreme" early blight-resistant hybrid tomato and its parents, NC EBR-3 and NC EBR-4. HortScience 34:745–746

Henning RG, Alexander LJ (1959) Evidence of existence of physio-logic races of *Alternaria solani*. Plant Dis Rep 43:298–308

Kalloo G, Banerjee MK (1993) Early blight resistance in *Lycopersicum esculentum* Mill. transferred from *L. pimpinellifolium* (L.) Mill. and *L. hirsutum* f. *glabratum* Mull. Gartenbauwissenschaft 58:238– 239

Locke SB (1948) A method for measuring resistance to defoliation diseases in tomato and other *Lycopersicon* species. Phytopathology 38:937–942

Locke SB (1949) Resistance to early blight and Septoria leaf spot in the genus *Lycopersicon*. Phytopathology 39:829–836

Nash AF, Gardner RG (1988) Tomato early blight resistance in a breeding line derived from *Lycopersicon hirsutum* PI 126445. Plant Dis 72:206–209

O'Leary DJ, Shoemaker PB (1983) Components of resistance for to-mato early blight. Phytopathology 73:803

Pandey KK, Pandey PK, Kallo G, Banerjee MK (2003) Resistance to early blight of tomato with respect to various parameters of disease epidemics. J Gen Plant Pathol 69:364–371

Payne RW, Harding SA, Murray DA, Soutar DM, Baird DB, Welham SJ, Kane AF, Gilmour AR, Thompson R, Webster R, Wilson GT (2002) GenStat for Windows, 6th edn. VSN, Oxford

Peralta IE, Knapp S, Spooner DM (2005) New species of wild tomatoes (*Solanum* Section *Lycopersicon*: Solanaceae) from northern Peru. Syst Bot 30:424–434

Poysa V, Tu JC (1996) Response of cultivars and breeding lines of *Lycopersicon* spp. to *Alternaria solani*. Can Plant Dis Surv 76:5–8 Rotem J (1966) Variability in *Alternaria porrii* f. sp. *solani*. Israel J Bot 15:48–57

Rotem J, Reichert I (1964) Dew – a principal moisture factor enabling early blight epidemics in a semiarid region of Israel. Plant Dis Rep 48:211–215

Sherf AF, MacNab AA (1986) Vegetable diseases and their control. Wiley, New York

Thirthamalappa, Lohithaswa HC (2000) Genetics of resistance to early blight (*Alternaria solani* Sorauer) in tomato (*Lycopersicum esculen-tum* L.) Euphytica 113:187–193

Vakalounakis DJ (1983) Evaluation of tomato cultivars for resistance to Alternaria blight. Ann Appl Biol 102:138–139

Vloutoglou I (1999) Evaluation of tomato cultivars and hybrids for resistance to *Alternaria solani* infection. Test Agrochem Cult 20:48– 49

**Early Blight Disease of Tomato**
***Edited by:*** **Virendra Kumar**
**ISBN: 978-93-5056-879-8**
***Edition:*** **2017**
***Published by:*** **Discovery Publishing House Pvt. Ltd., New Delhi (India)**

# Screening of Tomato Genotypes against Early Blight in Natural Epiphytotic Condition

[1]V. Kumar, [2]R.C. Gupta, P.C. Singh[1], R.P. Singh[1] and J. Singh[2]

## ABSTRACT

Early blight of tomato caused by Alternaria solani a serious disease throughout the country as well as in tropical and subtropical countries of the world. The maximum disease severity occurs during February to March at the time of peak crop growth. To find out the resistant source sixty seven tomato genotypes were screened during the cropping season viz. 2003-2004 and 2004-2005 in the month of February-March under natural epiphytotic condition. EC-508765, & EC-538994 and few cultivars i.e. RCMT-1, KS-118, H-88-78-sps-3, EC-538393 were found moderately resistant. Few other lines like DT-1, SKUT-2, ZTH-1037, Bio-wonder and VLT-87 were also found moderately resistant but became susceptible at late stage progress in both the year. Disease intensity was recorded up to 100% in many varities.

**Keywords:** (Early blight, Alternaria solani, genotype/ Cultivar, PDI).

Vegetable crop have an important place in the agricultural economy in India. Tomato (*Lycopersicon esculentum* Mill.) is one of the most popular and widely grown vegetable in the world ranking second in importance to potato including India. (1). Early blight of tomato caused by *A. solani* (Ellis & Martin) Sorauer is the most destructive disease of tomato in tropical and sub tropical countries. Diseases are one of the most limiting factors for production of tomato. It also reduces quantity and market value. There are several fungal , bacterial, viral and nematode diseases which are associated with tomato. Alternaria affects the whole plant parts such as leaves, stem, and fruits. Yield loss of tomato fruit was 78% at the disease intensity of 72% with each 1% increase in the intensity reducing tomato yield by 1.36% has been reported (4). Management of Early blight with chemicals is not effective under weather conditions favourable for epidemics. Moreover, spray of fungicides is not feasible because the disease always appears at fruit maturity when the crop is almost ready to be harvested. The residual effect of fungicides causes health hazards to human being. Growing

1 Department of Botany, Udai Pratap Autonomous College Varanasi India
2 Department of Mycology and Plant Pathology, Institute of Agricultural Sciences, Banaras Hindu University, Varanasi India

resistant varieties is the only effective and feasible technique for early blight management. Most of the available resistance sources are not in practical use due to several unacceptable qualitative and quantitative attributes. It is not easy to transfer resistant characteristics into cultivated varieties. However a few commercial cultivars with a moderate but useful degree of resistance have been released (6). Keeping in a view the above facts, the present study was undertaken to sreen some tomato genotypes against the early blight infection at Indian Institute of Vegetable Research Farm, Varanasi.

### Materials And Methods

Total sixty seven cultivars were screened against early blight resistant during the year 2003-2004 and 2004-2005 in the month of February - March under natural epiphytotic conditions. The seedling of tomato was raised separately in nursery and 25 days old tomato seedlings were transplanted in first week of December.In each plots 20 seedlings were maintained of each varieties with 45 × 60 cm spacing. Average disease severity of early blight was recorded after 60 days of transplanting. Ten plant from each plot was randomly selected, and scored individually using 0-5 rating scale based on leaf area, stem, and fruit parts covered by a blight symptoms. Disease incidence was recoded on the basis of percent-infected leaves, and stem. The scoring of disease intensity was recorded as reported by Pandey *et al.*, (6) the data were taken 3 times at 10 days periodical interval i.e. 107 DAT,116 DAT and 126 DAT to see the disease progress of early blight. Percentage disease index (PDI), and area under disease progress curve (AUDPC) (Shaner, and Finney (8), Johnson, and Wilcoxson (5), Campbell, and Madden (2) were calculated as follows:

The mean value of the PDI from first to last observations was also calculated. Host plant reaction was classified based on the mean PDI value as highly resistant (0-5%) resistant (5.1–12%), moderately resistant (12.1–25%), moderately susceptible (25.1-50%), susceptible (50.1-75) highly susceptible (>75%). These methodologies were applied for the plant under natural epidemics in the field conditions.

$$\text{PDI} = \frac{\text{Sum of all rating}}{\text{Total no. of observations} \times \text{Maximum rating grade}} \times 100$$

**Table 3.1 Varietal reaction against early blight under field conditions**

| Mean PDI value | | Progress of PDI (2003-2004) | | | Progress of PDI (2004-2005) | | |
|---|---|---|---|---|---|---|---|
| 0-5 rating scale 0-5 | Reaction HR | 107 DAT | 116 DAT | 126 DAT | 107 DAT | 116 DAT | 126 DAT |
| 5.1-12 % | R | EC- 508765, EC- 538394 | EC-508765, EC-538394 | EC-508765, EC-538394 | EC-508765, EC-538394 | EC-508765, EC-538394 | EC-508765, EC-538394 |
| 12.1-25% | MR | RCMT-1,KS-118,H-88-78-sps-3,EC-538393 | RCMT-1, KS-118, H-88-78-sps-3, EC-538393 | RCMT-1, KS-118, H-88-78-sps-3, EC-538393 | RCMT-1, KS-118, H-88-78-SPS-3, EC-538393 | RCMT-1, KS-118, H-88-78-sps-3, EC-53839 | RCMT-1, KS-118, H-88-78-sps-3, EC-53839 |

| | | | | | | | |
|---|---|---|---|---|---|---|---|
| 25.1-50% | MS | VNR-43, JKTH-3054, Praveen, SMTH-203, S-108, ZTH-1039, Bio-wonder, ARTH-3, TH-317, VRTH-1, ZTH-1037, SMTH-202, TH-10848, Hy6-108, JKTH-3053, VLT-34, ATL-9744, DT-1, SKUT-2, VLT-87, NDTS-2001-02, JTL-2, and KDTS-61 | | | VNR-43,Rishi-7, JKTH-3054, Praveen, SMTH-203, S-108, ZTH-1039, Bio-wonder, TH-1, ARTH-3, TH-317, VRTH-1, ZTH-1037, SMTH-202, TH-10848, Hy-6-108, JKTH-3053, VLT-34, ATL-9744, DT-1, SKUT-2, VLT-87, NDTS-2001-02, JTL-2, KDTS-61 | | |
| 50.1-75% | S | | VNR-43, Rishi-7, JKTH-3054, Praveen, BSS-422, SMTH-203, S-108, Rishi-II, VNR-15, ZTH-3037, JKTH-3064, ZTH-317, SMTH-31, ZTH-1039, TH-1, ARTH-3, NTH-976, Hg-10848, TH-01462, NTH-960, TH-317, VRTH-1, SMTH-202, NTH-01462, TH-10848, ARTH-1, TH-012, Hy6-108, JKTH-3053, DVRT-2, BT-107, Punjab Upama, BT-201, VLT-8, VLT-34, ATL-9744, BT-120, Sel-1, BT-1, SKUT-2, VLT-87, NDTS-2001-02, ZTH-1037, SMTH-202, TH-10848, Hy6-108, JKTH-3053, VLT-34, ATL-9744, DT-10, JTL-2, KS-16, KDTS-61 and TH-977 | | | VNR-43, Rishi-7, JKTH-3054, Praveen, BSS-422, SMTH-203, S-108, RIshi-II, VNR-15, ZTH-3037, JKTH-3064, ZTH-317, SMTH-31, ZTH-1039, TH-1, ARTH-3, NTH-976, Hg-10848, TH-01462, NTH-960,TH -317, VRTH-1, SMTH-202, NTH-01462, TH-10848, ARTH-1, TH-012, Hy-6-108, JKTH-3053, DVRT-2, VT-107, Punjab upama, BT-201, VLT-8, VLT-34, ATL-9744, VT-120, Sel-1, BT-1 SKUT-2, VLT-87, NDTS-2001-02, ZTH-1037, SMTH-202,TH-10848, Hy6-108, JKTH-3053, VLT-34, ATL-9744, VT-1, SKUT-2, VLT-87, NDTS-2001-02, DT-10,JTL-2, KS-16, KDTS-61, and TH-977 | |

| >75% | HS | | | VNR-43, Rishi-7, JKTH-3054, Praveen, BSS-422, SMTH-203, S-108, Rishi-III, VNR-15, ZTH-3037, JKTH-3064, ZTH-317, SMTH-2002, ZTH-1039, Bio-wonder, TH-1, ARTH-3, NTH-976, Hg-10848, TH-017, BSS-419, TH-01462, COTH-1,NTH-960, TH-317, VRTH-1, ZTH-1037, SMTH-202, DTH-41, NTH-01462, TH-10848, AQRTH-1, BSS—412, TH-012, Hy6-108, VNR-1, JKTH-3053, DVRT-2, CO-3, BT-107, Punjab upama, HADT-3,VLT-82, BT-201, VLT-8, VLT-34, ATL,9744, BT-120, DARL-65, KDTS-71, Sel-1, DT-1,SKUT-2, VLT-87, NDTS-2001-02, DT-10, JTL-2,Arka Vikash, KS-16, KDTS-61, TH-977 | | | VNR-43, Rishi-7, JKTH-3054, Praveen, BSS-422, SMTH-203, S-108,Rishi-III, VNR-15, ZTH-3037, JKTH-3064, ZTH-317, SMTH-2002, ZTH-1039, Bio-wonder, TH-1, ARTH-3,NTH-976, Hg-10848, TH-017, BSS-419, TH-01462, COTH-1, NTH-960, TH-317,VRTH-1, ZTH-1037, SMTH-202, TH-10848, ARTH-1,BSS-412, TH-012, Hy6-108,VNR-1, JKTH-3053,DVRT-2, CO-3, BT-107, Punjab upama, HADT-3, VLT-82, BT-201, VLT-8, VLT-34,ATL-9744, BT-120, DARL-65, KDTS-71, Sel-1,DT-1, SKUT-2, VLT-87, NDTS-2001-02, DT-10, JTL-2, Arka Vikas, KS-16, KDTS-61, TH-977 |
|---|---|---|---|---|---|---|---|

## Results

In order to find out the resistant source against the early blight, available cultivars of tomato were screened during 2003-2004 and 2004-2005 under the natural epiphytotic conditions, where the disease severity remained very high during the cropping season. Disease severity was recorded using 0-5 rating scale on randomly selected plants, and finally per cent disease index was calculated for each tomato cultivars. The data were taken 3 times at periodical intervals to see the disease progress of early blight and has been presented in Table 3.1. Among the 67 genotypes of tomato, the maximum number of cultivars were found highly susceptible, only two lines such as EC-508765 and EC-538394 were found resistant and four lines viz. RCMT-1, KS-118, H—88-78-sps-3 and EC-

538393 were found moderately resistant in all three observations, remaining 61 genotypes such as VNR-43, JKTH-3054, Praveen, SMTH-203, S-108,ZTH-1039, Bio-wonder etc. (Table-1) were found moderately susceptible and became susceptible during the first and second observations in both of the years respectively. But due to disease progress it become highly susceptible against early blight in third observation, where disease intensity was recorded very high and reached up to 100% in both of the successive year.

**Discussion**

The observation given in the table1 clearly revealed that all these test tomato cultivars showed highly susceptible reaction on 3rd observation taken at least stage of crop. Previous data taken during 1st, and 2nd observations revealed that few tomato cultivars were moderately susceptible but later due to disease progress it became highly susceptible against early blight. The third observation was taken in first week of April and during the period high humidity and high temperature ranging from 80% – 95% R.H. and temperature was in between 25-28°C. High humidity and high temperature was found most congenial for spreading of the disease. So that disease intensity was recorded very High up to 100% in third observation. Stevenson and Pennypacker (9) also reported that when the ambient Temperature was near 25°C and relative humidity 96 per cent, the conidia of *A. solani* germinated most rapidly, it was the major cause of the increasing the disease intensity. Therefore this temperature and humidity was found more suitable for increasing the disease severity. The severity of the disease recorded 100% in first year of cropping season while in second year the PDI value was recorded slightly lesser.

Initially few lines like DT-1, SKUT-2, ZTH-1037, Bio-wonder, and VLT-87 were found moderately susceptible but became susceptible at later stage. The disease index in temp. material varied from 32 to 74 per cent in 1st observation taken after 107 days of transplanting in the second week of February 2004 and 2005 the disease index increased between 51.33-82.66 per cent within next ten days. However, disease severity was comparatively very high on the same materials during 1st week of April, and varied between 71-100 per cent. The high disease severity was recorded in first year (2003-2004) cropping season as compared to year 2004-2005. Few cultivar's such as VNR-15, TH-017, TH-317, ZTH-103, TH-10848, TH-012, Hy6-08 and VNR-1. The disease severity was recorded 100% in first year of cropping season while in second year the PDI value was slightly low. Castro *et al.* (8) observation the effect of inoculums concentration of *A. solani* (0.625; 1.25; 5.0; and 1 × $10^3$ conidia/ml) on the resistant of tomato cultivar's Santa Clara ( Susceptible ), CNPH-353, an NCEBR-2 (resistant) under green house conditions. The concentration at $10^4$ conidia/ml made it possible to distinguish resistant, and susceptible genotypes of the tomato studied. But our experiment was carried out its natural epiphytotic condition so it is completely different from natural screening of tomato genotypes. In a separate study Prasad, and Naik (7) reported that the nine genotypes (Arka-Alok, Arka -Abha, Arka Meghali, Arka Sourabh, IIHR-305, IIHR -308, IIHR -2266, IIHR -2285, and IIHR - 2288) were resistant , 11 genotypes were moderately resistant to the Pathogen.

An insight into the results obtained revealed that generally, no cultivars showed complete resistant to the disease even though few lines showed partial or incomplete resistant during the year 2004, as crop age increased disease intensity was also increased. Similar types of observations were recorded by Pandey *et al.*(6)during artificial inoculations of the pathogen in polyhouse conditions. They found, tomato cultivars CLN - 2071- C, CLN - 2070-A, BSS -174 and DTH-41 as slow blighting resistance against four pathogenic isolate of *A. solani*. The present findings emphasized the need for further evaluation of more number of lines against early blight to find the resistance sample, which can be used , a donor source for breeding of disease resistance programme in future.

## REFERENCES


BOSE, T. K. ; J. KABIR; T. K. MAITY; V. A. PARTHASARATHY, and M.G. SOM 2002. "Vegetable Crops" Volume-1, pp.69 (1-154).

CAMPBELL, C.L., L.V. MADDEN 1990. Introduction to plant disease epidemiology, John Wiley, and Sons Inc. New York. 165p.

CASTRO, M.E.A.;G.M.CHAVES; L. ZAMBOLIM; C.D. CRUZ, and D.J.H. SILVA 1999. Effect of inoculums bconcentration on the resistance of tomato to Alternaria solani . Fitopathologia Brasileira, 24(3): 463-465.

DATAR, V.V. AND MAYEE, C.D. 1985. Chemical management of early blight of tomato. Journal of Maharastra Agricultural Unversities, 10: 3, 278-280.

JOHNSON, D.A., AND R.D. WILCOXON 1982. A table of area under disease progress curves. Technical Bulletin, Texas Agricultural Experiment Station, Texas, 122 p.

PANDEY, K.K.; P.K. PANDEY; GAUTAM KALLOO, and M.K. BENERJEE 2003. Resistance to early blight of tomato with respect to various parameters of disease epidemics. *Journal of General Plant Pathology,* **69** (6): 364-371.

PRASAD, Y., and M. K. NAIK 2003. Evaluation of genotypes, fungicides, and plant extracts against blight of tomato caused by Alternaria solani. Indian Journal of Plant Protection, 31 (2): 49-53.

SHANER, G., and R.E. FINNEY 1977. The effect of nitrogen fertilization on the expression of slow mildewing resistance in knox wheat. Phytopathology, 67: 1051-1056.

STEVENSON, R.E., and S.P. PENNYPACKER 1988. Effect of radiation, temperature, and moisture on conidial germination of *Alternaria solani. Phytopathology* **78:** 7, 926-930.

**Early Blight Disease of Tomato**
*Edited by:* Virendra Kumar
ISBN: 978-93-5056-879-8
*Edition:* 2017
*Published by:* Discovery Publishing House Pvt. Ltd., New Delhi (India)

# Evaluation of Different Germplasms/Cultivars of Tomato against Early Blight (*Alternaria solani*) in Field Conditions and by Artificial Inoculation Method: A Review Article

[1]Virendra Kumar, [2]Faiza Naeem, [3]Ajay Kumar

## ABSTRACT

An experiment was conducted for evaluation of tomato germplasm in field conditions and by artificial inoculation method in polyhouse conditions against early blight for two successive years at tomato farm of Swar region of Rampur district during cropping season from February to March. The total 141 tomato germplasms/cultivars were screened, including wild accessions, exotic collection, indigenous cultivars and advanced lines. Among the 141 germplasms, 5 wild accessions viz. EC-520057, EC-520058, EC-520059, EC-52061 and EC-501583 exhibited complete resistant against early blight and 10 lines viz. RCMT-1, LA-40-40-1, KS-118, H-88-78-3, IIVR-Sel-2, H-88-78-1, EC-538394, EC-538404, NCEBR-4 and EC-508765 found moderately resistant. The 36 cultivars were found moderately susceptible where disease severity was recorded up to 70%. The 55 cultivars were found to be susceptible and 35 were reported as highly susceptible where disease severity recorded up to 100% under the field screening. In another set of experiment spore suspension of having the three different cfu levels *i.e.* 125, 185 and 245 were sprayed on pot experiment under polyhouse conditions on 25 cultivars of tomato to check susceptibility of tomato plant, the higher values of cfu (i.e. 245 cfu) of A. solani were able to break the immunity of plants, in which KDTS-71, DVRT-1-2, CO-3, PANT-T-3 and VFN-8 were found to be highly susceptible to early blight in field screening as well as polyhouse conditions.

**Keywords:** (Early blight, Alternaria solani, genotype/Cultivar, PDI).

## Introduction

Early blight is the most important disease of tomato in India and caused by two pathogens *i.e. Alternaria solani* and *Alternaria alternata* f. sp. *lycopersici*. It is also a common problem in United Kingdom, Australia and United States. Symptoms of early blight appear on all above ground parts of the plant. The disease appears

1 Regional Pesticides Testing Laboratory, Ministry of Agriculture, Government of India, Department of Agriculture and Co-operation, Directorate of Plant Protection, Quarantine & Storage, Kanpur, India.

2 Govt. Raza P.G. College, Rampur, India.

3 Department of Botany, Kashi Naresh Govt. P.G. College, Gyanpur, India.

first as spots on leaflet; spots are circular to angular, dark brown to black and range from pin head to 4 mm in diameter. Leaf spots are scattered, brown with conspicuous concentric rings surrounded by chloratic halo on their outer margin due to host specific toxin produced by the pathogen. The stem lesions are usually restricted elongations and sunken. The fruit symptoms initiate generally at the end of February and radiate between attachment of calyx and fruit and are dark brown depressed, firm with distinct concentric rings (**Plate 1(b)**). Mostly disease appears in vegetative phase of the plant growth before flowering and is more prevalent between flowering to fruit ripening and continue till the crop completely senescent.

Tomato crop is damaged due to severe infection of *A. solani* every year in India. The yield loss of tomato fruit recorded is 78% at 72% disease intensity of *A. solani* and each 1% increase in reduced tomato yield by 1.36%. The disease severity was recorded up to 90% [2] in Varanasi region. It is also one of the commonest causes of seedling blight or damping off in tomato, causing dark lesion in rootlets [2]. The genetic resources of all wild species of *Lycopersicon* spp. have been extensively exploited as resource of early blight resistance. [3] also re-ported that tomato cultivars CLN-2071, CLN-2070-A BSS-174 and DTH-7 with resistance expressed as slow blightening against four pathogenic isolates of *A. solani* were selected for cultivation in disease prone areas. Diseased intensity increased with the age of plant under same inoculum load. [4] identified the two resistant source lines IIHR-1939 (*L. pimpinellifoloum* L. 4394) and IIHR-1939 (*L. esculentum* NCEBR-1). No genetic resource is known within the cultivated species of tomato. However, resistant accessions have been identified within related wild species of tomato, in particular the green fruited species *L. hirsutum* and the red fruited species *L. pimpinellifoloum*. A number of control measures were suggested by different researchers for minimizing the disease losses but the use of resistant cultivars remained the most reliable and economical one [5]. Non-judicial use of fungicides adds human and environmental hazards. Thus, availability of resistant to moderately resistant cultivars may reduce the dependency on fungicides and can also be an effective component of inte-grated disease management. Therefore the present study was undertaken for the screening of tomato cultivars for incidence of early blight under field condition as well as polyhouse conditions by artificial inoculation method.

## Materials and Methods

### *Field Screening*

The present investigation was carried out during the winter season in Swar region of Rampur District of Uttar Pradesh, India, at tomato farm with total 141 germplasms/cultivars of tomato. The seedlings of tomato were collected from Indian Institute of Vegetable Research (IIVR), Varanasi and were raised separately in nursery and 25 days old tomato seedlings were transplanted in first week of December in both of the successive years. In each plot, 20 seedlings were maintained of each variety with 40 × 60 cm spacing. Disease severity of early blight was recorded after 126 days of transplantation. 10 plants from each plot were randomly selected and scored individually using 0 – 5 rating scale based on leaf area, stem and fruit parts covered by blight symptoms. Per cent disease index was recorded as by [6] [7] and [8] were calculated as follows:

The mean value of PDI from first to last observations was also calculated according to [9]. Host plant reaction was classified based on the mean PDI value as highly resistant (0 - 5 rating scale).

$$\text{PDI} = \frac{\text{Sum of all rating} \times 100}{\text{Total No. of observation} \times \text{Maximum rating grade}}$$

The disease incidence was recorded as by [9]. The data were taken in the month of March on the basis of PDI values. The host plant reaction was classified as resistant (0%) if no sign of blight symptoms appeared, moderately resistant (1% - 25%) if blight symptoms appeared approx 25%, moderately susceptible if blight symptoms appeared in between (26% - 50%), susceptible if symptoms appeared between (51% - 75%) and highly susceptible if blight symptoms appeared in between (76% - 100%) on above ground parts of the plants. These methodologies were applied for the plants under natural epidemic in field conditions as well as in polyhouse experiment.

## Screening of Germplasms/Cultivars in Polyhouse Condition

In order to confirm the immunity of the cultivars an experiment was conducted under polyhouse conditions. In pot experiment, against 25 germplasms/ cultivars of tomato (**Table 1**) at three cfu level of spore suspension of *A. solani* ( *i.e.* 125, 185 and 245 cfu) were standardized for inoculation purposes. For this purpose five representa-tives of each cultivar of tomato were taken from each resistant, moderately resistant, moderately susceptible, susceptible and highly susceptible varieties, by previously mentioned methods of screening. Seedlings of the cultivars were raised in pot filled with sterilized soil (**Plates 1(c)- (e)**). Inoculations were done by different levels of cfu of fungal spore suspension on the one month-old-seedling. Ten days old culture of *A. solani* was taken to prepare spore suspensions which were isolated from native tomato leaf samples and it was grounded in 50 ml of sterilized distilled water with the help of sterilized pestle and mortar. It was filtered with sterilized muslin cloth in a clean conical flask aseptically. $cfu_s$ of culture of *A. solani* suspension were measured on Potato dextrose, rose Bengal, agar medium and standardized three different cfu levels. For maintaining the humidity, a humidifi-er was set up in this chamber around the pot seedlings of tomato and the temperature was maintained for the de-velopment of the symptoms. The percent disease incidence was rated as suggested by [9]. The data were taken on $9^{th}$ day to see the immunity of the different cultivars of tomato.

**Table 4.1 PDI values of different cultivars at three cfu level under polyhouse condition**

| Cultivars | PDI values | | | Reaction |
|---|---|---|---|---|
| | At 125 | At 185 | At 245 | |
| EC-520057 | 0.0 | 0.0 | 0.0 | Resistant |
| EC-520058 | 0.0 | 0.0 | 0.0 | Resistant |
| EC-520059 | 0.0 | 0.0 | 0.0 | Resistant |
| EC-520061 | 0.0 | 0.0 | 0.0 | Resistant |
| EC-520083 | 0.0 | 0.0 | 0.0 | Resistant |
| EC-538154 | 12.0 | 22.0 | 23.0 | Moderately resistant |
| FEB-4-1 | 11.5 | 18.0 | 20.0 | Moderately resistant |
| PDVR-14 | 13.0 | 16.5 | 24.0 | Moderately resistant |
| NCEBR-4 | 10.0 | 13.6 | 18.0 | Moderately resistant |
| H-88-78-5 | 14.0 | 16.5 | 23.5 | Moderately resistant |
| IIVR-Sel-2 | 30.0 | 38.0 | 44.0 | Moderately susceptible |
| H-88-78-1 | 28.0 | 36.0 | 45.0 | Moderately susceptible |
| EC-508765 | 36.0 | 42.0 | 48.5 | Moderately susceptible |
| RCM-1 | 40.5 | 46.0 | 49.0 | Moderately susceptible |
| DVRT-2 | 27.0 | 33.0 | 44.0 | Moderately susceptible |
| Punjab chhuhara | 52.5 | 65.0 | 74.0 | Susceptible |
| Arka-Saurabh | 58.0 | 64.0 | 72.0 | Susceptible |
| IIVR-Sel-3 | 56.0 | 60.5 | 68.5 | Susceptible |
| DARL-63 | 57.5 | 68.5 | 71.5 | Susceptible |
| VLT-34 | 53.5 | 63.3 | 67.3 | Susceptible |
| KDTS-71 | 98.5 | 99.0 | 100.0 | Highly susceptible |
| DVRT-1-2 | 79.3 | 86.5 | 89.0 | Highly susceptible |
| CO-3 | 100.0 | 100.0 | 100.0 | Highly susceptible |
| PANT-T-3 | 78.0 | 88.3 | 98.5 | Highly susceptible |
| VFN-8 | 81.0 | 88.3 | 100.0 | Highly susceptible |

(a) (b)

(c) (d)

(e) (f)

**Plate 4.1: (a) Circular spot with concentric rings; (b) Apical infection on fruits; (c)-(e) Three susceptible varieties of tomato for pathogenicity test; (f) *In vivo* infection on tomato as stem girdling with sunken lesion.**

## Results

### *Weather and Disease Development*

Symptoms of early blight were observed within the two week of transplanting as dark brown lesion with concentric rings initially on lower leaves. Stem lesions appeared much later followed by infection on fruits in last week of February

(**Plate 1(a)** & **Plate 1(b)**). The disease developed gradually and spread across the whole field assisted by humidity and higher temperature defoliation and infection was more sever in last week of February, when relative humidity (R.H.) were highest up to 89% in first year. The total rainfall recorded 0.00 m and tem-perature 26.7°C with 7.2 hrs sunshine was most favourable for the disease development. Therefore the similar observations were recorded in fourth week of February during second year. The total rainfall recorded was 032.2 m and 26.2°C with 7.9 hrs sunshine most favourable for the disease development (**Table 2**).

### Reactions of Cultivars to Leaf Blight in Field Screening

In order to find out the resistant source against the early blight, available cultivars of tomato were screened in natural field conditions and polyhouse conditions, where the disease severity remained very high during the cropping season. Disease severity was recorded using 0 - 5 rating scale on randomly selected plants and finally PDI was calculated for each tomato cultivar. The data was taken 3 times at periodical intervals to see the disease progress of early blight and has been presented in **Table 3**. Among the 141 genotypes of tomato, the maximum number of cultivars were found highly susceptible, only five lines such as EC-501583, EC-520058, EC-520061, EC-520059, and EC-520057 were found resistant in natural field conditions and ten tomato germplasms *i.e.* RCM-1, LA-4040, KS-118, H-888-78-3, IIVR- Sel-2, H-8-78-1, EC -538394, EC-538404, NCEBR-4 and EC-508765 were found moderately resistant. Thirty six germplasms viz. DVRT-2, VTG-87, DARL-64, SKUAT-2, DT-2, PANT-T-7, JTP-02-7, ATL -97-44, DARL-63, IIVR-SEL-3, VLT-34, BT-120, DT-1, DT -10, ARKA VIKASH, BT-136, NDTS-2002-3, H-86-3, LA-4012-1, F-5013-3, LA-17-1, F-7045-1, F-6012-1, F-701-1, F-7025-1, F-5013-4, F-4036-1, F-6050-1, F-6102-1, Punjab Chhuhara, Arka -Saurabh, IST-7, Shalimar, LA-7421, Naptune and Swarna Vaibhav were found to be moderately susceptible in field screening. While fifty five were found to be susceptible and thirty five were found to be highly susceptible in field conditions (**Table 3**).

### Reaction of Cultivars to Leaf Blight in Polyhouse Conditions

The twenty five cultivars of tomato were tested against *A. solani* at the three cfu levels of spore suspension (*i.e.* 125, 185 and 245 cfu) under the polyhouse conditions. Among them the five wild accessions *i.e.* EC-501583, EC-520058, EC- 520061, EC-520059, and EC-520057 were showing complete resistant and the per cent disease index were recorded as 0%. The ten cultivars, EC-538154, FEB-4 -1, PDVR-14, NCEBR-4, H-88-78-5, IIVR-Sel-2, H-88-78-1, EC-508765, RCM-1 and DVRT-2 were found to be moderately resistant where the PDI were recorded up to 10% - 49% at all three $cfu_s$ and five (Punjab chhuhara, Arka-Saurabh, IIVR-Sel-3, DARL-63 and VLT-34) were susceptible where PDI were recorded between 52.5% - 74%. The five cultivars (KDTS-71, DVRT-1-2, CO-3, PANT-T-3 and VFN-8) were found to be highly susceptible where PDI were recorded in be-tween 78% - 100% at all tested cfu levels (**Table 1** and **Figure 1**).

**Table 4.2: Agro-meteorological data recorded at Swar region of district Rampur U.P. India, during first year and second year**

| First year | | Temperature (°C) | | RH (%) | | Sunshine Hour | Total rainfall (mm) | Evapo-ration (mm) |
|---|---|---|---|---|---|---|---|---|
| St week | Period | Max | Min | Max | Min | | | |
| 6 | FEB 05-11 | 26.7 | 11.5 | 89 | 58 | 7.2 | 000.0 | 2.3 |
| 7 | FEB 12-18 | 29.5 | 13.7 | 81 | 41 | 9.0 | 000.0 | 2.8 |
| 8 | FEB 19-25 | 31.1 | 15.6 | 76 | 38 | 9.8 | 000.0 | 3.7 |
| 9 | FEB 26-04 | 30.6 | 14.0 | 76 | 36 | 8.0 | 000.0 | 3.3 |
| **Second year** | | | | | | | | |
| 6 | FEB 05-11 | 22.2 | 13.1 | 89 | 70 | 3.6 | 035.6 | 1.6 |
| 7 | FEB 12-18 | 23.1 | 12.1 | 81 | 55 | 6.2 | 030.6 | 1.9 |
| 8 | FEB 19-25 | 26.1 | 9.9 | 80 | 43 | 10.0 | 001.4 | 2.7 |
| 9 | FEB 26-04 | 26.2 | 13.0 | 80 | 50 | 7.9 | 032.2 | 2.9 |

## Discussion

The observations given in the **Table 4.2** clearly reveal that all these test tomato cultivars show resistant (R), moderately resistant (MR), moderately susceptible (MS), susceptible (S) and highly susceptible (HS) reactions at all $cfu_s$ *i.e.* at 125, 185 and 245. The third observation was taken from first week of February to last week of February during first and second years and during the periods of high humidity and high temperature conditions ranging from 76% - 89% R.H. and temperature was in between 26°C - 30°C. High humidity and high tempera-ture were found most congenial for spreading of the disease. So, at high humidity and high temperature disease intensity was recorded very high up to 100%. [10] also reported that when the ambient temperature was near 25°C and relative humidity was 96%, the conidia of *A. solani* germinated most rapidly. Therefore,

**Table 4.3 Reaction of different germplasm/cultivars against early blight disease of tomato under field condition**

| Mean PDI value in % | Reaction | Genotype/cultivar (in field) |
|---|---|---|
| 0% | R | EC-501583, EC-520058, EC-520061, EC-520059, and EC-520057 **(05)** |
| 1% - 25% | MR | RCM-1, LA-4040, KS-118, H-888-78-3, IIVR-Sel-2, H-8-78-1, EC-538394, EC-538404, NCEBR-4 and EC-508765, **(10)** |
| 26% - 50% | MS | DVRT-2, VTG-87, DARL-64, SKUAT-2, DT-2, PANT-T-7, JTP-02-7, ATL-97-44, DARL-63, IIVR-SEL-3, VLT-34, BT-120, DT-1, DT-10, ARKA VIKASH, BT-136, NDTS-2002-3, H-86-3, LA-4012-1, F-5013-3, LA-17-1, F-7045-1, F-6012-1, F-701-1, F-7025-1, F-5013-4, F-4036-1, F-6050-1, F-6102-1, Punjab Chhuhara, ArkaSaurabh, IST-7, Shalimar, LA-7421, Naptune and Swarna Vaibhav **(36)** |

| | | |
|---|---|---|
| 51% - 75% | S | KDTS-71, RCMT-2, IMPROVED SHALIMAR-1, DNTS-2002-2, DARL-62, PB UPMA, PANT-T-3, PDT-3-1-1, VRT-42-1, F-6109-1, F-5010-1, NDTVR-60-1, F-4036-2, EC-519731-1, F-4049-1, H-86-1, TLH-30-1, F-70111-1, F-6014-2, DVRT-1-1, VRT-40-2, F-5070-2, LA-3947-1, 126PD-1, PDT-3-1, H-86-2, VRT-1-1, F-6010-1, F-5013-2, LA-4049-1, LA-405-1, F-5013-1, F-6004-1, F-6016-1, VRT-2-1, LA-3951-1, LA-303-1, VRT-35-1, LA-3997-1, F-40000002-1, F-5025-1, F-6021-1, F-6061-1, VRT-5-1, DVRT-1, F-7028-1, EC-519785-1, VRT-35-2, LA-3940-1, LA-3941-1, VRT-41-1, IIVR-41-1, IIVR-SEL-3, CH-3, and KS-16 **(55)** |
| 76% - 100% | HS | CO-3, FLB-2-2, EC-519730-1, FEB-4-2, H-88-1, F-6024-1, DVRT-1-2, VRT-32-1, EC-519769-1, F-6059-1, TLH-27-1, TLH-17-1, LA-3959-1, FEB-4-1, F-4012-1, F-5020-1, TH-806 (F2), H-86, SEL-7, LA-3971-1, F-4047-1, VRT-4-1, F-505-1, HAT-122-1, VRT-40-1, HAT-18-1, FEB-2-1, LA-3772-1, F-6022-1, PANT-T-3, F-7012-1, LA-3772-2, VRT-31-1, VFN-8 and EC-538401 **(35)** |

Where, R = resistant, MR = moderately resistant, MS = moderately susceptible, S = susceptible, HS = highly susceptible.

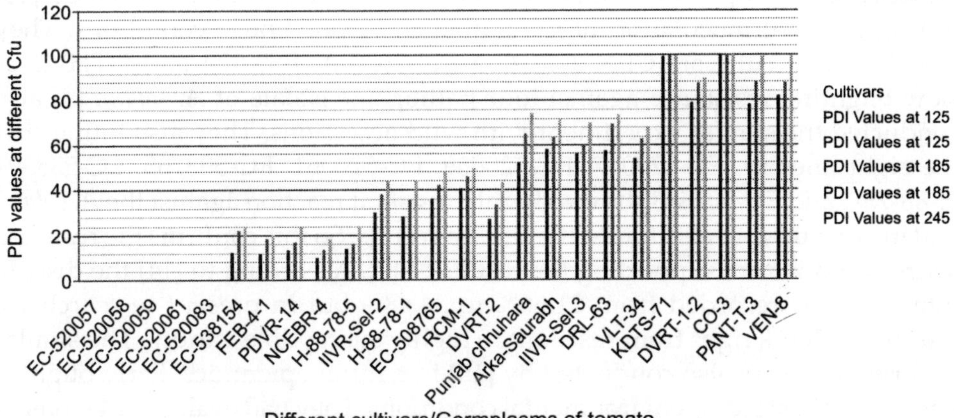


**Fig. 4.1 Per cent disease index (PDI) of different tomato cultivars/germplasm at three cfu$_s$ levels *i.e.*, 125 cfu, 185 cfu and 245 cfu.**

this temperature and humidity were found more suitable for increasing the disease severity. The severity of the disease was recorded 100% in few cultivars at high cfu value level (cfu 245) in KDTS-71, CO-3 and VFN-8. [11] observed effect of inoculums concentration of *A. solani* (0.625; 1.25; 5.0; and 1 × $10^3$ conidia/ml) on the resistant of tomato cultivars found to be, Santa Clara (Susceptible), CNPH-353, and NCEBR-2 (resistant) under green house conditions. The concentration at $10^{-4}$ conidia/ml made it possible to distinguish resistant and sus-ceptible genotypes of the tomato studied. But our experiment was carried out in its natural epiphytotic condition as well as artificial screening. In a separate experiment, [12] reported that the nine genotypes (Arka-Alok, Arka-Abha,

Arka -Meghali, Arka-Sourabh, IIHR-305, IIHR-308, IIHR-2266, IIHR-2285, and IIHR-2288) were resistant, and 11 genotypes were moderately resistant to the pathogen.

An insight into the results obtained revealed that generally, few cultivars showed complete resistant to early blight such as EC-501583, EC-520058, EC-520061, EC-520059, and EC-520057 (wild accessions) in field con-ditions and the same cultivars were found to be complete resistant in polyhouse conditions; even higher cfu level could not break the immunity of these line. It may be possible because the wild cultivars have some specific genes which are responsible for the resistance, that are needed to be studied. These resources may be utilized to make a resistant variety for plant breeder in future. In polyhouse conditions, we tested the germplasm against three $cfu_s$ of the pathogen. In this reference we had found that as the inoculums load of fungal spore increased, the PDI also increased but in case of wild accessions there was no effect of inoculums spore load. We are also observed that high humidity (up to 90%) and high temperature (up to 25°C - 28°C) were the most favourable for disease development. Similar types of observations were recorded by [13] during artificial inoculation of the pathogen in polyhouse conditions. They found tomato cultivars CLN-2071-C, CLN-2070-A, BSS-174 and DTH-41 as slow blighting resistance against four pathogenic isolate of *A. solani.* [9] also conducted the similar experiment with wild accessions. They also found that the eight lines *i.e.* EC-520057, EC-520059, EC-520061, EC-508765, EC-538394 H-88-78-1 and EC-501583 showed highly resistant reaction against the *A. solani,* and in our study we also found the similar results. So this confirms the resistant sources and we are supporting the results of [9]. According to [14] the disease intensity was recorded from 21.66% to 34.48% but in present re-search we found 0 to 100% right from resistant to highly susceptible variety. The similar experiments were also conducted by [15] in natural epidemics. Early blight is strongly influenced by environmental conditions. They had evaluated 44 tomato genotypes against early blight and found the highest early blight incidence in PS-1 (73.56%) and Kashi Amrit (71.12%) etc. We have also evaluated DVRT -1-2 (*i.e.* Kashi Amrit) and the PDI was recorded 89.0% (**Table 3** in HS Category). So this information may be utilized as a resistant source of tomato and may be beneficial to the farmers as a resistant source for tomato farming. The present findings emphasized the need for further evaluation of more number of lines against early blight to find the resistant sample. It should be screened at molecular levels and also it can be used, as a donor source for breeding of disease resistance program in future.

**Acknowledgements**

Authors are very much thankful to Dr. K. K. Pandey and Dr. P. K. Pandey, Division of crop protection, IIVR, Varanasi, India for providing different germplasms/cultivars to carry out present research work.

## REFERENCES

Datar, V.V. and Mayee, C.D. (1985) Chemical Management of Early Blight of Tomato. *Journal of Maharashtra Agri-cultural Universities*, **10**, 278-280.

Pandey, K.K., Pandey, P.K., Kalloo, G. and Benerjee, M.K. (2003) Resistance to Early Blight of Tomato with Respect to Various Parameters of Disease Epidemics. *Journal of General Plant Pathology*, **69**, 364-371. http://dx.doi.org/10.1007/s10327-003-0074-7

Bose, T.K., Kabir, J., Maithy, T.K., Parthasarathy, V.A. and Som, M.G. (2002) Vegetable Crops. Vol. 1, 1-154.

Thirthamallappa and Lohithaswa, H.C. (2000) Genetic and Resistance to Early Blight in Tomato. *Euphytica*, **13**, 187-193. http://dx.doi.org/10.1023/A:1003929303632

Keinath, A.A., DuBose, V.B. and Rathwell, P.J. (1996) Efficacy and Economics of Three Fungicidal Application Schedule for Early Blight and Yield of Fresh Market Tomato. *Plant Disease*, **80**, 1277-1282. http://dx.doi.org/10.1094/PD-80-1277

Shaner, G. and Finney, R.E. (1977) The Effect of Nitrogen Fertilization on the Expression of Slow Mildewing Resis-tance in Knox Wheat. *Phytopathology*, **67**, 1051-1056. http://dx.doi.org/10.1094/Phyto-67-1051

Johnson, D.A. and Wilcoxon, R.D. (1982) A Table of Area under Disease Progress Curve. Technical Bulletin, Texas Agriculture Experiment Station, Texas, 122 p.

Campbell, C.L. and Wilcoxon, L.V. (1982) Introduction to Plant Disease Epidemiology, John Wiley and Sons Inc. New York, 165 p.

Prabhash, C.S., Rajesh, K., Major, S., Ashutosh, R., Singh, M.C. and Mathura, R. (2011) Identification of Resistant Sources against Early Blight Disease of Tomato. *Indian Journal of Horticulture*, **68**, 516-521.

Virendra, K., Sanchita, H., Koshlendra, K.P., Rana, P.S., Achuit, K.S. and Prabhas, C.S. (2008) Cultural, Morphologi-cal, Pathogenic and Molecular Variability amongst Tomato Isolates of *Alternaria solani* in India. *World Journal of Microbiology and Biotechnology*, **24**, 1003-1009. http://dx.doi.org/10.1007/s11274-007-9568-3

Stevenson, R.E. and Pennypacker, S.P. (1988) Effect of Radiation, Temperature, and Moisture on Conidial Germina-tion of *Alternaria solani*. *Phytopathology*, **78**, 926-930. http://dx.doi.org/10.1094/Phyto-78-926

Castro, M.E.A., Chaves, G.M., Zambolim, L., Cruz, C.D. and Silva, D.J.H. (1999) Effect of Inoculums Concentration on the Resistance of Tomato to *Alternaria solani*. *Fitopathologia Brasileira*, **24**, 463-465.

Prasad, Y. and Naik, M.K. (2003) Evaluation of Genotypes, Fungicides, and Plant Extracts against Blight of Tomato Caused by *Alternaria solani*. *Indian Journal of Plant Protection*, **31**, 49-53.

Sunita, R., Ranbir, S., Sachin, G., Siddarth, D. and Razdan, V.K. (2015) Identification of Resistant Sources and Epi-demiology of Early Blight (*Alternaria solani*) of Tomato (*Lycopersicon esculentum*) in Jammu and Kashmir. *Indian Phytopathology*, **68**, 87-92.

Sunil, K. and Kartikeya, S. (2013) Screening of Tomato Genotypes against Early Blight (*Alternaira solani*) under Field Condition. *The Bioscan*, **8**, 189-193.

**Early Blight Disease of Tomato**
***Edited by:*** **Virendra Kumar**
**ISBN: 978-93-5056-879-8**
***Edition:*** **2017**
***Published by:*** **Discovery Publishing House Pvt. Ltd., New Delhi (India)**

# Identification of Resistant Sources and Epidemiology of Early Blight (*Alternaria solani*) of Tomato (*Lycopersicum esculentum*) in Jammu and Kashmir

[1]Sunita Rani, [1]Ranbir Singh, [1*]Sachin Gupta,
[2]Siddarth Dubey and [1]V.K. Razdan

## ABSTRACT

Field surveys were conducted during 2011 and 2012 to diagnose the symptoms of early blight disease (Alternaria solani) of tomato (Lycopersicum esculentum L.) in all vegetable-growing areas of Jammu Division of Jammu and Kashmir. The disease intensity and incidence varied from 21.66 to 34.13% and 10.48 to 18.56%, respectively. Progression of early blight disease in 15 genotypes of tomato in relation to different resistant components, viz. size of spot, disease index was studied under field and artificial conditions. Area under disease progress curve (AUDPC) calculated for field studies showed maximum AUDPC of 582.55 exhibited by Pusa Ruby. Three varieties, viz. CO3, Tomato Cherry and Heem Sohna were found moderately resistant, while Pusa Ruby, P-2 and Indam Vaishali were found susceptible under both field and artificial conditions. Maximum lesion size (11.33 mm) was recorded in Pusa Ruby and minimum (4.3 mm) in CO3 under artificial conditions. Weather factors (temperature, humidity and rainfall) were found to play a significant role in the development of early blight of tomato. Disease showed a progressive increase and maximum disease intensity was observed during 21st standard week in Pusa Ruby and minimum severity (12.42%) in CO3 during the same week. The disease intensity exhibited significant and positive simple correlation with minimum and maximum temperature and significant and negative correlation with maximum relative humidity. However, rainfall and minimum relative humidity showed non-significant positive and negative correlation, respectively. Step-wise regression equation was drawn for disease prediction.

**Keywords:** Alternaria solani, early blight, resistance, screening, tomato.

Tomato (*Lycopersicum esculentum* L.) crop is attacked by several pathogens, causing serious diseases. Among fungal diseases, early blight is a major one on tomato. It is caused by fungus *Alternaria solani* (Ellis & Martin) Sorauer. The

[1] Division of Plant Pathology, Sher-e-Kashmir University of Agricultural Sciences and Technology, Faculty of Agriculture, Main Campus, Chatha, 180 009, Jammu, Jammu & Kashmir, India.

[2] Department of Botany, University of Jammu, Jammu 180 006, Jammu & Kashmir, India.

disease is economically most important on tomato in USA, Australia, Israel, UK and India, where significant reduction in yield (35-79%) was observed (Basu, 1974; Datar and Mayee, 1982; Jones *et al.*, 1993). Although, early blight causes heavy losses to tomato in Jammu, there is no proper documentation of the status of disease. The disease in severe stage can lead to complete defoliation. It is most damaging on tomato in regions with heavy dew, rainfall, high humidity, and fairly high temperature (24-29°C). *A. solani* has the capability to grow over a temperature of 4-36°C (Pound, 1951). Epidemics can also take place in semi-arid climate where frequent and prolonged night dews occur (Rotem and Reichert, 1964). An extensive cultivation of susceptible cultivars and hybrids, increasing use of fungicides designed to suppress late blight or grey mould which may not effectively control early blight, and the close succession of tomato crops are important factors contributing to its epidemics. Atmospheric *Alternaria* spores, temperature and humidity are most closely correlated with the occurrence of this disease. An accurate forecast of disease in a geographical area allows for reduction in the use of fungicide treatments, preventing pollution of atmosphere, crops and fields (Frenguelli, 1998). The relationship between disease progression and weather variables is of paramount importance for an effective disease management. The rate of disease increase in fields and cumulative amount of disease over a season (expressed as AUDPC) provide useful overall measures of disease progress.

A number of control measures for minimizing the disease losses have been recommended by different workers but the use of resistant cultivars remains the most reliable and economical one (Keinath *et al.*, 1996). Non-judicial use of fungicides adds human and environmental hazards. Thus, availability of resistant to moderately resistant genotypes may reduce the dependency on fungicides and can also be an effective component of integrated disease management. Therefore, an attempt was made to know the status of early blight on tomato in different areas of Jammu Division in Jammu and Kashmir; to elucidate relationship between weather variables and disease progression and to identify sources of resistance through screening of cultivated tomato lines under artificial as well as natural conditions.

## Materials and Methods

### *Survey*

Fortnightly surveys were conducted during 2011 and 2012 to ascertain the status of early blight disease on tomato in Jammu Division. Five major vegetable-growing areas in three blocks of Jammu, *viz.* Akhnoor, Marh and Vijaypur, were identified for survey. Observations on disease incidence and intensity on foliage as well as fruits were taken at fortnightly intervals starting from the time of appearance of disease symptoms till harvesting (Datar and Mayee, 1986).

***Screening of germplasm***

The experiment was conducted at the Research Farm, Jammu, situated at 32.43$^0$N latitude, 74.54°E longitude and 327 m above mean sea-level. Fifteen germplasm/ varieties of tomato collected from various sources (Division of Vegetable Sciences and Floriculture, SKUAST-Jammu and local market) were evaluated for resistance to early blight under natural conditions. Plots of 2m × 2m size were prepared and four weeks old seedlings were transplanted at a spacing of 60 cm × 45 cm. Recommended doses of N and P were applied. The experiments were laid out in a Randomized Block Design with three replications of each treatment. All the recommended practices except application of fungicides for cultivation of tomato was followed in order to raise a good crop (DEE, Jammu, 2006). Twelve plants of each germplasm/variety were randomly selected and tagged for recording data on disease incidence and intensity 45, 60, 75 and 90 days after transplanting. Disease intensity using 0-5 scale and categorization for varietal reaction was made as per Datar and Mayee (1986).

Host plant reaction based on the mean Per cent Disease Intensity (PDI) was classified as resistant (0.0-9.0), moderately resistant (10.0-25.9), moderately susceptible (26.0-50.9), susceptible (51.0-75.9) and highly susceptible (< 76%). Early blight on tomato is more prevalent during January-April in northern India when it receives congenial condition for its perpetuation. Diseased samples were collected from tomato plots during this period. *Alternaria solani* (early blight pathogen) was isolated from leaves, twigs and fruits of tomato. The pathogen was identified based on spore morphology, septation and pigmentation (Neergard, 1945; Ellis, 1971; Kumar *et al.*, 2008) and was purified by hyphal tip method. The pathogen was multiplied and maintained in potato dextrose agar (PDA) medium.

Artificial screening was done to confirm the field screening during 2011 and 2012. However, under artificial conditions, five-week-old seedlings of each variety/ germplasm were transplanted in earthen pots containing sterilized soil. The seedlings in pots were inoculated by spraying conidial suspension of *A. solani* ($10^6$ spores $ml^{-1}$). Inoculated plants were covered with clear polyethylene bags for 72 h immediately after inoculation to allow infection (Bokshi *et al.*, 2003). The severity of disease on foliage was recorded after every five days by visualizing the area of necrotic spot as per Datar and Mayee (1986).

***Disease assessments and data analysis***

The effect of temperature, relative humidity and rainfall on development of early blight on tomato was studied under field conditions at Research Farm, Chatha, during both the years. The experiment was laid out in RBD with four replications in plots of 2m × 2m size. Observations on disease incidence and intensity were recorded at weekly intervals on randomly selected four plants of each plot following Datar and Mayee (1986). The averages of all weather parameters during each standard week were considered while calculating their effect on disease intensity in terms of correlation and regression analysis. In order to calculate the regression coefficient, maximum temperature, minimum temperature, mean temperature, maximum relative humidity (morning and evening) and rainfall were symbolized as $X_1$, $X_2$, $X_3$, $X_4$ and $X_5$, respectively. The effect of various environmental factors on disease progress was estimated using step-wise regression analysis. The AUDPC was computed using formula of Wilcoxson *et al.* (1975), who quantified the AUDPC as *A*-value:

$$AUDPC = \sum_{i=1}^{k} \frac{1}{2}(y_i + y_{i+1}) \times d$$

where $y_i$ is disease incidence at *ith* day of evaluation, *k* is number of successive evaluations and *d* is interval between *i* and *i*-1 evaluation of disease. Statistical analysis was performed using statistical package SPSS-14.0 version.

## Results and Discussion

### *Occurrence of disease*

The early blight on tomato was observed in all the tomato-growing areas of Jammu region. Per cent disease intensity (PDI) varied from 21.66 to 34.13% with an overall mean of 27.73%, while disease incidence varied from 10.48 to 18.56% with an overall mean of 13.31% at all the locations. In earlier studies, Kanjilal *et al.* (2000) found that early blight on tomato was the most predominant disease with the crop losses of 70-100% in West Bengal, whereas Abhinandan *et al.* (2004) observed that early blight on tomato ranged between 8.2-49.5% at the Tapa and Bababakala locations of Punjab. Yield losses of 0.76 t/ha have been reported in tomato fruits infected by early blight by Poly and Srikanta (2012). The present investigations indicated variable disease incidence as well as disease intensity at different locations. The reason for this discrepancy may be associated with prevalent environmental and/or pathogen factors. Change in weather variables and amount of initial inoculum of *A. solani* may be responsible for varying disease intensities at different locations (Vander-Walls *et al.*, 2003). Lower disease at some locations could be attributed to balance dose of fertilizer, wide spacing besides rapid disposal of debris of previous crop (Duhan and Suhag, 1990).

### *Screening of germplasm*

A total of 15 germplasm/varieties were transplanted and screened against early blight disease under natural epiphytotic conditions. The germplasm/varieties recorded highest disease intensity 90 days after transplanting (DAT) (Table 1). The intensity of disease ranged from 3.72% to 31.36% in CO3 and Pusa Ruby, respectively, 45 DAT. At 60, 75 and 90 DAT, the intensity of disease was maximum, i.e. 39.55%, 50.25%, 56.05% respectively in Pusa Ruby, while it was minimum, i.e. 8.06%, 11.12%, 12.42% 60, 75 and 90 days after transplanting, respectively in CO3. Maximum disease intensity was recorded in Pusa Ruby, followed by P-2 (53.84%). However, minimum disease intensity was observed in CO-3 (12.42%). It was found that there was no significant variation among Maharaja 3004, H-86, GS-2082 and S-22 in respect of disease intensity. During screening, it was observed that symptoms of early blight appeared on all above the ground parts of plants.

Leaf spots were scattered, brown to dark brown in colour with concentric rings. As the natural inoculum pressure increased, the spots coalesced and enlarged during April. Chlorotic halo was also observed around the spots in most of the genotypes. The stem lesions were usually restricted to one side of the stem and become elongated and sunken. Mature stem lesion clearly showed concentric rings. Fruit symptoms gradually progressed on apical portion of fruits as dark brown, depressed, firm with distinct continuous rings. The disease was more prevalent at fruit ripening stage and continued till the crop completely reached to senescence. Generally, early blight of tomato was common during January-April (when average temperature varied from 15 to 30°C).

**Table 5.1 Disease intensity of early blight on tomato in different germplasm under field conditions during 2011 and 2012**

| Genotype | 45 DAT | 60 DAT | 75 DAT | 90 DAT | AUDPC | Varietal reaction |
|---|---|---|---|---|---|---|
| Maharaja3004 | 11.18 (19.45) | 19.62 (26.27) | 25.72 (30.46) | 28.14 (32.00) | 285.91 | MS |
| H-86 | 11.24 (19.64) | 19.78 (26.38) | 25.73 (30.46) | 28.17 (32.02) | 290.59 | MS |
| GS-2082 | 19.98 (26.52) | 29.66 (32.98) | 38.32 (38.23) | 41.73 (40.22) | 433.50 | MS |
| CO-3 | 3.72 (11.01) | 8.06 (16.37) | 11.12 (19.44) | 12.42 (20.59) | 114.02 | MR |
| Pusa Ruby | 31.36 (34.03) | 39.55 (38.95) | 50.25 (45.13) | 56.05 (48.47) | 582.55 | S |
| Navodya | 14.82 (22.61) | 21.42 (27.53) | 26.84 (31.18) | 29.57 (32.90) | 305.70 | MS |
| Tomato Cherry | 9.22 (17.65) | 17.74 (24.89) | 22.51 (28.29) | 24.96 (34.94) | 251.08 | MR |
| DVRT-2 | 20.85 (27.16) | 26.36 (30.86) | 32.97 (35.02) | 36.65 (37.22) | 377.61 | MS |
| Indam Vaishali | 28.44 (32.20) | 36.31 (37.02) | 46.69 (43.08) | 53.02 (46.90) | 560.21 | S |
| P-2 | 29.47 (32.85) | 36.91 (37.38) | 47.04 (43.28) | 53.84 (46.90) | 549.32 | S |
| S-22 | 19.18 (25.94) | 29.66 (32.98) | 37.57 (37.79) | 42.05 (40.44) | 431.07 | MS |

| | | | | | | |
|---|---|---|---|---|---|---|
| Heem Sohna | 11.87 (20.12) | 18.09 (25.15) | 23.07 (28.66) | 25.89 (30.54) | 259.56 | MR |
| Karina | 16.29 (23.74) | 28.24 (32.06) | 34.92 (36.20) | 39.71 (39.07) | 409.98 | MS |
| Vijeta | 24.28 (29.50) | 31.14 (33.90) | 38.96 (38.60) | 44.21 (41.65) | 456.83 | MS |
| Century-12 | 25.80 (30.51) | 34.45 (35.91) | 41.70 (40.20) | 46.99 (43.25) | 488.82 | MS |
| Range | 3.72-31.36 | 8.06-39.55 | 11.12-50.25 | 12.42-56.05 | | |
| SE(m)± | 0.33 | 0.41 | 0.46 | 0.26 | | |
| $CD_{0.05}$ | 0.96 | 1.19 | 1.32 | 0.76 | | |

Figures are the average of two years data and the figures in parentheses indicate transformed angular values.

**Table 5.2 Quantification of early blight disease on different tomato germplasm under artificial conditions**

| Germplasm | Average lesion size (mm) | | |
|---|---|---|---|
| | 7 DAI* | 12 DAI | 17 DAI |
| Maharaja 3004 | 3.00 | 4.67 | 5.67 |
| H-86 | 2.67 | 4.33 | 5.33 |
| GS-2082 | 3.67 | 6.00 | 8.33 |
| CO-3 | 2.33 | 4.00 | 4.67 |
| Pusa Ruby | 4.67 | 8.33 | 11.33 |
| Navodya | 2.33 | 3.67 | 5.00 |
| Tomato Cherry | 2.67 | 4.33 | 5.33 |
| DVRT-2 | 2.33 | 4.00 | 5.33 |
| Indam Vaishali | 3.67 | 5.00 | 8.67 |
| P-2 | 2.33 | 6.00 | 7.33 |
| S-22 | 2.67 | 5.00 | 6.33 |
| Heem Sohna | 2.00 | 6.33 | 5.33 |
| Karina | 2.33 | 4.33 | 5.67 |
| Vijeta | 3.33 | 6.33 | 7.67 |
| Century-12 | 3.33 | 4.67 | 8.33 |
| SE(m)± | 0.43 | 0.39 | 0.92 |
| $CD_{0.05}$ | 1.25 | 1.15 | 2.7 |

*Days after inoculation.

Confirmation of field screening was done through artificial screening. Although, concentration of inoculum was constant for all the genotypes during the inoculation process, differential reactions of genotypes suggest variable potential of germplasm against *A. solani*. The disease symptoms were observed 2-3 days after inoculation and maximum lesion size (11.33 mm) was recorded after 17 days inoculation (DAI) in Pusa Ruby and minimum (4.67 mm) in CO-3. It can be concluded that none of the germplasm screened was observed to be resistant. The CO3, Tomato Cherry and Heem Sohna were found moderately resistant, whereas Century-12, Vijeta, S-22, GS-2082, Karina, DVRT-2, Navodya, H-86 and Maharaja 3004 were found moderately susceptible (Table 1). The earliest and most severe infection was observed on Pusa Ruby, P-2 and Indam Vaishali, indicating that these are most susceptible.

The area under disease progress (AUDPC) most suitable criterion to determine disease progress for polycyclic foliar pathogens like *Alternaria solani* where resistance is governed by quantitative trait loci (Jeger and Viljanen-Rollinson, 2001). Further, Christ (1991) demonstrated that AUDPC is best criterion to compare early blight severity on different cultivars. Therefore, AUDPC was also calculated for different genotypes. The results indicate that maximum AUDPC (582.55) was observed on Pusa Ruby, while minimum (114.02) on CO3. Our results are in corroboration to Paula and Oliveira (2003) who also concluded that epidemics were best represented by AUDPC and can be further helpful in evaluation of control strategies and prediction of future disease levels.

Three germplasm were found as moderately resistant under natural field screening as well as under artificially inoculated conditions. The disease severity increased with growth of plants. It has been observed that even on susceptible plants, younger leaves are usually free from early blight symptoms, whereas older and lower leaves may be greatly affected and necrotized by the fungus (Johanson and Thurston, 1990). The suggestion of Chaerani and Voorrips (2006) is worth mentioning who opined that genotypes exhibiting similar type of reaction under both natural and field conditions gives more reliable state for selecting the resistant or tolerant genotypes as there may be cases of disease escape under natural field condition due to environmental or some other reasons. Varietal differences in number and size of lesions in early blight have been reported by Barksdale (1968).

Our results are also in conformity with the finding of Datar and Mayee (1981) who reported Pusa Ruby variety of tomato as susceptible to early blight. The varying degrees of resistance of different germplasm against early blight disease has been reported by many workers (Pandey and Pandey, 2002; Prasad and Naik, 2003). The results are in also in conformity with the studies of Upadhyay et al. (2009) who reported 'EC520061' to be resistant; 'NCEBR 4', 'FEB 4' and 'DVRT 2' to be moderately susceptible and other genotypes as either susceptible or highly susceptible.

**Correlation of disease intensity with weather parameters**

Tomato crop grown in *rabi* season indicated that early blight incidence started in March. During 15 MSW, there was maximum increase in the development of disease in all the genotypes, where minimum and maximum temperatures (15.5°C and 29.8°C), minimum and maximum relative humidity (41.9 and 70.4%) and rainfall of 9.6 mm were found to be most favourable for the development of disease. Marginal increase in disease intensity was observed during rest of the meteorological standard weeks suggesting that the most vulnerable stage of the crop was 45-60 days after transplanting (Table 3).

Development and progress of disease exhibited significant and positively simple correlation with maximum temperature ($r$ = 0.868, 0.856, 0.866, 0.895, 0.888, 0.840, 0.808, 0.889, 0.916, 0.919, 0.860, 0.879, 0.844, 0.887 and 0.875), minimum temperature ($r$ = 0.869, 0.859, 0.868, 0.902, 0.892, 0.851, 0.825, 0.904, 0.929, 0.930, 0.870, 0.899, 0.864, 0.906 and 0.904) and significant and negative correlation with maximum relative humidity (r = –0.719, –0.725, –0.714, –0.744, - 0.731, –0.684, –0.683, –0.731, –0.752, –0.756, –0.717, –0.710, –0.718, –0.730, –0.712) in all the 15 genotypes/varieties. Thus, erratic trend of significant and

**Table 5.3 Correlation between disease intensity and weather parameters on different tomato genotypes**

| Genotype | Rainfall | Correlation with relative humidity | | Correlation with temperature | |
|---|---|---|---|---|---|
| | | Maximum | Minimum | Maximum | Minimum |
| Maharaja 3004 | 0.275 | -0.719* | -0.474 | 0.868** | 0.869** |
| H-86 | 0.297 | -0.725* | -0.476 | 0.856** | 0.859** |
| Golden Seed | 0.281 | -0.714* | -0.489 | 0.866** | 0.868** |
| CO-3 | 0.248 | -0.744* | -0.487 | 0.895** | 0.902** |
| Pusa Ruby | 0.176 | -0.731* | -0.553 | 0.888** | 0.892** |
| Navoday | 0.282 | -0.684* | -0.481 | 0.840** | 0.851** |
| Tomato Cherry | 0.300 | -0.683* | -0.422 | 0.808** | 0.825** |
| DVRT-2 | 0.255 | -0.731* | -0.516 | 0.889** | 0.904** |
| Indam Vaishali | 0.216 | -0.752* | -0.555 | 0.916** | 0.929** |
| P-2 | 0.170 | -0.756* | -0.577 | 0.919** | 0.930** |
| S-22 | 0.246 | -0.717* | -0.493 | 0.860** | 0.870** |
| Heem Sohna | 0.278 | -0.710* | -0.504 | 0.879** | 0.899** |
| Karina | 0.253 | -0.718* | -0.482 | 0.844** | 0.864** |
| Vijeta | 0.205 | -0.730* | -0.545 | 0.887** | 0.906** |
| Century-12 | 0.237 | -0.712* | -0.485 | 0.875** | 0.904** |

*Correlation is significant at 5% level of significance

**Correlation is highly significant at 5% level of significance

non-significant values could not yield any significant relationship between weather variables and disease progress.

**Table 5.4 Step-wise regression of disease intensity of early blight of tomato with weather parameters**

| Variety | Regression Equation | $R^2$ |
|---|---|---|
| Indam Vaishali | $Y = -3.05 + 2.58 X_1$ | 0.86 |
| P-2 | $Y = 2.65 + 2.21 X_1$ | 0.86 |
| Pusa Ruby | $Y = 5.93 + 2.20 X_1$ | 0.79 |

$X_1$ = Minimum Temperature
Y = Disease intensity

Since, simple correlation did not yield any substantial relationship between weather variables and disease progress, step-wise regression equations were fitted for the prediction of disease intensity under the given set of environmental conditions. Multiple correlation coefficients indicated strong relationship between disease intensity and weather parameters in three susceptible genotypes, *viz.* Indam Vaishali, P-2 and Pusa Ruby and it was observed that minimum temperature was mainly responsible for disease development (Table 4).

Further, elimination of variables from the best-fitted equations revealed that among various abiotic factors, minimum temperature was mainly responsible for the development of early blight on tomato. In conclusion, as stated throughout the entire work, temperature is the factor that most affects the development and progression of disease severity. A higher minimum temperature produced an increase in disease severity. However, rainfall and minimum relative humidity did not show any significant effect for disease development. The present study is in agreement with Gupta and Paul (2001) who reported that availability of abundant moisture during the growth period followed by warm and dry weather conditions are most conducive for early blight development of potato. Our results also corroborate to those of Hjelmroos (1993) who reported a strong positive correlation between spore concentration and temperature and found that *Alternaria* is a saprophytic genus with an optimal development at 22-28°C. A negative correlation of *A. solani* with rainfall and humidity has been observed by Sabariego *et al.* (2000). Apart from congenial weather factors, maturity of crop during this period is another reason for maximum disease severity. Degree of susceptibility to *A. solani* infection under artificial inoculation conditions increases with the age of tomato plant (Pandey and Pandey, 2003). The present studies give us an insight into the status of early blight of tomato in Jammu, resistant sources to early blight and its progression and development in relation to different weather variables.

# REFERENCES


**Abhinandan, D., Randhawa, H.S. and Sharma, R.C.** (2004). Incidence of *Alternaria* leaf blight in tomato and efficacy of commercial fungicides for its control. *Annual Biol.* **20**: 211-218.

**Barksdale, T.H.** (1968). A method of screening for resistance to early blight on tomato seedling. *Phytopathology* **58**: 883-888.

**Basu, P.K.** (1974). Measuring early blight, its progress and influence on fruit losses in nine tomato cultivars. *Canadian Pl. Dis. Survey* **54**: 45-51.

**Bokshi, A., Morris, S. and Deverall, B.** (2003). Effects of benzothiazole and acetylsalicylic acid on â-13-glucanase activity and disease resistance in potato. *Plant Pathol.* **52**: 22-27.

**Chaerani, R. and Voorrips, R.E.** (2006). Tomato early blight (*Alternaria solani*): the pathogen, genetics and breeding for resistance. *J. Gen. Plant. Pathol.* **72**: 335-47.

**Christ, B.J.** (1991). Effect of disease assessment method on ranking potato cultivars for resistance to early blight. *Plant Dis.* **75**: 353-356.

**Datar, V.V. and Mayee, C.D.** (1981). Assessment of losses in tomato yield due to early blight. *Indian Phytopath.* **34**: 191-195.

**Datar, V.V. and Mayee, C.D.** (1982). Conidial dispersal of *Alternaria solani* in tomato. *Indian Phytopath.* **35**: 68-70.

**Datar, V.V. and Mayee, C.D.** (1986). 'Potato'- *Alternaria solani In: Phytopathometry.* Marathwada Agriculture University, Parbhani, Maharahtra, India. 142 pp.

**DEE, Jammu** (2004). Solanaceous vegetables: In *"Package of Practices for Vegetable Crops"*, 3-7 pp. Directorate of Extension Education, SKUAST, Jammu.

**Duhan, J.C. and Suhag, K.S.** (1990). Alternaria leaf and pod blight of cauliflower. *Indian Phytopath.* **43**: 231-234.

**Ellis, M.B.**(1971). Demataceous Hyphomycetes. Commonweath Mycological Institute, Kew, England.

**Frenguelli, G.** (1998). The contribution of aerobiology to agriculture. *Aerobiologia* **14**: 95-100.

**Gupta, V.K. and Paul,Y.S.** (2001) *Diseases of Vegetable Crops*, pp. 7-25. Kalyani Publishers.

**Hjelmroos, M.** (1993). Relationship between airborne fungal spore presence and weather variables. *Grana* **32**: 40-47.

**Jeger, M.J. and Viljanen-Rollinson, S.L.H.** (2001). The use of the area under the disease-progress curve (AUDPC) to assess quantitative disease resistance in crop cultivars. *Theoretical and Applied Genetics* **102**: 32-40.

**Johanson, A. and Thurston, H.D.** (1990). The effect of cultivar maturity on the resistance of potato to early blight caused by *Alternaria solani*. *American Potato J.* **67**: 615-23.

**Jones, J.B., Jones, J.P., Stall, R.E. and Zitter, T.A,** (1993). *Compendium of Tomato Diseases*. St Paul, Minnesota, USA: American Phytopathological Society.

**Kanjilal, S., Samaddar, K.R. and Samajpati, N.** (2000). Field diseases and potential of tomato cultivation in West Bengal. *J. Mycopathol. Res.* **38**: 121-123.

**Keinath, A.P., DuBose, V.B. and Rathwell, P.J.** (1996). Efficiency and economics of three fungicidal application schedules for early blight control and yield of fresh market tomato. *Plant Dis.* **80**:1277-1282.

**Kumar, V., Haldar, S., Pandey, K.K., Singh, R.P., Singh, A.K. and Singh, P.C.** (2008). Cultural, morphological, pathogenic and molecular variability amongst tomato isolates of *Alternaria solani* in India. *World J. Microbiol. Biotechnol.* **24**:1003-1009.

**Neergard, P.** (1945). Danish Species of *Alternaria* and *Stemphylium*. Oxford University Press, London.

**Pandey, P.K. and Pandey, K.K.** (2002). Field screening of different tomato germplasm lines against *Septoria, Alternaria* and Bacterial disease complex at seedling stage. *J. Mycol. Plant Pathol.* **32**: 233-235.

**Pandey, K.K. and Pandey, P.K.** (2003). Survey and surveillance of vegetable growing area for prevalence of major diseases in this region. *Vegetable Science* **30**: 128-134.

**Paula, R.S. and Oliveira, W.R.** (2003). Resistência de tomateiro (*Lycopersicon esculentum*) ao patógeno *Alternaria solani*. *Pesquisa Agropecuária Tropical* **33**: 89-95.

**Poly, S. and Srikanta, D.** (2012). Assessment of yield loss due to early blight (*Alternaria solani*) in tomato. *Indian J. Plant Prot.* **40**: 195-198.

**Pound, G.S.** (1951). Effect of air temperature on incidence and development of early blight disease of tomato. *Phytopathology* **41**: 127-135.

**Prasad, Y. and Naik, M.K.** (2003). Evaluation of genotypes, fungicides and plant extracts against early blight of tomato caused by *Alternaria solani*. *Indian J. Plant Prot.* **31**: 49-53.

**Rotem, J. and Reichert,** I. (1964). Dew - a principal moisture factor enabling early blight epidemics in a semiarid region of Israel. *Pl. Dis. Reptr.* **48**: 211-15.

**Sabariego, S., Diaz, C. and Alba, F.** (2000). The effect of meteorological factors on the daily variation of airborne fungal spores in Granada (southern Spain). *International J. Biometeorol.* **44**: 1-5.

**Upadhyay, P., Singh, P.C., Sinha, B., Singh, M., Kumar, R., Pandey, K.K. and Mathura, R.** (2009). Sources of resistance against early blight (*Alternaria solani*) in tomato (*Solanum lycopersicum*). *Indian J. Agric. Sci.* **79**: 752-753.

**Vander-Walls, J.E., Korsen, L., Aveling, T.A.S. and Denner, F.D.N.** (2003). Influence of environmental factors on field concentrations of *Alternaria solani* conidia above a South African potato crop. *Phytoparasitica* **31**: 353-364.

**Early Blight Disease of Tomato**
*Edited by:* Virendra Kumar
**ISBN:** 978-93-5056-879-8
*Edition:* 2017
*Published by:* Discovery Publishing House Pvt. Ltd., New Delhi (India)

# Study of Variability and Sporulation by Isolates of *Alternaria Solani* of *Lycopersicon Esculentum* (Mill.)

[1]Virendra Kumar, [2]Koshlendra Kumar Pandey,
[3]Kaushlesh Kumar Mishtra

## ABSTRACT

Alternaria solani was studied on various parameters of cultural characters such as radial growth, pigmentation, pH, temperatures sporulation and differential host response. Among five isolates maximum radial growth was found in Sh isolates (75.2 mm) while minimum in Va isolates (56.5 mm). The maximum thickness of conidiogenous hyphae was recorded in Va isolate (9.56 m) and minimum (1.7 m) in Mi, Ba and Sh. Alternaria solani grew well on Czapek dox agar medium and Jenson medium. The maximum average radial growth was recorded 54.7 mm on PDA. The optimum temperature was recorded 25°C with pH 7.5 for the pathogen. Pigmentation varied from brown to black color on these media, light yellow to black color at different temperatures and gray to brown color on different pH ranges. The sporulation was not found at any tested media, pH and temperatures except host decoction media. A method of inducing sporulation on host decoction media has been developed. Now it is possible to produce mature conidia in culture under aseptic condition in 20-25 days at 28°C and pH 6.5. Septation of conidia were found to be greater in number from infected tomato leaves and fruits.

**Keywords:** *Alternaria solani*, early blight, resistance, screening, tomato.

## Introduction

The genus Alternaria is a large and important group of pathogenic fungi which cause significant number of important diseases on a wide range of agronomic and horticultural plants. *A. solani* (Ellis and Martin) Jones and Grout is most important pathogen causing severe early blight disease every year in tomato. It is one of the damaging as well as destructive disease of tomato. Due to this disease, about 80% yield loss was recorded in experimental field and severity

[1] Regional Pesticides Testing Laboratory, Directorate of Plant Protection Quarantine and Storage, T-2 Ratan Lal Nagar, Kanpur, U.P. India.

[2] Division of Seed Technology, Central Potato Research Institute (CPRI), Shimla, India

[3] Wheat Improvement Project, JNKV, Zonal Agriculture Research Station, Powerkheda, Hoshangabad, M.P., India

varies from 15-90 per cent (Pandey *et al.,* 2003). Information on *in vitro* aspects pertaining to pathogenic variability, factors influencing the mycelial growth and sporulation are limited. The fungus is readily cultured on artificial media such as potato dextrose agar where it produces a deeply yellow pigmented gray/ black hairy colony. But among the different species of Alternaria, the *Alternaria solani* does not produce spore readily under laboratory conditions. It is easy to recognize *Alternaria* sp. by the morphology of their large conidia. They are catenate or solitary typically ovoid often beaked, pale brown to brown, multi-celled and muriform. (Ellis 1971). Several workers have attempted to increase sporulation by various methods. These methods have included exposure of fluorescent light, exposure of UV light, exposure of sun light, dehydration of medium and chemical treatment of culture (Douglas and Pavek, 1971). For Example Rath and Padhi (1973) reported that the sporulation in *Alternaria solani* in three days old culture on solid media exposing direct sunlight for 10 minutes and incubation at 20-25 $^{O}$C temperature increased sporulation. Klimesova and Prasik (1989) reported that UV radiation had pronounced effect on five selected characters (length, Width, color, necrosity and length of the conidial beak) of these conidium. Distinct differences were found in 5 harbarium specimens of *Alternaria alternata* compared with corresponding isolates in cultures. These observations demonstrated the importance of studying the relation between natural material and their prospective cultures in order to assess correctly the general variability of the species. Pandey and vishwakarma (1999) have studied the morphological variability of the conidia of *Alternaria alternata* on culture media. He further reported the pathogenic isolates of *Alternaria alternata* reduced in its conidium and beak size from natural host to culture. A few workers viz. Rath and Padhi (1973), Stevenson and Pennypacker (1988), Sodlauskiene *et al.* (2003), Prasad *et al* (1973) and Rodriguez and Santana (1991) tested the isolates of *Alternaria* on particular temperatures for observing the cultural characters and sporulation of *A. solani*. The present study is completely different from previous workers. In this study cultural, morphological and an efficient method, proven consistently to induce sporulation in numerous isolates of *A. solani* has been developed. This makes it possible to produce spores under aseptic conditions in 20-25 days on host decoction media.

### Materials and Methods

*A. solani* was studied on various parameters of cultural and morphological variability such as radial growth, pigmentation, pH, temperatures, sporulation and pathogenic variability along with differential host response of pathogen on tomato. These all sets of experiments have been discussed as follows-Cultural and morphological variability of different isolates of *A. solani* on PDA. Five selective isolates of *A. solani* were taken for representing Varanasi (Va), Mirzapur (Mi), Robertsganj (Ro), Shillong (Sh) and Bangalore (Ba) of different zones of the country. The cultures were already maintained in laboratory. All these isolates were tested for their cultural and morphological variations on Potato dextrose agar (PDA) medium only. For each isolates 5 Petri plates were poured with potato dextrose agar medium. After solidification of the medium 5 mm culture bits of each isolates were inoculated onto the PDA Petri plates by maintaining the aseptic conditions. These inoculated Petri plates were kept in BOD at 25 ± 1°C for growth. The data was recorded after 3 days of inoculation and radial growth was measured per day upto $9^{th}$ day.

The thickness of conidiogenous hyphae of different isolates were measured by calibrations through ocular and stage micrometer. The growth rate, cultural, and morphological characters were studied. In another experiment three types of nutrient media *viz.* ASM (*Alternaria* sporulation medium), freshly prepared V-8 juice agar, and readymade available V-8 juice agar medium (Hi-media) containing asparagine was taken for above mentioned five isolates for the cultural and morphological study. Pathogen was incubated at 25±1°C for 11 days. The growths of different isolates of *A. solani* were measured on these medium and the variability were recorded. For cultural and morphological variability of *A. solani* on different nutrient media, pH and temperatures, pure culture of one pathogenic isolate of *A. solani* was grown on fourteen different synthetic, semi-synthetic and natural media *i.e.* V-8 juice medium (V-8 JM), Malt extract agar (MEA), Corn meal agar (CMA), Potato dextrose rose bengal agar (PDRBA), Casein hydrolysate medium (CHM), Richard synthetic agar (RSA), Oat meal agar (OMA), Rose bengal chloramphenical agar (RBCA) Potato dextrose agar (PDA), Czapek dox agar (CDA), Jenson media (JM), Asthana and Hawker medium (AHM), Malt extract potato dextrose agar (MEPDA) and *Alternaria* sporulation medium (ASM) for the study of cultural and morphological variability.

These media were prepared as per standard composition (Dhingra and Sinclair 1995). Twelve pH ranges *i.e.* 4.0, 4.5, 5.0, 5.5, 6.0, 6.5, 7.0, 7.5, 8.0, 8.5, 9.0 and 9.5 were adjusted through pH meter (Thermo Orion) by adding few drops of either HCl or NaOH solution in PDA medium. Five different temperatures *i.e.* 15°C, 20°C, 25°C, 30°C and 35°C were maintained in BOD incubator separately. PDA was selected as standard basal medium for both temperature and pH study. Ten days old culture of *A. solani* was inoculated on PDA with 5 mm culture disc and incubated at 25°C for the study of variability on various pH ranges and the same size of culture bits were taken for various temperatures range. Five replication of each set of experiment maintained for each test media, pH and temperatures. The data of radial growth rate, pigmentation and colony character were recorded after 3 days of inoculation and continued up to $9^{th}$ day. The experimental data was subjected to statistically analysis using factorial CRD design. Sporulation of *A. solani* on host decoction media:- The following *three* combination of host decoction medium were prepared and tested for the sporulation of *A. solani.*

**Preparation of host decoction media:** The tomato leaf extract and fruit juice were prepared by grinding in a mixer and it was filtered with a muslin cloth. Then the juice was centrifuged at 8000 rpm for 10 minutes at room temperature. The supernatant was taken as medium preparation at each step.

**Ist combination of host decoction media:** 20 ml of 1 % autoclaved agar was poured in a Petri plates and after solidification, the freshly prepared tomato leaf extract was passed through bacterial proof filter in each agar plates under aseptic condition. Then 7 days of old culture bits (5 mm size) of *A. solani* was inoculated on this Petri plates and incubated at 25 ± 1°C and data were recorded after every 7 days intervals upto 21$^{th}$ day.

**IInd combination of host decoction media:** 200 ml ripe tomato fruit juice as well as tomato leaf extract were taken in flask separately which contains 5 g of celite powder in both and it was centrifuged at 8000 rpm for 10 minutes at room temperature. The supernatant was taken as medium. 2 g. of Agar and 2 g. of Sucrose were added in this supernatant and pH is adjusted to 6.5. Then it was autoclaved at 15 lbs for 15 minute, after sterilization of 0.1% $CaCO_3$ was mixed in this medium under aseptic condition. It was poured in Petri plates and again 2 ml of freshly prepared tomato fruit juice and leaf extract added separately onto the Petri plates through bacterial proof filter. Then 7 days of old culture bits of *A. solani* (5 mm size) were inoculated on this Petri plates and incubated at 25 ± 1°C. The observations were recorded after every 7 days intervals upto 21$^{th}$ day.

**IIIrd combination of host decoction media:** The tomato juice was extracted from ripe and semi-ripe fruits separately. The whole juice was transferred in a conical flask which contains 5 g of celite powder and centrifuged at 8000 rpm for 10 minutes at room temperature. The supernatant was taken as medium. The total volume of the medium maintained up to 250 ml after adding 1% agar and 1% dextrose in it. Before pouring of this medium 0.5 % $CaCO_3$ powder was added in this medium and inoculation was done as mentioned in Ist and IInd combinations of host decoction media. These all combinations of host decoction medium were tested more than three times for the sporulation study of *A. solani.*

### Comparative study between conidial morphology of *A. solani* from host decoction media and infected host tissues

Conidial morphology of *A. solani* was studied from different parts of infected plant such as leaves, stem, and fruits.

Temporary slides were prepared separately from these parts of plant tissue. The horizontal septa, vertical septa, and septa in beak of different conidia were counted from infected host tissue for the study in morphological variability of conidia. The same tissues were incubated in BOD for 12 hours at 25 ± 1°C in moisture box and again data of conidial morphology was taken after incubation. The temporary slides were prepared in lacto phenol by scrapping of the infected tissue. The comparative study of conidial morphology had done in both cases *i.e.* from culture spore and host spores of *A. solani.*

## Results

### Variability of *A. solani* on PDA

The five isolates of *A. solani* exhibited significant variation for their cultural character, pigmentation and per day growth rate. Colonies of different isolates of the pathogen varied from white to dark black, circular to irregular, smooth to rough, with or without concentric zonation. The radial growth varied from 56.5 to 75.2 mm after 9 days of incubation. The pigmentation varied from brown to brownish black (Table 1). Maximum radial growth was 75.2 mm of Sh isolate while lowest growth was 56.5 mm in Va isolate. Radial growth was almost similar to Ro, Mi, Sh isolates. The variability in radial growth among these isolates has been presented in Fig. 1 from $4^{th}$ day to $9^{th}$ day. Periodical radial growth of these five isolate was recorded every day from $4^{th}$ to $9^{th}$ day of incubation which revealed that fastest growth was between $5^{th}$ to $7^{th}$ days in Ro, and Mi isolate. Sh isolate reflected maximum growth at initial stage between 4-5 days, and later on between 8-9 days. (Table 2) media *i.e.* ASM, V-8 juice agar, and

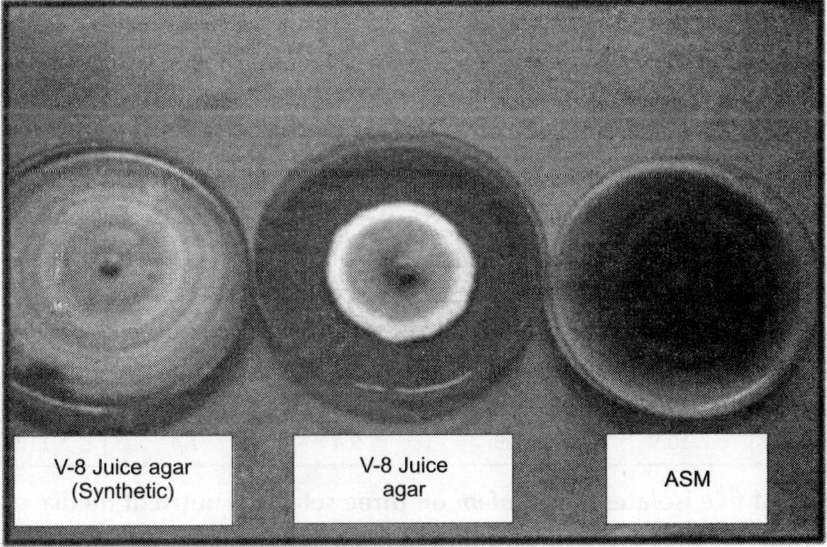


**Plate 1a Variability of Sh Isolates on three selective media**

V-8 juice agar (synthetic) which containing asparagine. Pathogen was incubated at 25±1°C for 11 days. The growth patterns observed significantly different for the test isolates. Radial growth of *A. solani* varied from 24.33 mm to 52.83 mm on a ASM, 25.50 mm to 53.33 mm on V-8 juice agar medium and 26.50 mm to 48.51 mm on V-8 juice agar synthetic medium (Table 3). All the isolates were significantly different from each other. The maximum radial growth of Mi, and Ba isolate were recorded on V-8 juice agar medium while Va, and Sh on V-8 juice agar synthetic. Although all five isolates of *A. solani* were pathogenic culture but great variability in radial growth were recorded within the isolate as well as among these three media. ASM did not supported formation of conidia under the present test condition (Plate 1a).

**Table 6.1 Cultural, morphological variability and sporulation of different isolates of *A. solani* on PDA**

| Isolates | Pigmen-tation | Average radial growth (mm) days after inoculation | | | | | | Width of Conidio-gnous hyphas (m) | Mycalial growth/colony character | | | | Sporulation |
|---|---|---|---|---|---|---|---|---|---|---|---|---|---|
| | | 4th | 5th | 6th | 7th | 8th | 9th | | Circular irrigular | Smooth/ rough | Growth rate | Zonation | |
| Pa | Brown | 29.9 | 39.8 | 48.5 | 50.2 | 58.5 | 9.58 | Irregular | Smooth | 4.4 | | No | |
| Ro | Black brown | 31.0 | 40.5 | 51.0 | 62.7 | 66.5 | 72.8 | 1.7 | Irregular | Rough | 6.9 | Without xonation | No |
| Mi | Brownish black | 30.5 | 38.7 | 51.8 | 58.3 | 66.7 | 72.9 | 1.7 | Circular | Smooth | 7.0 | Without zonation | No |
| Ba | Brownish black | 25.4 | 32.7 | 41.5 | 49.6 | 59.7 | 64.5 | 1.17 | Circular | Smooth | 6.5 | Concentric zonation | No |
| Sh | Black brown | 30.1 | 41.0 | 49.9 | 56.3 | 63.7 | 75.2 | 1.17 | Irregular | Smooth | 7.5 | Concentric zonation | No |

**Table 6.2 Average radial growth rates of different isolates of *A. solani***

| Isolates | Average radial growth (mm) per day after inoculation | | | | |
|---|---|---|---|---|---|
| | 4-5 days | 5-6 days | 6-7 days | 7-8 days | 8-9 days |
| Va | 9.9 | 9.2 | 7.2 | 6.0 | 9.7 |
| Ro | 9.5 | 10.5 | 11.7 | 3.8 | 6.3 |
| Mi | 8.2 | 12.9 | 6.7 | 8.4 | 6.2 |
| Ba | 7.3 | 8.8 | 8.1 | 10.1 | 4.8 |
| Sh | 10.9 | 8.9 | 6.4 | 7.4 | 11.5 |

**Variability of five isolates of *A. solani* on three selective nutrient media**

It was observed that the five different isolates of *A. solani* were significantly different in each other on three different Sporulation was not recorded on these selective media. The thickness of conidiogenous hyphae varied from 1.17 to 9.56 m. Minimum thickness of conidiogenous hyphae observed in Sh, Ro, Mi, and Ba isolate *i.e.* 1.17 m. The maximum thickness of conidiogenous hyphae was observed in Va isolate. (Table 1) The fastest growth rate after 9 days of incubation was recorded 7.5 mm in Sh isolate and slowest growth rate was recorded 4.4 mm in Va isolate. Irregular margin, dark brown, smooth, velvety, with zonation was recorded in Va isolate; smooth, Irregular margin, black brown without zonation colony in Ro isolate; circular, smooth margin, fluffy, slight velvety, brownish black, without zonation in Mi isolate; circular margin, fluffy, depressed center with concentric zonation, brownish black colony in Ba isolate, and irregular margin, gray periphery, black brown with concentric zonation colony character was recorded in Sh isolate. (Table 6.1)

**Table 6.3 Variability in radial growth of *A. solani* isolates on selected nutrient media**

| Isolates | Radial growth (mm) | | |
|---|---|---|---|
| | A.S.M. | V-8 uice Agar | V-8 uice Agar (Synthetic) |
| Va | 24.33 | 25.50 | 26.50 |
| Ro | 52.83 | 47.03 | 48.51 |
| Mi | 44.50 | 52.50 | 42.50 |
| Ba | 46.50 | 53.33 | 41.00 |
| Sh | 42.93 | 43.36 | 45.70 |
| C.D. at | 3.24 | 2.72 | 2.48 |

## Variability of *A. solani* on different nutrient media

The variability in radial growth was closely observed on fourteen different nutrient media. The maximum average radial growth (54.74 mm) was recorded on CDA medium followed by JM (50.14 mm). Both media were significantly different to each other. However, JM and PDA (48.5 mm) were significantly at par to each other. CHM (46.5 mm), AHM (45.8 mm) and RSA medium (45.3 mm) were significantly at par to each other and statistically belong to third group in supporting maximum mean radial growth of *A. solani*. (Fig. 1 and Plate 1b) Maximum radial growth of *A. solani* on $9^{th}$ d of incubation was recorded 77.0 mm on CHM. The radial growth varied between 74.6 to 77.0 mm on CDA, JM, RSA, AHM and CHM on $9^{th}$ day. PDA also supported very good radial growth of 70.7 mm. Lowest growth was recorded on Malt extract agar medium followed by V-8 JM. The slow growth on synthetic V-8 JM may be due to asparagine) Sporulation was not recorded on different nutrient media.

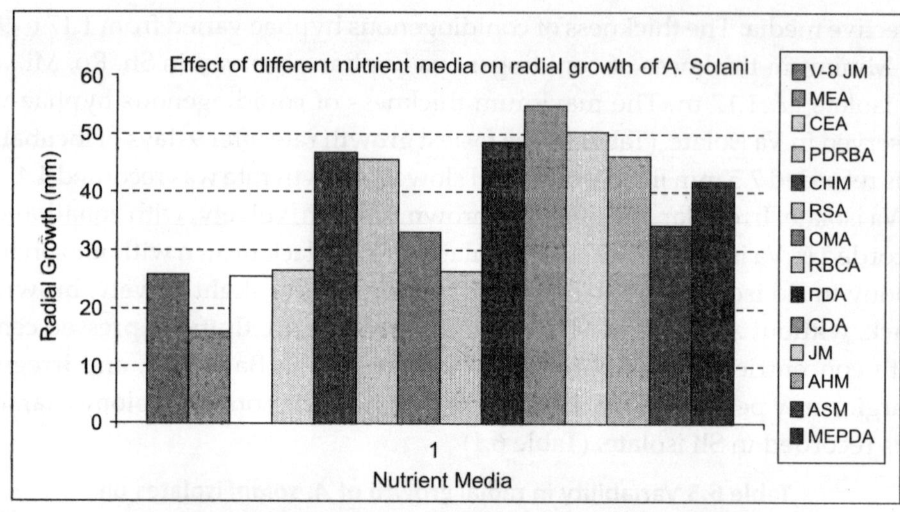


**Fig. 6.1 Effect of different nutrient media radial growth of *A. solani***

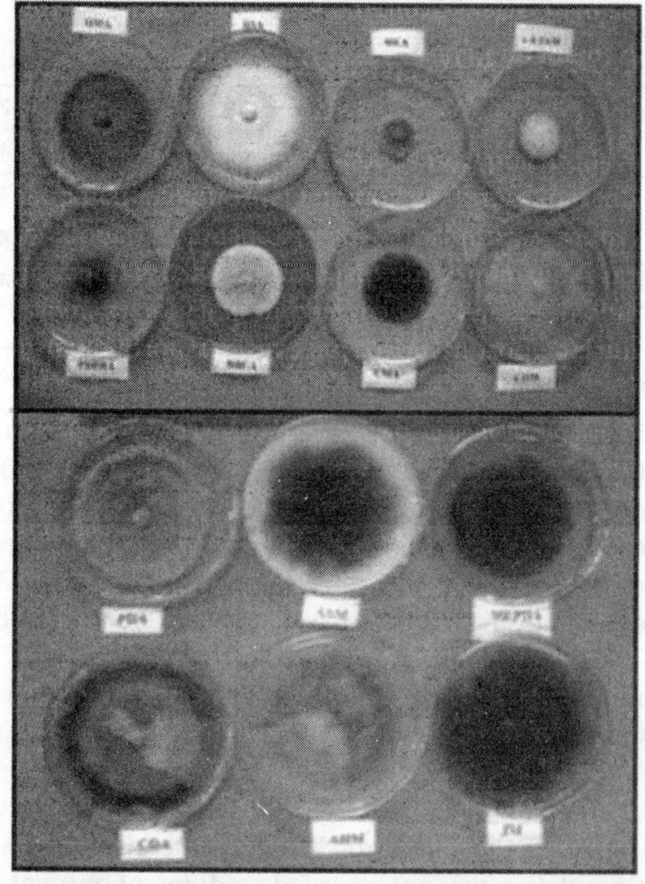

**Plate 1b Growth and Sporulation of *A. solani* on different nutrient media**

### Variability *A. solani* on different temperatures

Radial growth was found significantly different to each other at different temperatures. The most favorable temperature for growth of the pathogen was 25°C. Maximum average radial (48.65 mm) growth was recorded at 25°C temperatures while minimum average radial growth (25.97 mm) was at 35°C temperatures. (Fig. 6.2) The radial growth of *A.*

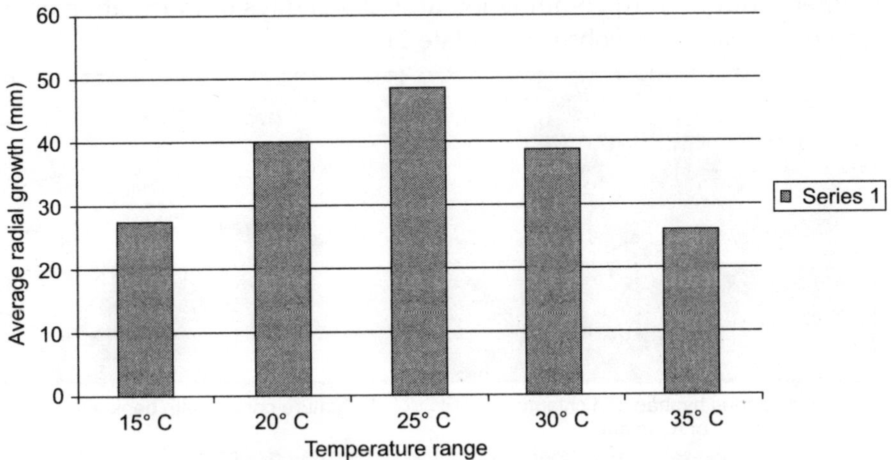


**Fig. 6.2 Effect of temperature on radial growth of *A. solani***

*solani* was maximum (70.0 mm) on 9th d of incubation. As the temperature decreased or increased from 25°C, the drastic growth reduction was observed. This trend of observation was continued from first observation (3rd day) to seventh observation (9th day). Inability of conidia production at any stage indicating that variable temperature range (15-35°C) cannot induce spore formation. (Fig. 6.2)

### Variability of *A. solani* on different pH

Behaviour of growth and colony character of *A. solani* was studied on different pH ranges between pH 4.0-9.5 on PDA at 25±1°C up to 9th days of incubation. Maximum radial growth 83.9 mm was recorded at pH 7.5 on 9th days. Maximum average radial growth was observed at pH 7.5 (52.54 mm) and minimum average radial growth was observed at pH 4.0 (18.67mm). Light acidic and slightly alkaline pH was suitable for the growth of *A. solani*. Apparent acidic (4.0) and alkaline pH (9.5) was reducing radial growth drastically and not Suitable for the growth of *A. solani*. Minimum radial growth was recorded 29.2 mm on 9th day at pH 4.0 highly significant on the growth of *A. solani*. The best suited pH was 7.5 for the growth of *A. so* where light brown pigment with zonation observed as colony characters. Colony characters varied from whitish gray to dark gray, dark brown with zonations at different pH. Sporulation did not observe under any pH ranges, which indicates that also variation in pH between 4.0 - 9.5 could not induce the sporulation in *A. solani* on PDA. Differences in radial growth were found significantly at different pH. This trend of observation was continued from first observation (3rd day) to seventh observation (9th day).

**Sporulation of *A. solani* on host decoction media:** Out of three combinations of the host decoction medium, third combination was found very effective for the good sporulation of *A. solani*. However sporulation were found in all set of experiments but in third combination after 20-25 days of inoculation a typical conidia of *A. solani* were observed (Plate 2).

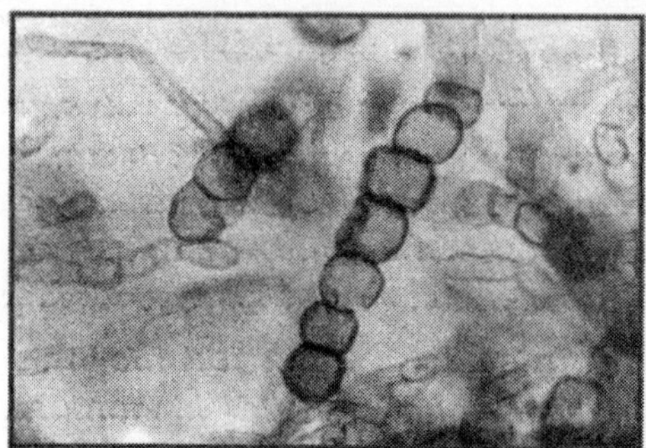

A: Conidiogenus hyphae and chlamydospore of A. solani

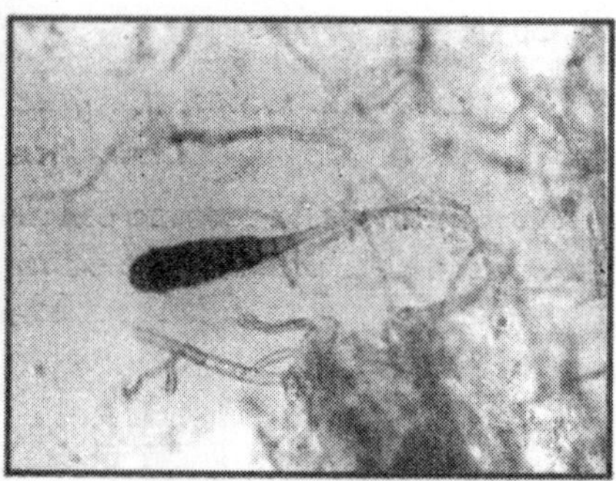

B: Mature conidia with beak and septa

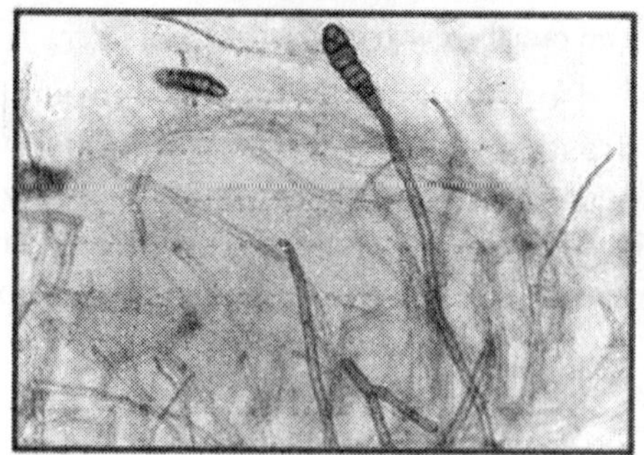

C: Mature conidia with beak and septa

D: A typecal A. Solani conidia having long beak

**Plate 2 Sporulation in *A. solani* on Host decoction media**

Neutral pH was also not promoting growth highly in comparison to pH 6.5 and 7.5. (Fig. 3) It is because of the complete balance of cationic and anionic charged nutrient particle, which does not readily made available to the growing fungi. The gradient charge may be zero at neutral pH hence there may be no movement of any nutrient material in the medium. Effect of period (days) and different pH ranges were Few conidiogenous hyphae were also produce in this media. (Plate 2A) The total host extracts either tomato juice or leaf extract were pass through bacterial filter under aseptic condition to prevent contamination and maintain heat sensitive vitamin and growth hormone and celite powder was added just for the removing of the colouring matter of tomato juice.

**Table 4 Septation of *A. solani* from different parts of host tissue and from host decoction media**

| | Infected host* | | | Incubated host* | | | From culture* | | |
|---|---|---|---|---|---|---|---|---|---|
| | Leaf | Stem | Fruit | Leaf | Stem | Fruit | Ist | IInd | IIIrd |
| No.of horizontal septa | 8.8 | 8.8 | 10.1 | 9.1 | 9.9 | 11.2 | 8.0 | 7.5 | 8.2 |
| No. of vertical septa | 1.0 | 1.3 | 2.1 | 2.4 | 1.9 | 2.0 | 1.3 | 1.8 | 1.6 |
| Septa in beak | 2.0 | 2.7 | 3.1 | 2.1 | 2.2 | 2.2 | 1.1 | 1.2 | 1.2 |

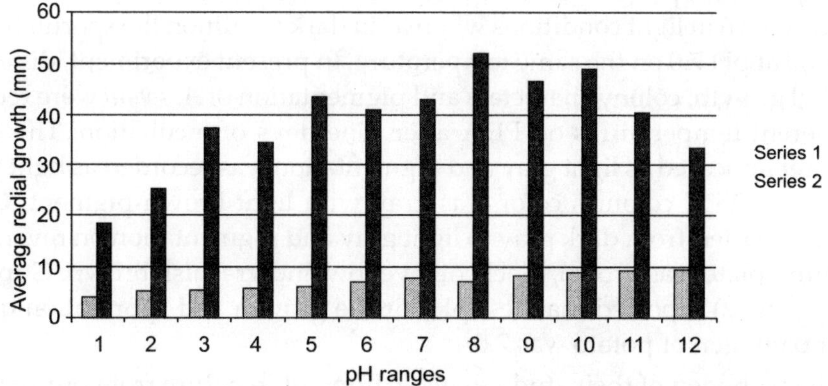


**Fig. 6.3 Effect of different pH ranges on radial growth of *A. solani***

Present findings clearly indicate that ripe tomato juice and $CaCO_3$ play very significant role in spore induction of *A. solani* as compared to leaf extract and unripe fruit juice. Shahin and Shepard (1979) developed an efficient technique for inducing profuse sporulation of *A. solani*. They had also used $CaCO_3$ with agar and were found good sporulation of 18-28 hours of inoculation and incubation of Petri plates at 28°C.

## Discussion

The present findings clearly indicate significant variability in the cultural characters of five isolates of *A. solani*. Sporulation was not recorded on PDA. Similar type of observation was taken by Klimesova and Prasik (1989) in case of *A. alternata*. Even after 9th d of incubation, differences in radial growth rate was found significantly on different nutrient media. CHM, RSA and AHM were almost similar for the periodical radial growth of the pathogen. PDA and JM were also similar in growth rate but the longer period of incubation, increases the intensity of conidiogenous hyphae formation. Variations in colony characters of the pathogen were also recorded on same fourteen nutrient media on 9th d.

Colony of *A. solani* was variable on these media. Blackish brown colony was recorded on V-8 JM, ASM and MEPDA. Whitish brown colony was on RSA, RBCA, AHM while light gray colony was observed on rest of the media. The velvety black colony was found in CMA, PDRBA, OMA.

Pigmentation on these media varied from brown yellowish to black. However, the concentric zonation was observed in some of the media from upper and lower sides. No spore production was observed in any of the above medium. However, only cultural variability was recorded among the different nutrient media. It is clear from the present findings that sporulation could not induced on the above tested media upto $9^{th}$ d of incubation at constant temperature of 25±°1C. Our findings corroborate the observation of Rath and Padhi (1973) where they reported that best growth was at 20-25°C temperature. Gupta and Nikhraj (1972) reported that best temperature for sporulation of *A. solani* was 22.5°C at pH 6 in light conditions whereas in dark condition the sporulation was reported at pH 7.0 on the same temperature. In present experiment, differences in radial growth, colony characters and pigmentation of *A. solani* were recorded at different temperatures on PDA after nine days of incubation. The colony character appeared as light gray and pigmentation was recorded as light yellow at 35°C. At 25°C colonies color was gray with light brown pigment. Colony character varied from dark gray to light gray and pigmentation on reverse side of culture plate was brown, black, oily yellow and greenish brown. Gupta and Nikhraj (1972) reported that best pH for the growth and sporulation of early blight pathogen of potato was 7.0.

The pathogen of their study may be different in nature from our pathogen because they had mentioned about sporulation and spore germination, which could not prove after several efforts in *A. solani*. Septation of a conidium was found to be greater in the incubated host as compared to natural host and culture. Maximum number of septation was found in infected tomato fruit tissue in both conditions viz. incubated, infected host and followed by spore from culture plates. The numbers of horizontal septa were recorded 4-11, vertical septa 1-4 and septa in beak recorded 1-5 in a conidium while from culture plates the number of horizontal septa 5-8, vertical septa1-2 and septa in beak 0-1 in a conidium and along beak in a conidium were also observed. (Table 4) It means septation of a conidium is reducing in culture medium as compare to natural host. Pandey and Vishwakarma (1999) also studied the pathogenic isolates of *A. alternata* reduced in its conidium and beak size from natural host of culture medium; therefore it is proving the results.

In present findings a well developed and maximum no. of septa recorded in tomato fruit which was incubated as 25±1°C because host nutrition is very important for size of spore. Our findings are similar to the observations of Ahmed (2002) he had reported that the no. of horizontal septa was 5-11 in the tomato leaf. In tomato fruit largest conidia observed in size and shape, because it has sufficient nutritional requirement for growth and development of the pathogen. Several workers Prasad *et al* (1973), Lukens and Horsfall (1973) Madan and Thind (1979), Stevenson and Pennypacker (1988), Ghosh and Gemawat (1979), Zhu *et al* (1985), Kvasnyuk (1985), Vakalounakis (1982) and Bernal *et al* (2002) have reported for sporulation by using different artificial media and other treatment. Prasad *et al* (1973) reported that sporulation was induced when fully grown *A. solani* cultures was dipped in or sprayed with sterilized distilled water, and kept partially covered at different temperatures. Cold water dips (4°C, 4 Min) or sprays at 4°C or 28°C followed by incubation at room temperature (13-26°C) in diffuse sunlight produced the spores within 0 hour. The cultures yielded a number of subsequent spore crops when scraped, and dipped after each conidial harvest.

Madan, and Thind (1979) had seen the role of trace elements on growth and sporulation of *A. solani*. Out of 20 trace elements tested Ca was determined for good sporulation in *A. solani*. Rodriguez and Santana (1991) reported sporulation on Yucca Glucose Agar, Malanga Glucose Agar and Sweet Potato Glucose Agar. Some researchers such as Kumagai and Oda (1969), Kaoru and Mitsuo (1970), Prasad and Dutt (1974), Singh (1967), Fourtouni *et al* (1998), Lukens (1962), Douglas and Pavek (1971) and Cotty (1987) have done work on effect of light for sporulation of *A. solani* and also its other species as *A. tegetica, A. alternate,* and *A. kikuchiana.* Kumagai and Oda (1969) found sporulation in *A. solani* only on exposure to irradiation by U. V. light followed by a period of darkness while Kaoru amd Mitsuo (1970) reported that effect of continuos white fluorescent light (340 mμ and 365m μ) exposed with short distance on culture plates of *A. solani* increased the spore production on three selective nutrient media i.e. V-8 juice medium, pear leaf juice medium and dry apricot V-8 juice medium. We have also studied sporulation on V-8 juice medium but only conidiogenous hyphae were found on both PDA and V-8 juice medium. Therefore the present work is completely different from earlier workers. Our finding shows that sporulation was not found on PDA, Alternaria sporulation medium, V-8 juice agar and v-8 juice agar (synthetic) without any light treatments. But successfully sporulation is induced in host decoction media. These host decoction combinations for conidial formation of *A. solani* was observed suitable and further standardization of temperature and pH and different carbon and calcium sources required getting.

## Acknowledgments

We wish to thanks Dr. P.K. Pandey, Ex. Head, Crop Protection Division, Indian Institute of Vegetable Research, Varanasi U.P., India for his constant encouragements, valuable suggestions and comments to carry out these research works. Source required getting more sporulation. Instead of sources required getting.

## REFERENCES


Ahmad, S., 2002. Conidial morphology of *Alternaria solani*, and its variation in tomato. *Annals of Agricultural Research* (23), p 514-515.

Bernal. A, Martinez, B., Perez, S., and Rivas, E., 2002. A method for inducing *in vitro* sporulation of isolates of *Alternaria solani. Centro Agricola* Cuba, (29),p 88-89. Cotty, J. P.1987. Modulation of sporulation of *Alternaria tagetica* by bcarbon di oxide. *Mycologia* (74), p 508-513. Dhingra, O.D. and Sinclair, J.B. 1995. Basic Plant Pathology *Lewis Publishers London*. p.392.

Douglas, D.R. and Pavek, J.J. 1971. A efficient method of inducing sporulation of *Alternaria solani* in pure culture. Phytopathology (61), p 239.

Ellis, M.B, 1971. Dematiaceous Hyphomycetes. Common Wealth Mycological Institute, Kew, England, p. 464-497.

Fourtouni, A., Mentos. Y., and Christias, C., 1998. Effect of UV- B radiation on growth, pigmentation and spore production in phytopathogenic fungus *Alternaria solani* Cannadian Journal of Botany (76), p 2093-2099.

Gemawat, P. D., and Gosh, S. K., 1979. Studies on the physiology of growth of *Alternaria solani*. *India Journal of Mycology and Plant Pathology*, (9), p 138-139.

Gupta, D.P. and Nikhraj, N.S., 1972. Host relations in *Alternaria* blight of potato germination of spore. *Journal of Bihar Botanical Society* (1),p 22-26.

Kaoru, O. and Mitsuo, N. 1970. Effect of light on sporulation of *Alternaria kikuchiana* TANAKA. *Ann. Phytopathol Soc Japan* (36), p 11-16.

Klimesova, M. and Prasil, K. 1989. Morphological variability of conidia of *Alternaria alternata* (Hyphomycetes).

*Novitates-Botonicae Universitatis Carolinae*. (5) 7-27. Kumagai, T. and Oda, Y. 1969. Blue and near ultraviolet reversible photoreaction in conidial development of the fungus,Alternaria Tomato. *Dev. Growth Differ* (11) pp . 130-142.

Kvasynyuk, N. Y. 1985. Sporulation intensity, and pathogenecity of *Alternaria solani* (Ell. and Mart.) Sor. Isolates. *Mikologiya-i-Fitopatologiya* 19: (2), p 148-150.

Lukens, R.J., and Horsfall. J.G. 1973. Processes of sporulation in *Alternaria solani* and their response to metabolic inhibitors. Phytopathology (63), p 176-182.

Madan, M., and Thind, K.S., 1979. Role of trace elements on the growth, and sporulation of *Alternaria solani*, and *Alternaria chartarum*. Proceedings of the Indian National Science Academy-B, 45: (6), p 628-632.

Pandey, K.K., and Vishwakarma. S.N. 1999. Morphological, and symptomatological variations in *Alternaria alternata* causing leaf blight in brinjal. *Indian J of Myco and Plant Pathol* (29) 350-354.

Pandey, K. K., Pandey, P.K., Kalloo, G. and Banerjee, M.K. 2003. Resistance to early blight of tomato with respect to various parameters of disease epidemics. *J of Gen. Plant Pathol* (69) 364-371.

Prasad, B., Dutt, B.L., and Nagaich, B.B. 1973. Inducing sporulation in Alternaria solani I. Effect of water treatment. *Mycolpathologia et Mycologia Applicata* (49) 141-146. Rath, G.C. and Padhi, N.N. 1973. Sporulation of *Alternaria solani* in pure culture. *Indian Phytopathology*, (26), p 495-501.

Rodriquez, A.C.M. and Santana, R. 1991. Effect of new culture media and temperature on the growth *in vitro* of *Alternaria solani*. *Centro Agricola* (18), p 86-88.

Shahin, E.A. and Shepard. J.F. 1979. An efficient technique for inducing profuse sporulation of *Alternaria* species. Phytopathology, (69),p 618-620.

Singh, B. M. 1967. Inducing sporulation of different strain of Alternaria solani II effect of ultra violet light.*Mycopathologia* (32), p 163-171.

Sodlauskiene, A and Surviliene, E, 2003. Influence of environmental conditions upon the development of *Alternaria* genus fungi *in vitro*. *Sodininkyste ir Darzininkyste,* (22), p. 160-166.

Stevenson, R.E. and Pennypacker, S.P. 1988. Effect of radiation, temperature and moisture on conidial germination of *Alternaria solani*. *Phytopathology* (78), p. 926-930.

Vakalounakis, D.J. 1991. Control of early blight of greenhouse tomato, caused by *Alternaria solani* by inhibiting sporulation with ultraviolet-absorbing vinyl film. *Plant Disease,* (75), p 795-797.

Zhu, Z. Y., Huang, X.M., and Li, Y.H. 1985. An efficient technique for inducing profuse sporulation of *Alternaria solani* in pure culture. *Acta Mycologica Sinica* 4: (3), p. 180-184.

**Early Blight Disease of Tomato**
***Edited by:*** **Virendra Kumar**
**ISBN: 978-93-5056-879-8**
***Edition:*** **2017**
***Published by:*** **Discovery Publishing House Pvt. Ltd., New Delhi (India)**

# Source of Resistance against Early Blight (*Alternaria solani*) in Tomato (*Solanum lycopersicum*)

[1]Priti Upadhyay, [2]Prabhash C. Singh, [3]B. Sinha, [4]M. Singh, [5]Rajesh Kumar, [6]K.K. Pandey, [7]Mathura Rai

Early blight incited by Alternaria solani (Ellis and Martin) Sorauer is one of the most damaging diseases of tomato [Solanum lycopersicum L. (Pevalta tt al. 2005), previously Lycopersicum esculentum Mill.]. The earliest symptoms of early blight are small, dark, necrotic lesions, usually on the leaves, which progress upward as the plants grow older. Huge yield losses occur due to early blight disease in tomato every year. The disease starts appearing from seedling stage till fruiting stage. Though fungicide use is effective control, hut economically not feasible in all areas of the world and may not be effective under weather conditions favourable for epidemics. Moreover, fungicides also cause environmental pollution and health hazards to human beings and animals. Development of resistant cultivars is the most economical and sustainable control measure of early blight Hence, die present work was planned to identify sources of resistance against early blight in tomato genotypes, which could provide a broader genetic base to facilitate the development of resistant cultivars.

A total of 14 germplasm/lines were used in mis screening during winter (rabi) season of 2006-07 and 2007-08. Tomato seeds were grown in nursery and 4-week old seedlings were transplanted in pots and grown under natural conditions at Indian Institute of Vegetable Research (IIVR), Varanasi, India. Three plants of each germplasm from 3 replications were taken for evaluation for resistance to Alternaria solani, A Varanasi isolate of Alternaria solani was propagated en Potato Dextrose Agar (PDA) in 90-mm Petridishes. The dishes were incubated at 25UC under a cool-white fluorescent diurnal light with 12 hr photoperiod for 10-15 days Todays old mycelial culture with thickening of conidiogeneu hyphae

1 Research Scholar (email: upadhyay.preeti@gmail.com).
2 Research Associate (email: prabhashiivr@gmail.com).
3 Professor (email: bsinha_vns@yahoo.co.in), Department of Genetics and Plant Breeding.
4 Principal Scientist (email: singhvns@gmail.com).
5 Senior Scientist (email: rajes74@gmail.com).
6 Principal Scientist (email: kkpiivr@gmail.com) Divisionof Plant Protection, IGFRI, Jhansi.
7 Director (email: mathura.rai@gmail.com)

and chlamydospore-like structures having proper aggressiveness and potential as described by Pandey et al, (2003) was used for inoculation. The plants were inoculate with a concentration of 157 cfu/ml inoculums during the screening process. Plants were transferred to growth chambe-and grown at temperature range of 23°-28°, with a 12K photoperiod. During the late seedling stage (6-7 weeks old) plants were individually spray-inoculated with A. sates 'Varanasi isolate*. All inoculated plants were kept moist K maintaining more than 95% relative humidity (RH) and L-30°C temperature for continuous 3 days. The plants were-closely observed each day after inoculation. In subsequent step, relative humidity was reduced to 85% and plants wert maintained at 12 hr photoperiod. The relative humidity light and temperature were controlled by a computer-regular system. This resulted in fee proper development of disease symptoms, *i.e.* distinct concentric rings and blighter. Disease severity was scored on 0-5 point scale as suggested by Pandey et al. (2003) and per cent disease incidence (PDI was calculated following McKinney (1923) formula. After 7 days of inoculation, plants were individually evaluated disease scoring and further all inoculated plants transferred in screen house to expose them to sunlight, dew and other diurnal weather changes.

The host plant reaction was classified based on the mem PDI as described by Pandey et al. (2003) as highly resistance (0-5%), resistant (5.1-12%), moderately resistance (12.1-25%), moderately susceptible (25.1-50%), susceptible (50.1-75%) and highly susceptible (75%).

Plant response against A. salani was measured by observing symptoms developed after inoculation. Of the 14 tomato lines screened for resistance against early blight controlled conditions, 'EC 520061' was found to be resistance with mean PDI of 9.99%, and 'NC EBR 4' was moderate susceptible (with mean PDI of 43.33%). The plant type of NC EBR 4' is determinate (*sp*) with dense foliage cover. NC EBR 4 is a reported resistant line against early blight, however, during this experimentation, it was found to be moderately susceptible. 'EC 520061' is a wild habrocbaites) relative of tomato having small green fruits on clusters with indeterminate growth habit. Fruits and upper pan of plants are hairy. Rest of the genotypes was either susceptible or highly susceptible for early blight. The average PDI ranged from 6.66 to 86.67%. The reaction of tomato genotypes may vary depending upon the climatic conditions prevailing under field condition. Best expression of early blight symptoms are observed during January-March in Varanasi under field condition. Similar results have been reported by Foolad *et. al.*, (2000) where significant differences jinong genotypes in their response to A. solani infection in the field, greenhouse, and growth chamber experiments were served. In the field and greenhouse experiments, disease itsponse varied from near-complete resistance in some accessions of the wild tomato species, L. hirsutum, to complete susceptibility in some tomato cultivar. Godika *et al.* (2001) reported that the incidence of Alternaria blight on leaves of Indian mustard increased when sown after 15 October under Rajasthan condition, however, infection on pods was decreased, probably due to rise in temperature and lowered humidity during pod formation.

These results suggested that screening against early blight disease provided information on new and broad source of resistance that could be useful to breeders hi order to develop improved cultivars with resistance against early blight. It was observed that 'EC 520061', the green-fruited wild species of tomato showed appreciable resistance and can be utilized in early blight breeding programme. However, there is need for further evaluation of more numbers of lines against early blight to find more resistant materials.

**Summary**

Fourteen tomato genotypes, representing two Solatium species were screened for resistance against early blight disease, Evaluations were conducted in growth chamber for disease severity and host resistance of the plants. 'EC520061' (S. habrochaites) showed resistance against infection, 3 genotypes 'NCEBR 4', 'FEB 4' and ' VRT 2' were moderately susceptible, while other genotypes were found either susceptible or highly susceptible. The resistant material found in this study is useful in the tomato improvement programme, especially for early blight disease.

## REFERENCES

Foolad M R, Ntahimpera N, Christ B J and Lin G Y. 2000. Comparison of field, greenhouse, and detached-leaflet evaluations of tomato germplasm for early blight resistance. Plant Disease **84**: 967-72.

Godika S, Pathak A K and Jain P K. 2001. Integrated management of alternaria blight (Alternaria brassicae) and white rust (Albugo Candida) diseases of Indian mustard (Brassica jwtcea). Indian Journal of Agricultural Sciences **71** (11); 733-5.

Mckinney H H. 1923. Influence of soil temperature and moisture on infection of wheat seedling by Helminthosporium sativum. Journal of Agriculture Research **26**; 195-217.

Pandey K K, Pandey P K, Kalloo G and Banerjee M K. 2003. Resistance to early blight of tomato with respect to various parameters of disease epidemics. Journal of General Plant Pathology **69**: 364-71,

Peralta IE, Knapp S and Spooner D.M. 2005. New species of wild tomatoes (Solanum Section Lycopersicon: Solanaceae) from Northern Peru. Systematic Botany **30** (2): 424-34.

**Early Blight Disease of Tomato**
*Edited by:* Virendra Kumar
**ISBN:** 978-93-5056-879-8
*Edition:* 2017
*Published by:* Discovery Publishing House Pvt. Ltd., New Delhi (India)

# Efficacy and Safety of Some Plant Extracts against Tomato Early Blight Disease Caused by *Alternaria solani*

[1]A.S. Derbalah, [2]M.S. El-Mahrouk, [3]A.B. El-Sayed

**ABSTRACT**

In an attempt to establish new control practices with low mammalian toxicity and low persistence in the environment against plant pathogens, crude extracts of seven plant species (Cassia senna, Caesalpinia gilliesii, Thespesia populnea var. acutiloba, Chrysanthemum frutescens, Euonymus japonicus, Bauhinia purpurea and Cassia fistula) were evaluated against Alternaria solani in tomato under laboratory and greenhouse conditions. Furthermore, GC-MS analysis was carried to identify the biologically active components of the most effective extract against A. solani. Moreover, the safety of the most effective extract was evaluated with respect to histological changes in treated rats' organs. The results showed that, B. purpurea was most effective plant extract against'early blight pathogen under laboratory and greenhouse conditions. The GC-MS analysis for the most effective plant extract showed the presence of different bioactive chemical components than known by its antifungal activity. The most effective plant extract showed low toxicity on rats relative to control. The results revealed that, the using of plant extracts can be regarded as effective and safe control of A solani in tomato.

**Keywords:** Extract, control, pathogen, fungicides, tomato.

## Introduction

More than 800 million people in developing countries do not have adequate food supplies and at least 10% of food is lost due to plant diseases (Strange and Scott, 2005). Plant diseases are caused by pathogens such as fungi, bacteria, nematodes and viruses. Compared to other plant parasites, fungi cause the greatest impact with regard to diseases and crop production losses either foliage or post harvest losses of fruits and vegetables through the decay resulted from fungal plant pathogens.

[1] Department of Pesticides.
[2] Department of Horticulture, Faculty of Agriculture, Kafr-El-Sheikh University, 33516, Egypt.
[3] Institute of Plant pathology Research, Agriculture Research Center, Egypt.

Tomato *(Lycopersicon esculentum* Mill.) is an important vegetable crop grown throughout the world. Tomato early blight disease caused by *Alternaria solani* become the most destructive in all over the world and yield losses up to 80% (Singh, 1985; Mathur and Shekhawat, 1986; Chandravanshi *et al.,* 1994). The control of tomato early blight disease has been almost exclusively based on the application of chemical pesticides. Several effective pesticides have been recommended against this pathogen but they not considered a long-term solution, due to concerns of expense, exposure risks and the hazards of its residues. Moreover, the development of resistance of pathogenic fungi towards synthetic pesticides is a great problem that can affect significantly the efficacy of chemical fungicides. Thus to find safe, efficacious and environmentally friendly fungicides considered as source of major concern (Mdee *et al.,* 2009). Presently, the search for natural products with novel uses, particularly related to pest management is very important task. The use of plant extracts has been shown to be eco-friendly and effective against many plant pathogens (Khallil, 2001; Hawamdeh and Ahmad, 2001; Saadabi, 2006; Gachomo and Kotchoni, 2008; Thobunluepop, 2009; Latha *et al.,* 2009; Moslem and El-Kholie, 2009; Duru and Onyedineke, 2010). Most of these substances were evaluated in order to find a safe alternative control methods to the human and the environment. Therefore, research should focus not only on the efficacy of botanical extracts against the target pests but also their safeties on human health in demand. Although, the assessment of enzymes activity in the blood is generally a sensitive measure of compounds toxicity than histopathological changes that can be assessed within a shorter time. The tissue alterations considered a confirmatory and supporting diagnostic role in the case of certain abnormalities in blood sampling (Cornelius *et al,* 1959). Most of the selected extracts in this study were known by their natural origin and safety to human heallh (Park *et al,* 2005; Panda and Kar, 1999). Moreover, no evidence of teratogenic or genotoxic activity has been detected by using of plant extracts to control pests (Mengs *et al,* 2004; Mitchell *et al,* 2006). This is besides the fact these plants are available in high amount in Egypt.

Therefore, the present work was designed to investigate the efficacy of certain plant extracts against the early blight pathogen, caused by *A. solani,* under laboratory and greenhouse conditions. This study has also to identify of the biologically active components of the most effective plant extract against the tested plant pathogen. Finally, it has been done to evaluate the toxicity of the most effective plant extract on rats with respect to histology changes in treated rats' organ relative to control.

## Materials and Methods

**Plants and preparation of crude extracts:** The leaves of seven medicinal plant species *(Cassia senna, Caesalpinia gilliesii, Thespesia populnea* var. *acutiloba, Chrysanthemum frutescens, Euonymus japonicus, Bauhinia purpurea* and *Cassia fistula)* were collected from a local nursery at Kafr El-Sheikh, Monofia, Gharbia and Alexandria Governorates, Egypt. *C. senna* (Alexandrian Senna) belonging to the family Fabaceae, is native to tropical Africa and cultivated in Egypt and Sudan. *C. gilliesii* (bird of paradise) belonging to the family Fabaceae, is native to tropical America, mainly Argentina and Uruguay. *T. populnea* var. *acutiloba* (Portia Tree) belonging to the family Malvaceae, is native to South Africa. *C. frutescens* (marguerite daisy) belonging to the family Asteraceae, is native to the Canary Islands. *E. japonicus* (Japanese Spindle) belonging to the family Celastraceae, is native to Japan, Korea and China. *B. purpurea* (Purple camel's foot) belonging to the family Fabaceae, is native to South China. *C. fistula* (Cassias) belonging to the family Fabaceae, is native to southern Asia. The different leave samples were oven dried for 24 h at 70°C and then, finely ground into a powder using a blender. Each sample (25 g) was extracted twice with 300 mL of methanol at room temperature for 2 days. The extracts were filtered through Whatman filter paper. The combined filtrate was concentrated to dryness by rotary evaporation at 40°C.

**Pathogen and plant cultivar source:** The *A. solani* isolated from tomato plant was obtained as culture slant from the Department of Mycology and Plant Disease Survey, Plant Pathology Research Institute, Giza Egypt. Tomato, *(Lycopersicon esculentum)* plant, cultivar Super Strain, was obtained from Legumes Department, Gemmiza Agriculture Research Station. Cultures were grown on potato dextrose agar in 9 cm diameter Petri dishes for 14 days and incubated at 28±1°C. The resultant fungal growth was providing the amount of water used amounts of sterilized distilled water for 2 min. The suspension was filtered through two layers of sterilized cheesecloth. The spore suspension was counted using a hemocytometer under the microscope and was adjusted to $10^6$ spores $mL^{-1}$ according to the methods described by Shahin and Shepared (1979).

**The tested fungicide:** The tested fungicide used in this study was metalaxyl with a trade name of vicomil 50% WP used at field rate of five 370 g $ha^{-1}$ and produced by Kafr-El-Zayat Company for chemicals and pesticides, Egypt This fungicide recommended for control early blight disease in vegetables crops in Egypt.

**Screening of plant extracts efficacy against *A solani* under laboratory conditions:** The seven extracts and metalaxyl were tested for their efficacy against *A. solani* in a completely randomized design. The efficacy of the tested plant extracts and fungicide was determined as percent of inhibition in the growth of selected fungus relative to the control treatment. Four concentrations for each plant extract (50, 100, 150 and 200 ppm) and four concentrations for the fungicide (1, 10, 25 and 50 ppm) were used. The required concentrations for plant extracts and fungicide were obtained by adding the appropriate amount of stock solution used to 60 mL portions of auto-calved PDA cooled to about 45°C. Four Petri dishes, 9 cm in diameter, were used as a replicate for each concentration of each treatment, including control. Control treatment was carried out without adding fungicide or plant extracts. Each dish was inoculated in the center with a disk (5 mm diameter) bearing the mycelium growth from *A. solani* culture (5 days old culture). The dishes were sealed with parafilm to avoid the evaporation of volatile compounds. The Dishes were incubated at 28°C until the full growth (mycelium reaching the edge of the plate) of the control treatment. The inhibition percentage of radial growth of *A. solani* was calculated using the formula suggested by Vincent (1947). Each the experiment (all concentrations for each treatment) was repeated three times. The inhibition percentage was calculated as shown in Eq. 1:

$$\%I = \frac{A - B}{A} \times 100 \quad (1)$$

where, A is the radial growth of the tested fungus in control, B is the radial growth of the tested fungus in treatment and %I is percentage of radial growth inhibition.

**Efficacy of the tested plant extracts against *A. solani* under greenhouse conditions:** These experiments were carried under greenhouse conditions. Seeds of tomato (L. *esculentum),* cultivar Super Strain were planted in 17 cm diameter plastic pots filled with 2 kg/each of unsterilized-loamy-clay soil. The plants were irrigated normally and the treatments were applied on the plants after 4 weeks from planting. The highest concentrations of tested plant extracts (150 and 200 ppm) were applied as foliar treatment on tomato early blight grown under greenhouse conditions. Metalaxyl was used as standard fungicide against *A. solani* at recommended dose level. Tomato plants in control were sprayed with water only at the same intervals used in plant extracts application. The tested plant extracts were applied twice, once at 15 days prior to inoculation with the pathogen and once 7 days before inoculation. The inoculation of tomato plants with *A. solani* spore suspension at concentration level of $10^6$ spore $mL^{-1}$ was carried out by sprayed it on tomato seedlings 10 days after transplanting using an atomizer. Inoculated seedlings were covered with black polyethylene bags for 48 h and kept in the green house at 30-32°C. Diseased plants were assessed weekly starting with the first symptom appearance till the end of the growing period. Twenty five leaves for every treatment were used to record the disease parameters according to the method of Awad (1980). Disease severity was assessed 8 days after inoculation according to the scale of Chirst (1991) and the efficacy of each treatment was calculated using Eq. 1:

$$\%\ \text{Efficacy} = \frac{\text{DSC-DST}}{\text{DSC}} \times 100 \quad (2)$$

Where:

DSC = Disease severity under control

DST = Disease severity under treatment

**Chemical composition of the most effective plant extract:** GC/MS analysis was carried to identify the components of the most effective plant extract *(B. purpurea)* according to the method described by Duarte-Almeida *et al.* (2004).

**Toxictty assessments:** The used adults Wistar male rats *(Rattus norvegicus)* with 8 weeks old and 80-100 g in weight were obtained from Faculty of Medicine, Tanta University. Wister rats were housed in wire cages under standard conditions with free access to drinking water and food The rats were kept in temperature-controlled room with 14 h light and 10 h dark cycles. The rats were given a standard diet as described by Romestaing *et al.* (2007). Before treatment, rats were left two weeks during feeding for adaptation. The animals were randomly divided into two groups each comprising of three animals.

The first group was for the treatment with the most effective plant extract (21 days) and the second group was for control. The most effective plant extract *(B. purpurea)* against the tested fungus were administered one time to rats orally at concentration level of 500 mg $kg^{-1}$ body weight Rats in control treatment were orally administrated with equal amount of almond oil. After 21 days of treatment, the rats were sacrificed under anesthesia. Then, specimens from kidney and lung were taken from each treatment and kept in neutral buffered formalin 10% for histopathological tests. The histopathology test was carried out at Histopathology Laboratory, Department of Histopathology, Faculty of Veterinary Medicine, Kafr El-Sheikh University according to the method described by Bancroft *et al.* (1996).

**Statistical analysis:** Data were subjected to the analysis of variance test and Newman-Keuls's multiple range test using a computer program SAS (Version 6.12, SAS Institute Inc., Cary, USA). The level of significance was 0.05.

## Results

**Effect of the tested plant extracts on radial growth of *A. solani*:** Seven plant species, belonging to the various families were selected and evaluated for their antifungal activity against *A. solani,* the causal of early blight disease in tomato. All the tested plant extracts at different concentration levels inhibited the radial growth of *A. solani,* relative to control. The leaf extract of *T. populnea var. acutiloba* was the most effective one against *A. solani* with the inhibition percentage of 79.4%, followed by *C. frutescens, C. gilliesii, C. senna, E. japonicus, B. purpurea* and *C. fistula* with inhibition percentages of 73.3%, 71.1, 67, 59.4, 56.4 and 54.2%, respectively (Table 1). However, the fungicide metalaxyl as a recommended compound against *A. solani* was still the most effective treatment compared to all tested botanical extracts. The efficiency of the tested botanical extracts was concentration dependent since it's toxicity against *A. solani* increased with the increasing of their concentrations level.

**Efficacy of plant extracts on tomato early blight pathogen under greenhouse conditions:** The protective action of the tested plant extracts relative

**Table 8.1: Efficacy of the tested plant extracts and metalaxyl against early blight disease pathogen *(A- solani)* under laboratory conditions**

| Treatments | Concentrations | Inhibition percentages |
|---|---|---|
| *C. senna* | 50 | 27.7a |
| | 100 | 34.5d |
| | 150 | 39.8i |
| | 200 | 39.4J |
| *C. giUiesii* | 50 | 32.3v |
| | 100 | 51.5fg |
| | 150 | 59.0m |
| | 200 | 73.3pq |
| *T. populnea* var. *acutiloba* | 50 | 24.8igh |
| | 100 | 31.6r |
| | 150 | 34.2c |
| | 200 | 56.4f |
| *C.jhttescens* | 50 | 32.7q |
| | 100 | 39.5fgh |
| | 150 | 45.5J |
| | 200 | 71.1L |
| *E. japonicus* | 50 | 25.5q |
| | 100 | 31.0u |
| | 150 | 33.9c |
| | 200 | 67.0fe |
| *B. purpurea* | 50 | 44. 7t |
| | 100 | 57.5L |
| | 150 | 68.8po |
| | 200 | 79.4s |
| *Cfstula* | 50 | 21.7ih |
| | 100 | 29.7o |
| | 150 | 41.9b |
| | 200 | 54.2e |
| Metalaxyl | 1 | 33.5c |
| | 10 | 68.7n |
| | 20 | 86.2k |
| | 50 | 98.0x |
| Control | 0 | 0.00y |

Lower case letters in this column indicate separation of means according to the Student Newman Keuls multiple range test ($p<0.05$)

to the recommended fungicide metalaxyl against *A. solani* in Tomato plant that evaluated under greenhouse conditions is shown in Table 2. The results showed that metalaxyl was the most effective treatment against *A. solani* followed by *C. gilliesi, T. populnes* var. *acertiloba, C. frutesscens, C. fistula, C. senna, B. purpurea*

**Table 8.2 Efficacy of the tested plant extracts and metalaxyl against early blight disease pathogen (A. *solani)* under greenhouse conditions**

| Treatments | Disease severity | % Efficacy | Disease severity | Efficacy |
|---|---|---|---|---|
| C. serma | 13.0d | 47.60 | 9.02cde | 66.00 |
| C. giUiesii | 10.8e | 56.47 | 9.46de | 64.31 |
| T. populnea var. acutiloba | 17.6b | 29.03 | 9.99cd | 62.31 |
| C.frutescens | 11.25e | 54.66 | 9.56d | 63.97 |
| E. japonic us | 15.4e | 28.00 | 10.85bc | 59.04 |
| B. purpurea | 9.7e | 61.00 | 8.07e | 69.55 |
| C. Jistula | 12.65d | 49.00 | 9.63cde | 63.67 |
| Metalaxyl | 7.57f | 69.50 | 5.24g | 80.20 |
| Control | 24.81 a | 0.00 | 26.50a | 0.00 |

Lower case letters in this column indicate separation of means according to the Student Newman Keuls multiple range test ($p<0.05$)

and *E. japnicus,* respectively either at concentration level of 150 or 200 ppm. The results also implied that the efficacy of the plant extracts was higher at a concentration level of 200 ppm than that of 150 ppm (efficacy was concentration dependent). There was no phytotoxicity of the tested plant extracts on tomato was observed Moreover, one of the most important notices that, there is no phytotoxicity of the tested plant extracts on tomato was recorded.

**Composition of the most effective botanical extract against** ***A solani:*** The identified compounds from the most effective botanical extract *(B. purpurea)*

**Table 8.3 The main constituents of *B. purpurea* extract identified by GC-MS analysis**

| Identified compounds | Retention time (min) | %Area |
|---|---|---|
| Eugenol | 8.37 | 5.80 |
| Alpha humulene | 9.15 | 2.56 |
| Myristicin | 9.71 | 0.88 |
| Elemicin | 9.90 | 0.69 |
| Tetradecanoic acid methyl ester | 11.17 | 0.66 |
| Tetradecanoic acid | 11.61 | 3.52 |
| Mone inositol | 11.97 | 8.73 |
| 2-methyl -1- thia cyclopentene | 12.05 | 5.09 |

| Acrylic acid | 12.19 | 6.60 |
|---|---|---|
| 4,6 Di-o-methyl-alpha d galactose | 12.43 | 4.15 |
| Methylthiolane | 12.57 | 5.47 |
| Pivalion | 12.61 | 5.20 |
| Pentadecanoic-4-methylethyl ester | 13.07 | 2.53 |
| n-hexadecanoic acid | 13.60 | 7.72 |
| 9,12,15 octadecatrienoic methyl ester | 15.13 | 2.56 |
| Phytol | 15.28 | 12.8 |
| Oleic acid | 15.70 | 3.18 |
| 9,12, 15 octadecanoic acid | 15.78 | 2.93 |

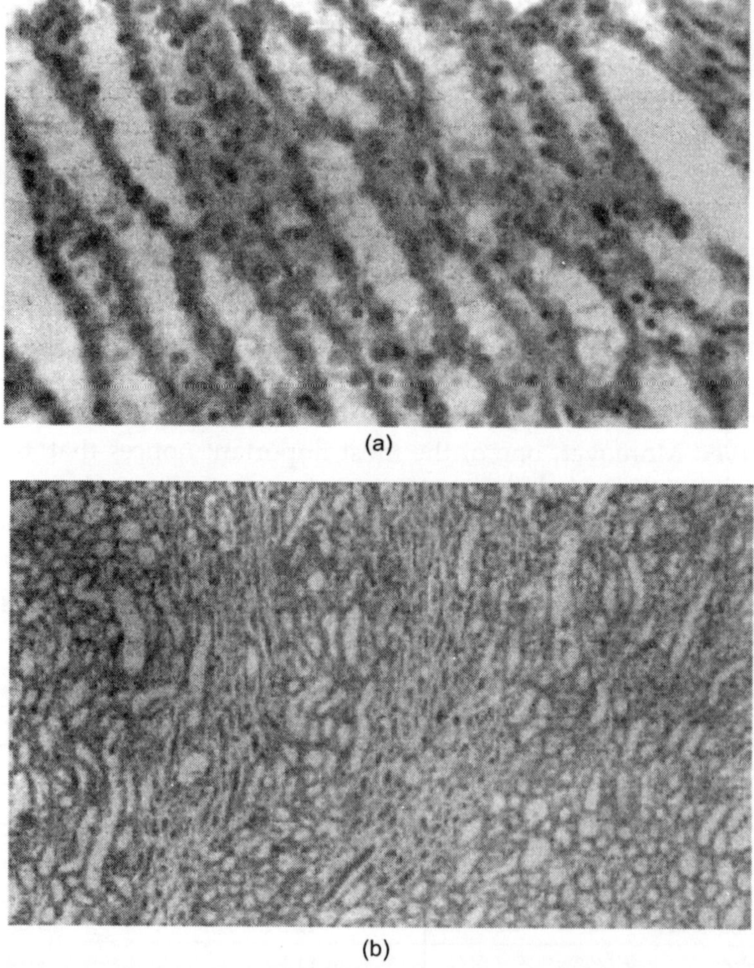

(a)

(b)

**Fig. 8.1 (a-b) Sections in kidney of rats treated with B. purpurea (b) at dose level of 500 mg kg$^{-1}$ after 21 days of treatment relative to control (a)**

against *A. solani* are given in Table 3. Eighteen compounds were identified from *B. purpurea* plant extract as shown in Table 3. The identified compounds are belonging to aldehydes, esters, alcohols and fatty acids.

## Toxicity evaluation

**The histopathological changes in the kidney:** The normal structure of kidney tissue was shown in Fig. 1(a). For the rats treated with *B. purpurea* extract at dose level of 500 mg $kg^{-1}$, the kidney tissue was the lung tissue is normal as control except for some collecting tubules (Fig. Ib).

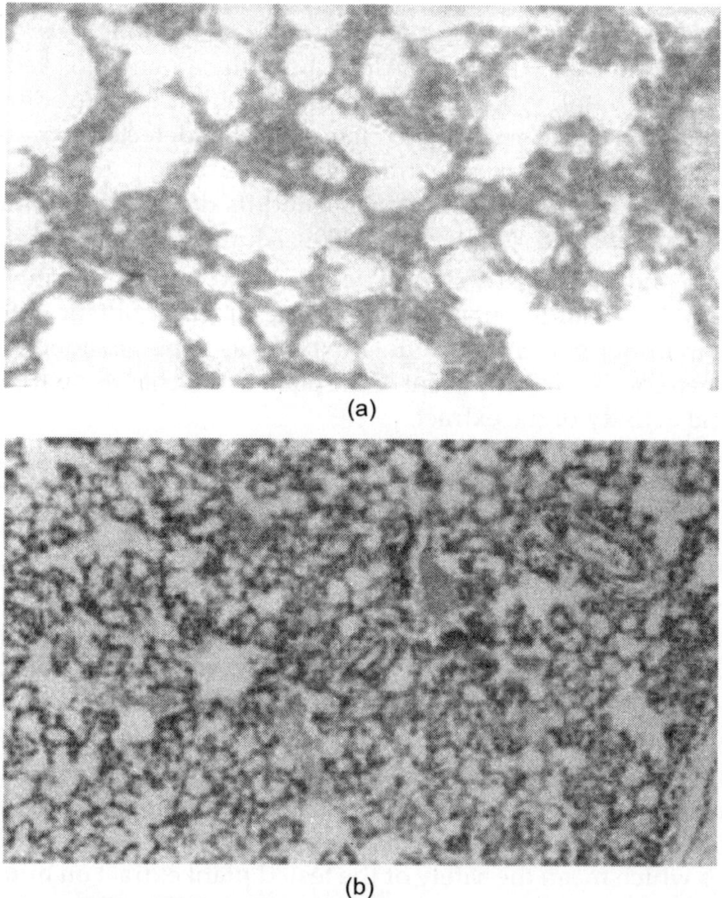

(a)

(b)

**Fig. 2 (a-b): Sections in lung of rats treated with *B. purpurea* (b) at dose level of 500 mg $kg^{-1}$ after 21 days of treatment relative to control (a)**

**The histopathological changes in the lung:** The normal structure of lung tissue was shown in Fig. 2a. For the rats treated with *B. purpurea* extract at dose level of 500 mg $kg^{-1}$, the tissue was normal as control with some lymphocytes infiltration and the blood vessels were observed to be engorged with blood (Fig. 2b). However, these changes still not significant relative to the normal tissue.

## Discussion

In the present study, the tested plant extracts showed antifungal activity against early blight pathogen in tomato. The efficacy of different plant extracts belonging to different species other than the tested botanical extracts against the *A. solani* either under laboratory or greenhouse conditions have been reported (Bergaoui *et al.*, 2007; Tegegne *et al.*, 2008; Chutia *et al.*, 2009; Latha *et al.*, 2009; Zaker and Mosallanejad, 2010). However, for the tested plant extracts especially the effective ones against early blight pathogen *A. solani,* this is considered the first report.

It was observed that, among the identified compounds from *B. purpurea* extract, some compounds such as, Alpha humulene , eugenol, tetradecanoic acid, oleic acid, Phytol, 9, 12, 15 oetadecanoic acid and n-hexadecanoic acid were detected with high percentages relative to other detected compounds. The antifungal activity of *B. purpurea* extract against A., *solani* pathogen may be due to the presence of the previous fatty acids and its derivatives (Hammer *et al.*, 2003; Bergaoui *et al.*, 2007; Chutia *et al.*, 2009; Ahmadi *et al.*, 2010).

Although, the antifungal activity of tested plant extracts is mainly attributed to its major compounds but the synergistic or antagonistic effect of one compound in minor percentage in the mixture has to be considered (Ragasa *et al.*, 2002). Therefore, each component of the plant extract has its own contribution on biological activity of the extract.

The essential oils in the tested plant extracts as antimicrobial agents considered at low risk for resistance development by pathogenic microorganisms. It is believed that it is difficult for the pathogens to develop resistance to such a mixture of components with, apparently, different mechanisms of antimicrobial activity *(Liu et al.,* 2008).

The botanical extracts as pest control agents present two main characters: the first is their safety to the people and the environment and the second is the less resistance development against it by the tested pathogen. Regarding to the safety, the toxicity evaluation of the most effective plant extract revealed that, there were some slight variations occurred sporadically in treated rats relative to control with the respect to enzymes markers and histopathology of treated organs. Moreover, the observed changes in the tissues were mostly uncorrelated with the dosages which mean the safety of the tested plant extract on human health. With the referring to resistance development, it is believed that, it is difficult for the insect to develop resistance to such a mixture of bioactive components with, apparently, different mechanisms of fungicidal activity (Liu *et al,* 2008).

## Conclusions

The fungicidal activity of the extracts against *A. solani* indicates the potential of some plant species as a natural source of fungicidal material. Antifungal activity was confirmed in all the tested plant species, although the results showed that different plant extracts varied in their effectiveness in inhibiting the mycelia growth of different pathogens tested. *In vivo* results under greenhouse confirmed and could be a viable option for controlling *A. solani* because leaves are available in all seasons and it is a world wide invasive species. The ability of using botanical products as alternative of chemical control of plant pathogens is possible. This approach can contribute in reducing the amount applied of fungicides and subsequently minimize its hazards to the environment and human health. Work in this regards should continuing on other invasive species on isolating antifungal compounds and on field trials with promising extracts or compounds. Also, further research is needed in order to obtain information regarding the practical effectiveness of essential oils to protect the plants or the plant products without toxic effects.

## REFERENCES

Ahmadi, F., S. Sadeghi, M. Modarresi, R. Abiri and A. Mikaeli, 2010. Chemical composition, *in vitro* anti-microbial, antifungal and antioxidant activities of the essential oil and methanolic extract of *Hymenocrater longiflorus* Benth., of Iran. Food Chem. Toxicol., 48: 1137-1144.

A wad, N.G.H., 1980. Studies on tomato collar rot caused by *A. solani.* M.Sc Thesis, Faculty of Agriculture Zagzig University, Egypt

Bancroft, J.D., A. Stevans andD.R. Turner, 1996. Theory and Practice of Histopathological Techniques. 4th Edn., Churchill Livingstone, Eidinburg, London, Melbourne, New York.

Bergaoui, A., N. Boughalleb, H.B. Jarmet, F. Harzallah-Shiric, M. El-Mahjoub andZ. Mighri, 2007. Chemical composition and antifungal activity of volatiles from three *Opuntia* species growing in Tunisia. Pak. J. Biol. Sci., 10:2485-2489.

Chandravanshi, S.S., B.P. Singh and M.P. Thakur, 1994. Persistence of different fungicides used against *AHernaria alternata* in tomato. Indian Phytopathol., 47:241-244.

Chirst, B.J., 1991. Effect of disease assessment methods on ranking potato cultivars for resistance to early blight Plant Dis., 75: 353-356.

Chutia, M., P.D. Bhuyan, M.G. Pathak, T.C. Sarmaand P. Boruah, 2009. Antifungal activity and chemical composition of *Citrus reticulatareticulate* Blanco essential oil against phytopathogens from North East India. LWT-Food Sci. Technol., 42: 777-780.

Cornelius, C.E., J. Bishop, J. SwitzerandE.A. Rhode, 1959. Serum and tissue transaminase activities in domestic animals. Cornell Vet, 49: 116-126.

Duarte-Almeida, J.M., G. Negri and A. Salatino, 2004. Volatile oils in leaves of *Bauhinia* (Fabaceae Caesalpinioideae). Biochem. Syst Ecol., 32: 747-753.

Duru, C.M. andN.E. Onyedineke, 2010. *In vitro* study on the antimicrobial activity and phytochemical analysis of ethanolic extracts of the mesocarp of *Voacanga qfricana.* Am. J. Plant Physiol., 5: 163-169.

Gachomo, E.W. and O. Simeon Kotchoni, 2008. Extract from drought-stress leaves enhances disease resistance through induction of pathogenesis related proteins and accumulation of reactive molecules. Biotechnology, 7: 273-279.

Hammer, K.A., C.F. Carson and T.V. Riley, 2003. Antifungal activity of the components of *Melaleuca alternifolia* (tea tree) oil. J. Applied Microbiol., 95:853-860.

Hawamdeh, A.S. and S. Ahmad, 2001. *In vitro* control of *Alternaria solani,* the cause of early blight of tomato. J. Biological Sci., 1: 949-950.

Khallil, A.R.M., 2001. Phytofungitoxic properties in the aqueous extracts of some plants. Pak. J. Biol. Sci., 4: 392-394.

Latha, P., T. Anand , N. Ragupathi, V. Prakasam and R Samiyappan, 2009. Antimicrobial activity of plant extracts and induction of systemic resistance in tomato plants by mixtures of PGPR strains and Zimmu leaf extract against *Alternaria solani.* Biol. Control., 50: 85-93.

Liu, W.W., W. Mu, B.Y. Zhu, Y.C. Du, F. Liu, 2008. Antagonistic activities of volatiles from four strains *of Bacillus* spp. and *Paenibacillus* spp. against soil-borne plant pathogens. Agric. Sci. China, 7: 1104-1114.

Mathur, K. andK.S. Shekhawat, 1986. Chemical control of early blight in kharif sown tomato. Indian J. Mycol. Plant Pathol., 16: 235-236.

Mdee, L.K., P. Masoko and J.N. Eloff, 2009. The activity of extracts of seven common invasive plant species on fungal phytopathogens. South African J. Bot, 75: 375-379.

Mengs, U., J. Mitchell, S. McPherson, R. Gregson and J. Tigner, 2004. A 13-week oral toxicity study of senna in the rat with an 8-week recovery period. Arch. Toxicol., 78: 269-275.

Mitchell, J.M., U. Mengs, S. McPherson, J. Zijlstra, P. Dettinar, R. Gregson and J.C. Tigner, 2006. An oral carcinogenicity and toxicity study of senna *(Tinnevelly senna* fruits) in the rat. Arch. Toxicol., 80: 34-44.

Moslem, M.A. and E.M. El-Kholie, 2009. Effect of neem *(Azardirachta indica* A. Juss.) seeds and leaves extract on some plant pathogenic fungi. Pak. J. Biol. Sci., 12: 1045-1048.

Panda, S. and A. Kar, 1999. *Withania somnifera* and *Bauhinia purpwea* in the regulation of circulating thyroid hormone concentration in female mice. J. Ethnopharmacol., 67: 233-239.

Park, S.H., S.K. Ko and S.H. Chung, 2005. *Euonymus alatus* prevents the hyperglycemia and hyperlipidemia induced by high-fat diet in ICR mice. J. Ethnopharmacol., 102: 326-335.

Ragasa, C.Y., J.O. Hofilena and J.A. Rideout, 2002. New Furanoid Diterpenes from *Caesalpinia pulcherrima.* J.Nat. Prod., 65: 1107-1110.

Romestaing, C., M.A. Piquet, E. Bedu, V. Rouleau and M. Dautresme *et al,* 2007. Long term highly saturated fat diet does not induce NASH in Wistar rats. Nutr. Metab., 4: 4-4.

Saadabi, A.M.A., 2006. Antifungal activity of some saudi plants used in traditional medicine. Asian J. Plant Sci., 5: 907-909.

Shahin, E.A. and J.F. Shepared, 1979. An efficient technique for inducing profuse sporulation of Altemaria species. Phytopathology, 69: 618-620.

Singh, R.S., 1985. Diseases of Vegetable Crops. Oxford and IBH Publishing Co., New Delhi, Pages: 346.

Strange, R.N. andP.R. Scott, 2005. Plant disease: A threat to global food security. Annu. Rev. Phytopathol, 43:83-116.

Tegegne, G., J. Pretorius and J. Swart, 2008. Antifungal properties of *Agapanthus africanus* L. extracts against plant pathogens. CropProtec., 27: 1052-1060.

Thobunluepop, P., 2009. Implementation of bio-fungicides and seed treatment in organic rice cv. KDML 105 farming. Pak. J. Biol. Sci., 12: 1119-1126.

Vincent, J.M., 1947. Distortion of fungal hyphae in the presence of certain inhibitors. Nature, 159: 850-850.

Zaker, M. andH. Mosallanejad, 2010. Antifungal activity of some plant extracts on *Alternaria alternata,* the causal agent of altemaria leaf spot of potato. Pak. J. Biol. Sci., 13: 1023-1029.

**Early Blight Disease of Tomato**
*Edited by:* Virendra Kumar
ISBN: 978-93-5056-879-8
*Edition:* 2017
*Published by:* Discovery Publishing House Pvt. Ltd., New Delhi (India)

# Control of Tomato Early Blight Disease by Certain Aqueous Plant Extracts

[1]Nashwa M.A. Sallam

## ABSTRACT

The objective of this work to study the effect of six plant extracts, Ocimum basilicum (Sweat Basil), Azadirachta indica (Neem), Eucalyptus chamadulonsis (Eucalyptus), Datura stramonium (Jimsonweed), Nerium oleander (Oleander) and Allium sativum (Garlic) against Alternaria solani in vitro and in vivo. In in vitro study the leaf extracts of D. stramonium, A. indica and A. sativum at 5% concentration caused highest reduction of mycelial growth of A. solani (44.4, 43.3 and 42.2%, respectively), while O. basilicum at 1 and 5% and N, oleander at 5% caused the lowest inhibition of mycelia growth of the pathogen. In greenhouse experiments the highest reduction of disease severity was achieved by fungicide (Ridomil Plus 50% WP, 15% metalaxy+35% Copper oxychloride, at 2 g L–1) 82.8% followed by the extracts of A. sativum at 5% and D. stramonium at 1 and 5% concentration. The greatest reduction of disease severity was achieved by Ridomil Plus 74.2% followed by A. sativum at 5% and the smallest reduction was obtained when tomato plant was treated with O. basilicum at 1 and 5% (46.1 and 45.2%, respectively). Fungicide, D. stramonium and A. sativum at 5% increased the fruit yield 85.7, 76.2 and 66.7% compared to infected control. All treatments, plant extracts and fungicide (Ridomil Plus), significantly reduced the early blight disease as well as increased the yield of tomato compared to infected control under field condition.

**Keywords:** *Alternaria solani*, plant extracts, antimicrobial activity, early blight, tomato.

## Introduction

Under Egyptian conditions tomato plants are vulnerable to infection early blight disease caused by *Alternaria solani* (Ellis and Martin) Sorauer (Abada *et al.*, 2008) which causes great reduction in the quantity and quality of fruit yield The *Alternaria* fungus can cause disease on all parts of the plant (leaf blight, stem collar rot and fruit lesions) and result in severe damage during all stages of plant development (Abada *et at.*, 2008).

---

[1] Department of Plant Pathology, Faculty of Agriculture, Assiut University, 71526 Assiut, Egypt

This disease is controlled mainly with agro chemicals. However, the world wide trend towards environmentally-safe methods of plant disease control in sustainable agriculture calls for reducing the use of these synthetic chemical fungicides. In an attempt to modify this condition some alternative methods of control have been adopted. Recent efforts have focused on developing environmentally safe, long lasting and effective biocontrol methods for the management of plant diseases. Natural plant products are important sources of new agrochemicals for the control of plant diseases (Kagale *et al.*, 2004). Furthermore, biocides of plant origin are non-phytotoxic, systemic and easily biodegradable (Qasem and Aau-Blan, 1996). It is now known that various natural plant products can reduce populations of foliar pathogens and control disease development and then these plant extracts have potential as environmentally safe alternatives and as components in integrated pest management programs (Bowers and Locke, 2004). A number of plant species have been reported to possess natural substances that are toxic to several plant pathogenic fungi (Goussous *et al.*, 2010). Dushyent and Bohra (1997) studied the effect of 11 different plant extracts on mycelial growth of *A. solani* and found that leaf extracts of some plants *i.e. Tamarix aphytta* and *Salsola baryosma* totally inhibited the growth of the pathogen *in vivo.* Also, Wszelaki and Miller (2005) reported that garlic extracts significantly reduced the early blight disease on tomato. Additionally, several plant extracts have shown antimicrobial activity against fungal pathogens under *in vitro* and *in vivo* conditions (Kagale *et al.*, 2004). Therefore, our present study investigated the efficacy of various Egyptian plants leaf extracts, *Ocimum basilicum, Azadirachta indica, Eucalyptus chamadulonsis, Datura stramonium, Nerium oleander and Allium sativum* for control of early blight of tomato under greenhouse and field conditions. The treatments were compared with a commonly used fungicide (Ridomil Plus).

## Materials and Methods

**Plant materials:** Seeds of tomato *(Solanum lycopericum* L.) cultivar Super Strain B were obtained from the Ministry of Agriculture, Egypt and used in this study. Seeds were sown in plastic pots, each of 30 cm diameter and containing a soil mixture consisting of sand 3 kg pot and 10 g slow-release fertilizer per kg (N.P.K 12: 4: 6). All pots were placed on a benchtop in a climate controlled greenhouse at 30 ± 5°C with 68-80% RH and watered as required

**Isolation and pathogenicity tests of the causal pathogen**: Six fungal isolates were isolated from naturally diseased tomato leaves and fruits showing blight symptoms. Pathogenicity tests *of Alternaria* sp. isolates were carried out under greenhouse conditions in 2007-2008 experiments in greenhouse of Plant Pathology Department, Faculty of Agriculture, Assiut University, Assiut, Egypt. The inoculum was prepared by growing each of the tested isolates on PDA medium at 27°C for 15 days. Then 10 mL of sterile distilled water was added to each plate and colonies were carefully scraped with a sterile needle. The resulting conidial suspension from each isolate was adjusted to SxlO$^6$ spores $mL^{-1}$ and used for inoculation of 20 tomato plants (cv. Super Strain B), using an atomizer. After inoculation, plants were covered with polyethylene bags for 48 h to maintain a high humidity conditions. After 48 h, bags were removed and plants were kept under greenhouse conditions. Pots were maintained in completely randomized design under glasshouse conditions. Two weeks after inoculation, disease severity was recorded The trial was repeated twice. The intensity of disease was recorded in each treatment following the score chart 0-9 scale (0-Healthy; 1 = 1 to 5%; 2 = 6to 10%; 3 = 11 to 25%; 5 = 26 to 50% and 7 = 51-75% 9 = >76% leaf area infected) proposed by Latha *etal.* (2009).

**Preparation of extracts:** Extracts from leaves of six plants namely, *O. basilicum, A. indica, E. chamadulonsis, D. stramonium, N. oleander* and A *sativwn* were collected from different parts of Assiut, Egypt and tested for their efficacy in reducing the mycelial growth of *A. solani in vitro* using the poisoned food technique (Schmitz, 1930). Ten grams of fresh leaf material of each plant species was collected, washed with water and crushed in a mortar and pestle by adding sterile distilled water at the rate of 10 mL $g^{-1}$ of plant tissue and the homogenates were centrifuged at 10000xg for 15 min at 4°C and the supernatant solutions were collected. The plant extract was diluted further to have 1 and 5% concentration (v/v). These fractions were sterilized using 0.2 m disposable syringe filters and used for assay of antimicrobial activity as described below.

The PDA media amended with five milliliters of aqueous leaf extract, 1 and 5%, of each plant extracts individually were inoculated with mycelial discs (9 mm diameter) taken from the advancing edges of 7 day-old pure cultures of *A. solani.* The control experiments had distilled water instead of plant extracts. The inoculated media were incubated at temperature 27±1 °C. Four plates were each treatment was used as a replicates. The diameter of the fungal colony was measured using a meter rule along two diagonal lines drawn on the reverse side of each Petri plate 7 days after inoculation. Each treatment was replicated three times with four plates per replication.

**Testing of plant extracts against early blight of tomato under greenhouse conditions:** Fungicide (Ridomil Plus 50% WP, 15% metalaxyl+35% Copper oxychloride, at 2 g $L^{-1}$) and plant extracts treatments at 1 and 5% were applied as foliar application, 30 mL on tomato plants, seven week olds and every 15 days up to 60 days of planting after two days from second spraying tomato plants were inoculated with 20 mL of *A. solani* suspension containing $5 \times 10^6$ cfu $mL^{-1}$. After inoculation, plants were kept in a climate chamber with 28°C day temperature and 85% relative humidity. Disease development was recorded 15 days after inoculation. Disease severity was recorded as described before. Greenhouse experiments were repeated twice.

**Testing of plant extracts on early blight of tomato under field conditions:** The field trials were conducted at the Experimental Farm of Faculty of Agriculture, Assiut University, Assiut, Egypt in 2008 and 2009 growing seasons. Field plots (3 × 3.5 m) comprised two rows and 5 plants/row arranged in a completely randomized block design. Three plots were used as replicates for each treatment as well as for the untreated control treatment. Application of plant extracts was carried out as in greenhouse experiments. Disease development was recorded 15 days after inoculation Disease severity was recorded as described before. Field experiments were repeated twice. At harvest time, the average accumulated yield was calculated for each treatments including untreated control. Ten plants from each replicate were harvested to assess the total yield of each treatment (tonha$^{-1}$).

**Statistical analysis:** All experiments were performed twice. Analyses showed no significant interaction between the two tests run for any of the treatment. Therefore, results from duplicate tests were combined for final analysis. Analyses of variance were carried out using MSTAT-C program version 2.10 (MSTAT-C 1991). Least Significant Difference (LSD) was employed to test for significant difference between treatments at $p = 0.05$ (Gomez and Gomez, 1984).

## Results

**Identification of the causal pathogen:** Six fungal isolates were obtained from naturally diseased tomato leaves and fruits showing blight symptoms and identified as *A. solani,* based on the morphological characteristics (Ellis, 1976).

**Pathogenicity tests:** Results in Fig. 1 indicate that all the tested isolates of *A. solani* were able to infect tomato plants causing typical early blight symptoms with different degrees of disease severity. Data indicate that isolates 1, 3 and 5 were highly pathogenic and caused the highest disease severity. Isolates 2 and 4 exhibited the lowest disease severity on tomato plants followed by isolate 6. On the basis of this result, isolate 1 was used in the following experiments.

**Effect of plant extracts on radial growth of A *solani'*:** Six plant species were selected and evaluated for the antimicrobial activity against *A. solani.* All the leaf extracts of tested plants at 1 and 5% concentration were effective in inhibiting the radial growth of *A. solani,* compared to control. The leaf extract of *D. stramonium, A. indica* and *A. sativum* at 5% concentration caused highest reduction of mycelial growth of *A. solani* (44.4, 43.3 and 42.2%, respectively), followed by *E. chamadulonsis* and *D. stramonium* at 1 % concentration. *O. basilicium* at 1 and 5% and *N. oleander* at 1% caused the lowest inhibition of mycelial growth of the pathogen. Overall the Ridomil Plus at 2 g L$^{-1}$ caused the highest reduction of the pathogen by 77.8% (Table 1).

**Effect of plant extracts on early blight incidence of tomato under artificial infection in greenhouse conditions:** The different concentrations of six plant extracts, *O. basilicum, A. indica, E. chamadulonsis, D. stramonium, N. oleander* and

*A. sativum,* significantly reduced the early blight diseases (Table 2). The greatest reduction 82.8% of disease severity was achieved by Ridomil Plus at 2 g LT[1]. The most effective treatments from plant extracts were *A. sativum* at 1 and 5% followed by *D. stramonium* at 1 and 5% concentration. The least reduction of disease severity was achieved by *O. basilicum* at 1% (35.2%). Other plant extracts treatments were moderately effective.

**Effect of some plant extracts on early blight incidence of tomato under field conditions:** All treatments, plant extracts and fungicide (Ridomil Plus at 2 g $L^{-1}$),

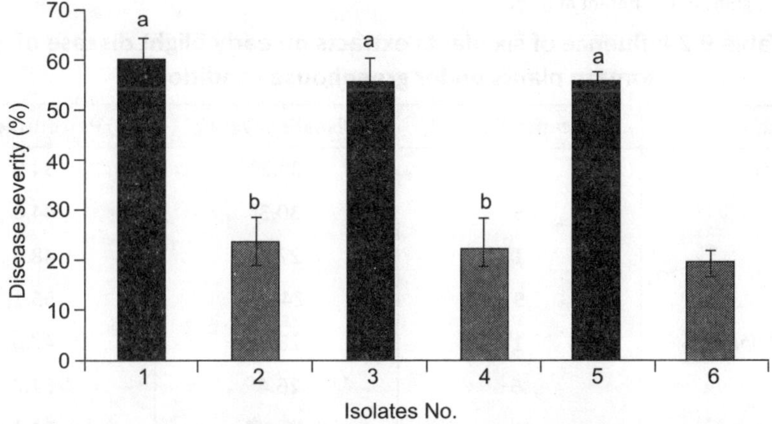


**Fig. 9.1 Pathogenicity tests of six isolates of *Alternaria solani* on tomato plants (cv. Super Strain B) under greenhouse conditions. Different letters indicate significant differences among treatments according to least significant difference test (p = 0.05). Means of standard deviation for twenty plants per treatment are shown**

**Table 9.1 *In vitro* effect of six plants extracts on the linear growth of *Alternaria solani***

| Treatments | Concentration (%) | Linear growth (%) | Percent reduction |
|---|---|---|---|
| *O. basilicum* | 1 | $7.0^{b}$ | 22.2 |
| | 5 | $6.9^{b}$ | 23.3 |
| *A. indica* | 1 | $6.2^{c}$ | 31.1 |
| | 5 | $5.1^{d}$ | 43.3 |
| *E. chamadulonsis* | 1 | $6.5^{c}$ | 27.8 |
| | 5 | $6.3^{c}$ | 30.0 |
| *D. stramonium* | 1 | $5.5^{d}$ | 38.9 |
| | 5 | $5.0^{d}$ | 44.4 |
| *Nerium oleander* | 1 | $6.9^{b}$ | 23.3 |
| | 5 | $6.1^{c}$ | 32.2 |

| | | | |
|---|---|---|---|
| *A. Sativum* | 1 | 6.1$^{c}$ | 32.2 |
| | 5 | 5.2$^{d}$ | 42.2 |
| Ridomil Plus g $L^{-1}$ | 2 | 2.0$^{e}$ | 77.8 |
| Control | | 9.0$^{a}$ | 0.0 |

A five milliliters of aqueous leaf extracts prepared from each of the plant sample was mixed with 45 mL of PDA medium (1 and 5%).[b] The percent inhibition of radial growth of A *solani* was calculated. Each treatment was replicated three times with four plates per repltcatioa Values in the column followed by the same letter are not significantly different at ($p$ = 0.05)

**Table 9.2 Influence of six plants extracts on early blight disease of tomato plants under greenhouse conditions**

| Treatments | Concentration (%) | Disease severity | (%) Percentreduction |
|---|---|---|---|
| *O. basilicum* | 1 | 35.2$^{b}$ | 34.9 |
| | 5 | 30.3$^{c}$ | 44.0 |
| *A, indica* | 1 | 27.8$^{c}$ | 48.6 |
| | 5 | 24.3$^{cd}$ | 55.1 |
| *E. chamadulonsis* | 1 | 28.7$^{c}$ | 47.0 |
| | .5 | 26.4$^{c}$ | 51.2 |
| *D. stramonium* | 1 | 19.4$^{de}$ | 64.1 |
| | 5 | 17.2$^{de}$ | 68.2 |
| *Nerium oleander* | 1 | 30.0$^{c}$ | 44.5 |
| | 5 | 25.9$^{c}$ | 52.1 |
| *A. Sativum* | 1 | 20.8$^{cd}$ | 61.6 |
| | 5 | 15.3$^{f}$ | 71.7 |
| Ridomil plus g $L^{-1}$ | 2 | 9.3$^{g}$ | 82.8 |
| Infected Control | | 54.1$^{a}$ | 0.0 |

The intensity of the disease was recorded in each treatment as proposed by Latha *et al.,* (2009). Values in the column followed by different letters indicate significant differences among treatments according to least significant difference test ($p$ = 0.05)

**Table 9.3: Influence of six plant extracts on early blight disease and yield of tomato under field conditions**

| Treatments | Concen-tration (%) | Disease severity C%) | Percent reduction | Yield (t $ha^{-1}$) | Percent increase (%) |
|---|---|---|---|---|---|
| *O. basilicum* | 1 | 46.1$^{b}$ | 21.1 | 2.7$^{cb}$ | 28.6 |
| | 5 | 45.2$^{b}$ | 23.6 | 2.8$^{cb}$ | 33.3 |
| *A. incSca* | 1 | 41.3$^{c}$ | 30.2 | 2.8$^{cb}$ | 33.3 |
| | 5 | 38.2$^{d}$ | 35.5 | 2.8$^{cb}$ | 33.3 |

| | | | | | |
|---|---|---|---|---|---|
| *E. chamadjlonsis* | 1 | 37.9$^{d}$ | 36.0 | 2.8$^{cb}$ | 33.3 |
| | 5 | 36.2$^{d}$ | 38.9 | 3.1$^{b}$ | 47.6 |
| *D. stramonium* | 1 | 28.4$^{f}$ | 51.0 | 3.1$^{b}$ | 47.6 |
| | 5 | 21.1$^{f}$ | 54.2 | 3.7$^{e}$ | 76.2 |
| *Nerium oleander* | 1 | 37.2$^{d}$ | 37.2 | 2.9$^{cb}$ | 38.1 |
| | 5 | 35.1$^{e}$ | 40.7 | 3.0$^{b}$ | 42.9 |
| *A. sctivum* | 1 | 27.3$^{f}$ | 53.9 | 3.2$^{b}$ | 52.4 |
| | 5 | 25.1$^{g}$ | 57.6 | 3.5$^{a}$ | 66.7 |
| Ridomil ptusgL$^{-1}$ | 2 | 15.3$^{h}$ | 74.2 | 3.9$^{a}$ | 85.7 |
| Infected control | | 39.2$^{e}$ | 0.0 | 2.1$^{d}$ | 0.0 |

Values in the column followed by different letters indicate significant differences among treatments according to least significant difference test ($p = 0.05$) significantly reduced the early blight disease under field conditions (Table 3). The greatest reduction of disease severity at 74.2% was achieved by Ridomil Plus at 2 g L$^{-1}$ followed by *A. sativum* at 5% and the least reduction was obtained when tomato plant were treated with *O. basilicum* at 1 and 5% (46.1 and 45.2 %, respectively). The other treatments were moderately effective.

**Effect of treatments on fruit yield:** Data in Table 3 indicate that the efficacy of the Ridomil Plus and plant extracts was reflected in the fruit yield produced. Plants sprayed with fungicide, *D. stramonium and A. sativum* at 5% increased the fruit yield 85.7, 76.2 and 66.7% respectively, compared to nontreated control. In contrast, *O. basilicum, A. indica, E, chamadulonsis* and *N. oleander* treatments increased the fruit yield moderately, ranged between 28.6 to 38.1% compared to infected control.

## Discussion

Our results indicated that all tested plant extracts, *Ocimum basilicum, Azadirachta indica, Eucalyptus chamadulonsis, Datura stramonium, Nerhan oleander andAllium sativum* and fungicide, Ridomil Plus 50% WP, caused significant reduction in the linear growth of *A. solani.* This reduction was gradually increased by increasing the concentration of extracts in the growth medium. Ridomil Plus was more effective than the plant extracts. Similar effect of various other plant products effective against *Alternaria* spp. have been reported by several workers (Latha *et al.*, 2009; Goussous *et al.*, 2010). Vijayan (1989) reported that the bulb extract of *A. sativum,* leaf extract of *Aegle marmelos* and flower extract of *Catharanthus roseus* inhibited the spore germination and mycelial growth of *A. solani.* The inhibitory effect of the fungicide on the growth of *A. solani* was reported by many researchers (Patil *et al.*, 2001; Abada *et al.*, 2008). The inhibitory effect of the tested plant extracts may be due to their direct toxic effect to the pathogen as reported by Vijayan (1989). Investigations on mechanisms of disease suppression by plant products have suggested that the active principles present in plant extracts may e'ither act on the pathogen directly (Amadioha, 2000), or induce systemic resistance in host plants resulting in reduction of disease development (Kagale *et al.*, 2004).

The greenhouse and field experiments indicated that foliar spray of tomato plants by plant extracts and fungicide resulted in significant reduction in early blight infection. However, the tested fungicide was more efficient than plant extracts. These results were similar to previous work on the role of plant extracts in fungal disease control. Several authors including Krebs *et al.* (2006), Curtis *et al.* (2004) and Latha *et al.* (2009) reported that plant extracts from 20 non-host plant species caused reduction of early blight disease and suppressed the mycelial growth of *A. solani.* All tested plant extracts treatments improved the yield of tomato plants compared to infected control.

In conclusion, present study demonstrated that many plant extracts, *O. basilicum,* A. indica, *E. chamadulonsis, D. stramonium, N. oleander* and *A. sativum,* can be used for the bio-control of early blight disease. Thus, this method of control can contribute to minimizing the risks and hazards of toxic fungicides, especially on vegetables produced for fresh consumption. Further research into these extracts will identify the active compounds responsible for their fungicidal activity.

## REFERENCES

Abada K.A., S.H. Mostafa and MR. Hillal, 2008. Effect of some chemical salts on suppressing the infection by early blight disease of tomato. Egypt. J. Applied Sci., 23: 47-58.

Amadioha, A.C., 2000. Controlling rice blast *in vitro* and *in vivo* with extracts of *Azadirachta indica.* Crop Prot, 19: 287-290.

Bowers, J.H. and J.C. Locke, 2004. Effect of formulated plant extracts and oils on population density of *Phytophthora nicotianae* in soil and control of Phytophthora blight in the greenhouse. Plant Dis. 88: 11-16.

Curtis, H., U. Noll, J. Stormann and A. J. Slusarenko, 2004. Broad-spectrum activity of the volatile phytoanticipin allicin in extracts of garlic *(Allium sativum* L.) against plant pathogenic bacteria, fungi and Oomycetes. Physiol. Mol. PlantPathol., 65: 79-89.

Dushyent, G. and A. Bohra, 1997. Effect of extracts of some halophytes on the growth *ofAlternaria solani.* J. Mycolo. Plant Parhol., 27: 233-233.

Ellis, M.B., 1976. More Dematiaceous Hyphomycetes. 1st Edn., Commonwealth Mycological Institute, Kew, Surrey, UK., pp: 507.

Gomez, K.A. andK. Gomez, 1984. Statistical Procedure for Agricultural Research. John-Wiley and Sons, Inc., New York.

Goussous, S.J., P.M. Abu-El-Samen and R.A. Tahhan, 2010. Antifungal activity of several medicinal plants extracts against the early blight pathogen *(Alternaria solani).* Archi. Phytopatholo. Plant Protect, 43: 1746-1758.

Kagale, S., T. Marimuthu, R. Nandakumar and R. Samiyappan, 2004. Antimicrobial activity and induction of systemic resistance in rice by leaf extract of *Datura metel* against *Rhizoctonia solani* and *Xanthomonas oryzae* pv. *oryzae.* Physiol. Mol. Plant Pathol., 65: 91-100.

Krebs, H., B. DomandH.R. Forrer, 2006. Control of late blight of potato with medicinal plant suspensions. Agrarforschung, 13: 16-21.

Latha, P., T. Anand, N. Ragupathi, V. Prakasam and R. Samiyappan, 2009. Antimicrobial activity of plant extracts and induction of systemic resistance in tomato plants by mixtures of PGPR strains and Zimmu leaf extract against *Alternaria solani.* Biol. Control., 50: 85-93.

MSTAT-C, 1991. A Software Program for the Design, Management and Analysis of Agronomic Research Experiments. Michigan State University, USA., Pages: 400.

Patil, M.J., S.P. Ukey and B.T. Raut, 2001. Evaluation of fungicides and botanicals for the management of early blight *(Alternaria solani)* of tomato. PKV Res. J., 25:49-51.

Qasem, J.R. andH.A. Aau-Blan, 1996. Fungicidal activity of some common weed extracts against different plant pathogenic fungi. J. Phytopathol., 144: 157-161.

Schmitz, H., 1930. Poisoned Food Technique. 2nd Edn., Industry of Engineering Chemical, London, USA., pp: 333-361.

Vijayan, M., 1989. Studies on early blight of tomato caused by *Alternaria solani* (Ellis and Martin) Jones and grout. M.Sc. Thesis, Tamil Nadu Agricultural University, Coimbatore, India.

Wszelaki, A.L. and S.A. Miller, 2005. Determining the efficacy of disease management products in organically-produced tomatoes. Plant Health Progress, (Online). 10.1094/PHP-2005-0713-01-RS.

**Early Blight Disease of Tomato**
***Edited by:*** **Virendra Kumar**
**ISBN: 978-93-5056-879-8**
***Edition:*** **2017**
***Published by:*** **Discovery Publishing House Pvt. Ltd., New Delhi (India)**

# Resistance of Two Tomato Species to Five Isolates of *Alternaria solani*

[1]Ali Ayaz Khan

**ABSTRACT**

Research studies were conducted in the green house to investigate the nature of pathogenicity of Alternaria solani, 6 isolates on two tomato species Lycopersicon asculentum and L. asculentum × L. hirsutum F1 hybrids and to describe the procedures by which it would be possible to determine the 5 isolates of Alternaria pathogenic action and progressive disease development. The results showed that the five isolates of Alternaria solani were non-pathogenic against the two tomato species tested in the experiment.

**Keywords:** Alternaria solani, Lycoparsicon spp., isolate, media, inoculum, haematocytometer.

## Introduction

Early blight of tomato is a fungal disease caused by *Alternaria solani* (Ellis & Martin) Jones and grout (Maiero *at al.,* 1 989). It is a three-phase disease, which can produce leaf spots, stem canker and fruit rot. But the foliar phase is the most common and destructive part of the disease. The disease is characterized by dark colored leaf spots that are necrotlc in the center and have concentric rings pattern seemingly associated with the periodic development of the fungus. When lesions expand and become more numerous, leaves are blighted and plants are prematurely defoliated.

Hence a number of cuttivars with this moderate but useful degree of resistance have been released (Barksdale and Stoner, 1977; Gardner, 1988; Nash and Gardner, 1 988a; 1988b). In developing a screening method for tomato early blight, considerable difficulty has been experienced in getting *Alternaria solani* to sporulate profusely in culture. In the past, several researchers used mycelial fragments as inoculation in their intensive screening and breeding methods. A few others relied on natural infection (Bashi and Rotem, 1974; Douglas, 1972). On the other hand, some researchers have been able to obtain sporulation in the lab (Barksdale, 1969; Maiero *et al.,* 1989; Nash, 1988; Nash and Gardner, 1988).

---

1 Agricultural Research Station (North) Mingora, P.O. Box-22, Saidu Sharif, Swat, NWFP, Pakistan

Maiero *et al*., (1989), grown twelve isolates on Lima bean agar for 6 days at 22 °C under normal diurnal light conditions. Aerial mycelium was scraped and the cultures were uncovered inverted and placed in diurnal light at ambient room temperature for 24 hour to induce sporulation-spores from all twelve isolates were mixed with distilled water to produce a spare suspension of 5000 spares/ ml. McCallan and Chan (Barksdale, 1 969) induced sporulation by growing cultures on PDA, scraping them and then putting them in a moist chamber with the lid on a jar and then placing them in a window sunlight. Barksdale (1969) induced sporulation by growing cultures on Lima bean agar (LBAI at about 23 °C in plastic petri dishes. Nash (1988) induced sporulation on LBA at about 23 °C. The aerial mycelia were flattened with a spatula and uncovered plates were inverted and exposed to eight hours of light at 23 °C, then twelve hours of dark at 19 °C. Conidia were harvested after twenty-eight hours by flooding cultures with d $H_2O$ and rubbing the surface lightly with a spatula.

Maiero *et al*. (1989), grown twelve isolates on Lima bean agar for 6 days at 22 °C under normal diurnal light conditions. Aerial mycelium was scraped and the cultures were uncovered inverted and placed in diurnal light at ambient room temperature for 24 hours to induce sporulation-spores from all twelve isolates were mixed with distilled water to produce a spore suspension of 5000 spores/ml.

The objectives of the study were to produce fungal spore inoculum for each five isolate in the laboratory and to study those conditions that would favor rapid systematic disease development on tomato seedlings *in vitro*.

## Material and Methods

**Plant material:** Two tomato, *L*. esculentum and *L. esculantumx L. hirustum* F1 hybrid sixty seedlings were produced in individual containers in the greenhouse. After thirty days the disease-free seedlings were transferred into 6 inches pots. The plants were watered as required. No fungicide was applied in any stage.

**Inoculum preparation and Inoculation:** Five isolations of *Alternaria solani were* collected from tomatoes blighted early in the field in the Lexington area. These isolates were grown on reconstituted lima bean agar (LBA) at about 23°C in 9 cm disposable plastic petri dishes. This procedure was similar to Nash and Gardner (1988) as mentioned previously, but with some modifications-one week old cultures were handled in the following pattern (Table 1). The isolated written on back of plate lid was discarded and mycelium flattened with flamed spatula, plates inoculated were inverted on tray for ten hours of light at 23°C then fourteen hours of dark at 1 9°C. The culture dish lids were removed but one plate of each isolate was not uncovered and then aerial mycelium was flattened with a spatula the cultures were inverted on racks one centimeter above a tray surface for slow drying in an incubator for ten hours at 23°C, then fourteen hours of dark at 19°C. The inverted plates were then covered with plastic and uncovered plates were also covered. It was observed that uncovered plates became dried under the above diurnal temperature.

**Table 10.1: Uncovering of culture**

| Isolate# | Good plates | Discarded plates | Success | % Morphology |
|---|---|---|---|---|
| 146 | 4 | 4 Sectored | 50 | Even |
| 147 | 4 | 2 Sectored 2 virus | 50 | Zonate |
| 148 | 7 | 1 Sectored | 87 | Even |
| 149 | 8 | — | 100 | Zonate |
| 150 | 7 | 1 Sectored | 87 | Zonate |

After thirty hours, the flattened cultures were flooded with d $H_2O$ and the surface rubbed lightly with a spatula. The spore suspension for each isolate from different plates was mixed together. The conidia suspension was then filtered through four layers of cheesecloth. Spore concentration was estimated with the aid of a haematocytometer to be 10,000 spores per milliliter of distilled water. This spore suspension contained about equal numbers of spores from each of the five isolates mentioned above. Inoculation in the greenhouse was accomplished with a hand sprayer, by atomizing the spore suspension on leaves up to the level that suspension water ran off the leaves. Two plants of each tomato variety in every block were sprayed only by clean water as a control. All plants were then covered with plastic bags and bind with rubber bands to provide a moist chamber. The plastic covers were removed after fifteen hours.

**Greenhouse) test for pithogvnictty:** Thirty plants of each accession were selected and grown as mentioned previously. The plants were placed in the greenhouse in five blocks, six plants of each variety in one block. When plants became six weeks old, then inoculation was accomplished by spraying three hundred milliliters of spore suspension (diluted) of five isolates per treatment or thirty millliters per plant on ten plants. Two plants in each block were sprayed only with water as check. Following inoculation, plants were covered with plastic bags and closed with rubber bands for fifteen hours. The uncovered plants were then sprayed by water daily in the evening to encourage lesion development. The disease data on the percentage of necrotic leaf area and tolerance to defoliation were recorded with the following: disease scale parameters; No, very slight, moderate, severe, extreme and complete defoliation.

## Results and Discussion

All the plants leaves were observed routinely for *Alternaria* disease development. We found that *Alternaria* disease spots were present only on *Lycopersion esculentum* leaves but were not significant and therefore, no defoliation of plants occurred (Table 10.2). Water spray *L. esculentum* (check) plants have no spots on the leaves and *L. esculentum* x *L. hirsutum* F1 plant leaves also have no spots.

**Table 10.2: Fungal inoculum and *Lycoparticon* species reaction**

| Treatments | *Lycoperticon* species | No. of plants | Reaction against *Attimarittcttni* |
|---|---|---|---|
| Water spray | *L. etculantum* | 5 | – |
| Water spray | *L. hinutum* | 5 | – |
| Fungal inoculum spray | *L. etculantum* | 25 | + |
| Fungal inoculum spray | *L. hirautum* | 25 | – |

– : No spots + : Spots

Symptoms of early blight are often difficult to obtain on young seedlings. It was reported by Marisa *et al.* (1989) that early blight is associated with physiological maturity of the plant; older, senescing leaves are more susceptible then young immature leaves. It was found that an air temperature of 1 6°C for two weeks following inoculation was more favorable for symptoms development (Pound, 1951). Moreover, as the susceptibility of tomato plants to infection by *A. solani* is determined by the age of the host (Rotem, 1 994). It was reported by Barksdale (1 969) that after one week of inoculation, the plants which received repeated moist periods, the lesions were about twice as large as those which received one initial incubation. It was found that the development of early blight symptoms on tomato plants is affected by inoculum concentration, leaf wetness duration, plant age and host susceptibility (Vloutoglou and Kalogerakis, 2000). In similar experiments Coffey and Marshall (1976), showed that early blight severity on young tomato plants increased from $5 \times 10^3$ to $8 \times 10^4$ conidia $ml^{-1}$. A positive relationship between inoculum concentration and symptom development has also been demonstrated for other *Alternaria* species (Vloutoglou, 1994). Vloutoglou and Kalogerakis (2000) showed that tomato cultivars become increasingly susceptible to *A. solani* infection as plants aged. It was also found in earlier experiments by Moore (1942) that susceptibility of tomato plants to *A. solani* infection was age dependent the pathogen caused color rot in seedlings and early blight in mature plants, whereas middle aged plants were relatively tolerant. Moreover Voutolou and Kalogerakis (2000) found that percentages of leaf area affected by the pathogen and defoliation increased with increasing leaf wetness duration up to 24 hours. As it was observed from the experimental results that no significant disease spots were present on the leaves of the two tomato species and as a result no defoliation of inoculated plants occurred and these findings will partially conform the Coffey and Marshall (1976) and Vloutoglou and Kalogerkis (2000), who showed that increased conidial concentration increased early blight severity on young tomato plants. Thus we assume that it is either tolerance of the two tomato species, inoculum concentration $ml^{-1}$ and/or the unattended chance factors might affected the controlled conditions in the greenhouse.

The results of the study showed that *Alternaria* disease screening for *Lycopersicon* species can be carried out in vitro by careful handling of the fungal isolates and hence forth inoculation of the plants for the early blight symptom development. Therefore, similar studies should be undertaken to develop best disease screening procedures and methods for different plants species *in vitro*.

## REFERENCES

Barksdale, T.H., 1969. Resistance of tomato seedlings to early blight. Phytopathology, 69:443-446.

Bashi, E. and J. Rotem, 1974. Adaptation of four pathogens to semi arid habitats as conditioned by penetration rate and germinating spore survival. Phytopathology, 64: 1036-9.

Coffey, M.D. and W.C. Marshall, 1976. The effect of early blight disease caused by *Alternaria solani* on shoot growth of young tomato plants. Ann. Appl. Biol., 80: 17-26.

Douglas, D.R. and J.J. Pavek, 1972. Screening potatoes for field resistance to early blight. Am. Potato J., 49: 1-6.

Gardner, R.G., 1989. Combining ability estimates for early blight resistance in tomato breeding lines. J. Am. Soc. Hort. Sci.

Gardner, R.G., 1990. Greenhouse disease screening facilitates breeding resistance to tomato early blight. Hort. Sci., 26: 222-223.

Hong, C.X. and B.D.L. Fitt, 1996. Effects of inoculum concentration, leaf age and wetness period on the development of dark leaf and pod sport *(Alternaria brassicae)* on oilseed rape *(Brassica napus}*. Ann. Appl. Biol., 127: 283-95.

Maiero, M., T.J. Ng and T.H. Barksdale, 1989. Combining ability estimates for early blight resistance in tomato. J. Am. Soc. Hort. Sci., 114: 118-121.

Maiero, M., T.J. Ng and T.H. Barksdale, 1990. Genetic resistance to early blight in tomato breeding lines. Hort Sci., 25: 344-346.

Moore, W.D., 1942. Some factors affecting the infection oftomato seedlings by *Alternaria solani* on tomato. Phytopathology, 68: 1354-8.

Pound, G.S., 1961. Effect of air temperature on incidence and development of the early blight disease of tomato. Phytopathology, 41: 127-35.

Rotem, J., 1994. The genus *Alternaria;* Biology epidemiology and pathogenicity. St-paul, Minnesota, USA. Am. Phytopathol Society.

Vloutoglou, I., 1999. Evaluation of tomato cultivars and hybrids for resistance to *Alternaria solani* infection. Ann. Appl. Biol., 134: 48-9.

Vlautoglou, I. and S.N. Kalogerakis, 2000. Effects of inoculum concentration, wetness duration and plant age on development of early blight *(Alternaria solani}* and on shedding of leaves in tomato plants. J. Pl. Pathol., 49: 339-345.

**Early Blight Disease of Tomato**
***Edited by:*** **Virendra Kumar**
**ISBN: 978-93-5056-879-8**
***Edition:*** **2017**
***Published by:*** **Discovery Publishing House Pvt. Ltd., New Delhi (India)**

# Performance Assessment of Tomato Advanced Lines to Late Blight and Early Blight under Natural Eiphytotics

[1]Nazrul Islam, Bimal Kumar Pramanik, [2]Md. Atiqur Rahman Khokon and M. Ashrafuzzaman

## ABSTRACT

Fifteen advanced lines of tomato including two check cvs. 'Manik' and 'BAR 1-10' were assessed under natural epiphytotics for their performance to late blight (Phytophthora infastans) and early blight (Alternaria solani). The highest late blight disease incidence was found in V-52 & V-21 5 and the lowest in V-378. Two lines were found resistant (V-426 & V-259), two moderately resistant (V-187 & V-386), two were tolerant (V-282 & V-422), four moderately susceptible (V-378, V-138, V-258 and BARI 10), three were susceptible (V-330, V-201 and Manik) and two highly susceptible (V-52 & V-216), but none was found highly resistant. In case of early blight V-259 showed the highest and V-215 showed the lowest disease incidence. On the basis of early blight disease intensity, one was found resistant (V-52), three were moderately resistant (V-1 38, V-201 and V-215), six were moderately susceptible (V-378, V-282, V-330, V-426, V-422 and Manik), four were susceptible (V-187, V-386, V-258 and BARI 10), one was highly susceptible (V-259) and none was found highly resistant.

**Keywords:** Performance, late blight, early blight, tomato lines.

## Introduction

Tomato (*Lycopersicon esculentum* Mill.) is one of the most nutritious vegetables. The average yield of this crop in Bangladesh is 2.76 ton/ha (BBS, 2000) which is very low as compared to other leading tomato producing countries (FAQ, 1999). This crop suffers from as many as 200 diseases in the world, of which 30 are routinely important (Watterson, 1986). Out of these diseases, late blight caused by *Phytophthora* infastans is quite important in Bangladesh (Talukdar, 1974) as 80-90% of its production may be damaged by this disease if control measures are not taken in time (Zahid *at al.,* 1993). Another most important disease is early blight, caused by *Alternaria solani.* Most of the cultivated varieties are susceptible to this disease and it can cause loss to the extent of 78% in fruit yield (Singh,

[1] Agricultural Research Station (North) Mingora, P.O. Box-22, Saidu Sharif, Swat, NWFP, Pakistan

1985). Under severe epiphytotics loss of fruits may be as high as 95% (Sridhara & Naik, 1 983). For healthy tomato cultivation use of resistant cultivars is gaining popularity because it is cheap, safe and easy way to manage diseases. It is imperative to screen tomato cultivar/lines against the above mentioned major diseases and thus research to locate resistant/tolerant genotypes.

On the above mentioned perspective the study was undertaken to assess performance of 1 5 tomato lines against late blight *(Phytophthora infestans)* and early blight *(Alternaria solani)* under natural epiphytotics.

## Materials and Methods

Fifteen tomato advance lines including 2 checks (Manik and BARI 10) were evaluated under natural field conditions at the field laboratory of the Department of Genetics and Plant Breeding, Bangladesh Agricultural University, Mymensingh during October 1999 to March 2000. The experimental field was well prepared into good tilth by ploughing and cross ploughing followed by laddering.

The recommend doses of urea, TSP & MP were applied during final land preparation 4 days before the transplanting of the seedlings (BARC, 1997). The experiment was laid out in RGB design with three replications. Each experimental field was divided into 15 small plots. Thus there were 45 unit plots for the study. The size of the unit plot was 8.4 sq.m. Seedlings were in 15 different seed beds. Twenty five days old healthy seedlings were transplanted in the experimental field. Twenty eight seedlings were transplanted per unit plot. The incidence of late blight and early blight was calculated by the formula:

$$\% \text{ incidence} = \frac{\text{No. of infected seedlings/plant}}{\text{Total no. of seedling/plant}} \times 100$$

The severity of the late blight infestation was recorded using a standard scale (Anonymous, 1985) and early blight infestation was recorded using the scale described by Vakalounakis (1983). For diagnosis collected diseased leaf samples were surface sterilized by dipping in 0.1 % HgCU for 30 seconds and rinsed in sterile water before placing in acidified potato dextrose agar medium in petridish with sterile forceps. The plated tissue were incubated at 20 ± 2°C for 7 days or more to allow associated organisms to grow. *Phytopthora infestens* was identified under a compound microscope following the keys out - lined by Alexopoulus (1961) and Ingram and Williams (1971). *Alternaria solani* was identified following the key out lined by Ellis & Gibson (1 975). Data on the % plants infected, % leaves infected and % leaf area infected due to the two diseases were recorded and were subjected to statistical analysis (ANOVA) following RCBD to determine the level of significance (Gomez and Gomez, 1983).

## Results and Discussion

The highest disease incidence, 97.62% was observed in the lines V-52 and V-215 in present experiment (Table 1). It was not unpromidented as Anonymous (1

997) reported that 100% late blight disease incidence may occur in different tomato varieties/genotypes. In check cultivar Manik, the disease incidence was 78.28%. which is in conformity with the report by Anonymous (1995) that per cent disease incidence in cultivar Manik could vary from place to place and also reported that disease incidence was 52.1% at Ishurdy and 100% at BINA farm, at Mymensingh in 1 994-95. The average per cent infected leaves per plant was found between 1 6.93 to 72.54 at 80 days after transplanting (Table 1). This resembled the findings of Anonymous (1 995). Cultivar Manik, in this study showed 59.20% leaves infected. The disease severity due to late blight in terms of per cent leaf area infected (LAD varied between 4.83 to 96.61 (Table 11.1).

**Table 11.1: Reaction of 15 tomato cultivars/lines against late blight under field conditions**

| Varieties /lines | % plant infected (incidence) | % infected leaves/ plant | % leaf area infected (LAI) |
|---|---|---|---|
| V-187 | 34.52 d-f | 46.35 cd | 22.86 fh |
| V-378 | 16.67 f | 35.35 de | 62.92 cd |
| V-282 | 46.43 d | 35.67 de | 36.50 e |
| V-136 | 70.24 be | 67.14 ab | 65 74 cd |
| V-330 | 86.91 ab | 64.60 ab | 75.29 be |
| V-52 | 97.62 a | 67. 17 ab | 96. 13 a |
| V-385 | 41.67 de | 27.46 ef | 13.63 gh |
| V-426 | 1905 ef | 19.18 ef | 4.83h |
| V-215 | 97.62 a | 72. 54 a | 96.61 a |
| V-258 | 28.57 d-f | 16 93 f | 67.65 cd |
| V-259 | 17.85 f | 20.90 ef | 4.96 h |
| V-201 | 80.95 ab | 63.93 ab | 4.96 h |
| V-422 | 50.00 cd | 53.44 be | 34.09ef |
| Manik | 78.28 ab | 59.20 a-c | 82.69 b |
| BARI 10 | 29.76 d-f | 27.16 ef | 59.24 d |
| LSD ($p = 0.01$) | 23 36 | 16.55 | 13.26 |

Means followed by the same letter(s) in a column are not significantly different at 1% level.

**Table 11.2: Reaction of 15 tomato cultivars/lines against early blight under field conditions.**

| Varieties /lines | % plant infected (incidence) | % infected leaves/ plant | %leaf area infected (LAI) |
|---|---|---|---|
| V-187 | 64.28a-d | 36.79 b | 62.00 a |
| V-378 | 70.24 a-c | 39.51 b | 38.83 b |

| V-282 | 54.76 b-c | 36.22 b | 36.34 b-d |
|---|---|---|---|
| V-138 | 33.33 f-h | 63.14 a | 18.75 c-e |
| V-330 | 28.75 gi | 42.46 b | 37. 59 be |
| V-52 | 10.53 ij | 10.38 c | 867e |
| V-385 | 5237c-f | 72.94 a | 64.46 a |
| V-426 | 69 05 a-c | 68. 15 a | 37 49 be |
| V-215 | 833 j | 17.95 c | 17.73 de |
| V-258 | 74 82 a | 79.31 a | 64 55 a |
| V-259 | 74 99 a | 73. 20 a | 80.75 a |
| V-201 | 25 00 hi | 35.93 b | 23.32 b-e |
| V-422 | 4523 d-g | 38.69 b | 41.52 b |
| Manik | 38.10 e-h | 46.11 b | 37. 10 be |
| BARI 10 | 73 74 ab | 67. 66 a | 67. 32 a |
| LSD ($p$ = 0.01) | 19.18 | 16 92 | 19.00 |

Means followed by the same letter(s) in a column are not significantly different at 1% level.

**Table 11.3: Reaction of tomato cultivars/lines to late blight *(Phyrophthora infestans)* and early blight *(Alwmaria solanfi)***

| Reaction | List of tomato cultivars/lines | |
|---|---|---|
| | Lata blight | Early blight |
| **Mighty resistant** | | |
| Resistant | V-426, V-269 | V- 62 |
| Moderated resistant | V-386, V- 187 | V- 138, V-201, V- 216 |
| Tolerant | V- 282, V- 422 | |
| Moderately susceptible | V- 378, V- 1 38, V-268, BARI-10 | V-378, V-282, V-330, V- 426, V-422, Manik |
| Susceptible | V- 330, V- 2 10, Manik | V-187, V-386, V-268, BARI- 10 |
| Hiqhlv susceptible | V- 62, V- 21 6 | V-269 |

In case of late blight of 0-6 scale (Anonymous, In case of early blight of 0-5 scale (Vakalounakis,
tomato. Cultivars/lines were classified using 1985)
tomato: Cultivars/lines were classified using 1983)

Anonymous (1996) also revealed such wide range of leaf area infection (7.2-100%). In check cv. Manik per cent leaf area infected observed was 82.69 (Table 1). This was very similar to the finding of Anonymous (1996), where it was 85.8%. Two genotypes (V-426 and V-269) were found to be resistant to late blight of tomato (Table 3 ) and one genotype (V-52) was found to be resistant to early blight of tomato (Table 3 ). Although the genotype V-52 was found resistant to early blight of tomato but found highly susceptible to late blight of tomato.

The result has similarity with the statements made by some author's findings and Institutions annual reports such as Mlungu (1996), Anonymous (1990a), Anonymous (1990b) and Kaur *at al.* (1988). Two genotypes (V-386 and V-187) were found moderately resistant (MR) to late blight (Table 3). Suhardi (1986) and Anonymous (1990b) reported that they located 6 and 12 tolerant entries/lines out of 27 and 58 entries/lines to late blight disease of tomato and the present study observed 2 genotypes (V-282 & V-422) tolerant (T) to tomato late blight out of 15 genotypes (Table 3). Anonymous (1989, 1990a, 1990b) reported that 2, 5 and 10 genotypes/entries were found moderately susceptible out of 11, 23 and 58 genotypes/entries and the present study observed 4 genotypes (V-378, V-138, V-258, BARI 10) moderately susceptible (MS) to late blight disease of tomato and 2 genotypes were found highly susceptible (V-52 and V-216) to late blight (Table 3). The observations are supported by Anonymous (1990b), Anonymous (1989) and Kaur at al. (1988). Three genotypes (V-138, V-201, V-215) were found to be moderately resistant, six genotypes (V-378, V-282, V-330, V-426, V-422 and cv. Manik) were found moderately susceptible, four genotypes (V-187, V-385, V-258, BARI 10) were susceptible and one genotype (V-269) was found highly susceptible to early blight of tomato (Table 11.4 ).

Begum (1 992) found 14 genotypes moderately resistant out of 40 genotypes. The highest incidence of early blight caused by Al tern aria so/an/ was found in advance line V-269 and the lowest incidence was found in V-215. The lowest and the highest per cent infected leaves/plant were observed in V-52 and V-268 respectively. The severity in terms of per cent leaf area infected due to early blight varied from 8.67 to 80.75. The lowest severity (% LAI) was found in V-62 and the highest severity (% LAI) was found in V-259 (Table 11.2).

Out of 15 advance genotypes none was found highly resistant to early blight. However one material (V-52) was found resistant, 3 (V-137, V-215, V-210) were moderately resistant, 6 (V-378, V-282, V-330, V-426, V-422 and Manik) were moderately susceptible, 4 (V-187, V-396, V-258 and cv. BAR I-10) were susceptible and one was highly susceptible(V-259) to early blight disease of tomato (Table 11.3).

Different workers found different percentages of resistant cuttivars/ genotypes in their respective studies. Sridhra ef al. (1983), Avdeev and Shcherbinin (1988), Begum (1992), Banerjee ef al. (1998a) and Banerjee et al. (1998b) found 9, 5, 9, 23 and 7 resistant lines to early blight respectively out of 38, 200, 40, 81 and 64 cultivars/genotypes.

Three genotypes (V-138, V-21 6 and V-201) were found to be moderately resistant (Tables 3) to early blight. In different screening 15,13 and 22 moderately resistant genotypes were obtained out of 40, 38 and 81 cultivars/lines by Begum (1992), Banerjee ef al. (1998a, 1998b) and Anonymous (1984).

It is interesting to note that among the fifteen test lines, no genotype was found to be resistant simultaneously to both Phytophthort and Alternaria. On the contrary the genotype which has shown considerable amount of resistance to Phytopathora infestans (viz. V-259, V-378 & V-426) suffered from very high incidence and severity of Alternaria blight. Among the tested lines V-216 was found to be susceptible to both the designated pathogens. The check cultivars, Manik and BAR 1-10 were also found to be susceptible to both of these major tomato diseases and these cultivars need replacement.

For that matter manipulation-recombination of resistant genes must be continued to breed new cultivars fairly resistant to both of these major pathogens without compromising the agronomic characters and market-qualities. The advanced test tomato lines V-378, V-426, V-269, V-216, V-52 could'be used as the sources of resistance.

## REFERENCES

Alexopoulos, C.J., 1961. Introductory Mycology. Second Edn., John Willey Sons. Inc., New York, London, p: 613

Anonymous, 1986. Plant disease scoring scale. Department of Plant Pathology, BARI, Joydebpur, Gazipur, p: 11.

Anonymous, 1989. Germplasm evaluation of tomato. Annual Report (1988-89). BARI, Joydebpur, Gazipur, p: 276.

Anonymous, 1990a. Screening of tomato varieties/lines against late blight. Annual Report (1989-90). BARI, Joydebpur, Gazipur, pp: 272-274

Anonymous, 1990b. Evaluation of some entries/lines of tomato for disease resistance. Annual Report (1989-90). BARI, Joydebpur, Gazipur, pp: 185-186

Anonymous, 1995. Field evaluation of advanced lines/varieties of winter tomato against late blight, mosaic and root-knot. Annual Report (1994-95). BINA, Mymensingh, pp: 197-199.

Anonymous, 1997. Field evaluation of advanced hybrid lines/varieties of winter tomato against late blight, mosaic and leaf curl. Annual Report (1996-97). BINA, Mymensingh, pp: 240-243.

Avdeev, Y.I. and B.M. Shcherbinin, 1988. Resistance of tomatoes to *Alternaria.* Tsitologiya I Genetika, 22: 21-27

Banerjee, M.K., Kalloo and P.S. Saini, 1998a. Screening of tomato varieties/advance lines against early blight under field condition. Annal. Agric. Bio. Res., 3: 39-44

Banerjee, M.K., M.L. Chhabra, A.P. Garg and P.S. Saini, 1998b. Screening of tomato genotypes against *Alternaria* blight under field conditions. Annal. Agric. Bio. Res., 3: 109-113

BARC., 1997. Fertilizer Recommendation Guide. Bangladesh Agril. Res. Coun. Farmgate, New Airport road, Dhaka-1215. p: 72.

BBS., 2000. Monthly Statistical Bulletin (July, 2000), Bangladesh Bureau of Statistics, Ministry of Planning, Govt. of Bangladesh, p: 55.

Begum, S.N., 1992. Screening of tomato genotypes for resistance to early blight caused by *Alternaria solani.* Bangla. J. Bot., 21: 131-133

Ellis, M.B. and I.A.S. Gibson, 1975. *Alternaria solani.* CMI Descriptions of pathogenic Fungi and Bacteria. No. 475

FAO., 1999. FAO Quarterly Bulletin of Statistics. Food and Agricultural Organization, Rome, 1 2: 79-80

Gomez, K.A. and A.A. Gomez, 1 993. Statistical Procedure for Agricultural Research. John Wiley and Sons, New York, 400-620

Ingram, D.H. and P.M. Williams, 1971. Advances in Plant Pathology. Academic press. Horcourt Brace Jovanocich Publishers, London, 7: 273

Kaur, *S., S.* Singh, J.S. Kanwar and D.S. Cheema, 1988. Variability in tomato for resistance to late blight under field conditions. Ind. Phytopathol., 41: 486-487

Mlungu, L.S., S.P. Reuben and J. Godwin, 1996. Early and late blight development of local and exotic tomato *(Lycopersicon esculentum)* germplasm collection under field conditions at Morogoro. Tanzinia Research & Training News Letter (Dar es Salam). 11: 9-14

Singh, R.S., 1985. Disease of vegetable crops. Oxford and IBM Publishing Co. New Delhi, p: 441

Sridhra, T.S. and L.B. Naik, 1983. Relative resistance of tomato cultivars to early blight. The Madras Agric. J., 70: 488-489

Talukdar, M.J., 1974. Plant Diseases in Bangladesh. Bangla. J. Agric. Res., 1: 71

Vakalounakis, D.J., 1983. Evaluation of tomato cultivars for resistance to *Alternaria* blight. Ann. Appl. Biol., 102: 138-139

Watterson, J.C., 1986. Diseases. The tomato crops. Edited by Atherton and Rudich. Chapman and Hall Ltd. NY. pp: 461-462

Zahid, M.I., K.D. Tapan and B.C. Chowdhury, 1993. Major Diseases of potato, tomato, brinjal, lady's finger and country bean and their control (In Bengali). Bangla Press. BARC, Dhaka. 20: 5s

**Early Blight Disease of Tomato**
***Edited by:*** **Virendra Kumar**
**ISBN: 978-93-5056-879-8**
***Edition:*** **2017**
***Published by:*** **Discovery Publishing House Pvt. Ltd., New Delhi (India)**

# Characterization of Tomato Accessions for Resistance to Early Blight

[1]Jose Fernando Jurca Grigolli, [2]Carine Rezende Cardoso

## ABSTRACT

The purpose of this study was to characterize 50 tomato genotypes of the Vegetable Genebank of the Federal University of Viçosa. They wer e evaluated together with the controls Débora, Fanny and Santa Clara, in a randomized block design with two replications. The experiment was conducted in a research field of the UFV, from February to May 2007. We evaluated the disease severity, which is the percentage of diseased leaf area. The severity values were transformed into area under the disease progress curve (AUDPC), improving the result visualization. The analysis of variance and grouping of AUDPC means by the Scott-Knott test at 5 % significance were performed. The accessions BGH-2081, BGH-2034, BGH-700, BGH-2057, BGH-2035, BGH-2054, BGH-2018, BGH-2065, BGH-2008, and BGH-2032 had a lower mean AUDPC than the controls and are therefore indicated for future breeding programs.

**Keywords:** Alternaria solani; Solanum lycopersicon; genebank; biotic stress; genetic resources; pre-breeding.

## Introduction

The plant diversity in the Solanaceae family is great and several species of economic importance, *e.g.,* tomato (Tambarussi et al. 2009) belong to it. Tomato is related to an intensive use of pesticides since numerous factors can cause significant crop losses, *e.g.,* pests and diseases (Schuelter et al. 2006). It is estimated that fungal diseases of tomato are responsible for a 30% increase in production costs in fungicides used to combat these diseases (Lopes and Santos 1994). Among the diseases, early blight, caused by the fungus *Alternaria solani,* is one of the most important and frequent diseases of the crop nation- and worldwide (Jones et al. 1991, Balbi-Peña et al. 2006). In plantations in the U.S.,

[1] Universidade Federal de Vicosa (UFA), Departmento de Fitotecnia, Av. P.H. Rolfs, s/n, Campus Universitario. 36.571.000, Vicosa, MG, Brazil. E-mail: jose_fernando_jg@yahoo.com.br

[2] UFV, Departmento de Fitopatologla

Australia, Israel, UK and India, these losses range from 35 to 78 % (Basu 1974, Datar and Mayee 1982). In Brazil, a disease survey in tomato areas in Minas Gerais stated that the incidence of early blight was one of the highest (88 %) and that 18 fungicide applications had to be sprayed during the crop cycle to control this disease (Vale et al. 1992).

The destructive power of the disease is considerable; it attacks leaves, stems and fruits, eventually defoliating the plants and reducing yield and fruit quality (Castro et al. 2000, Foolad et al. 2002, Chaerani et al. 2007). Increased susceptibility to early blight is usually associated with mature tissue, and is more common during the fruiting phase. Severe epidemics of the disease occur at physiological plant maturity, since older and senescing leaves are more susceptible (Barratt and Richards 1944, Barksdale 1971, Martin and Hepperly 1987, Nash and Gardner 1988, Maiero et al. 1990).

Although genetic resistance is the most efficient control method, there is still no tomato variety available with acceptable levels of resistance to early blight. As a result, the main control method involves the application of protective and systemic fungicides, raising production costs, besides being little effective in wetter periods (Holm et al. 2003). Furthermore, fungicides are often used at excessive doses, causing environmental contamination risks and health problems of workers and consumers (Batista et al. 2006). Generally, these fungicides are applied every 7-10 days, without taking the disease development or epidemiological conditions into consideration (Patterson and Nokes 2000).

Improvement programs from a base population with high genetic variability will increase the chances of establishing superior genotypes successfully in subsequent generations of selection (Hallauer and Miranda Filho 1988). These parents may be selected from old cultivars of the cultivated species as well as from wild species of the same genus represented in genebanks (Vallois et al. 1996). One of the main factors contributing to the low use of parents in breeding programs is that breeders are not aware of the genetic resources available in genebanks (Morales et al. 1997).

Thus, genebanks are important tools in plant breeding programs and should be used, as in this case, as gene sources to confer disease resistance to commercial tomato cultivars. With this purpose, the Federal University of Viçosa, supported by the Rockefeller Foundation, officially created the Vegetable Genebank of the Federal University of Viçosa (BGH - UFV) in 1966, the oldest in Latin America (Silva et al. 2001).

Thus, this study aimed to characterize 50 tomato accessions of the UFV genebank for resistance to early blight in order to detect useful genes for tomato breeding programs.

## Material and Methods

The experiment was conducted from February to May 2007 in a research garden of the Plant Science Department, of the university Federal of Viçosa (UFV), in Viçosa, state of Minas Gerais (lat 20 ° 45′ S, long 40 º 38′ W, and alt 690 m asl).

The following 50 tomato accession from the UFV Vegetable genebank were used: BGH-700, BGH-2000, BGH-2002, BGH-2003, BGH-2004, BGH-2006, BGH-2008, BGH-2013, BGH-2014, BGH-2016, BGH-2017, BGH-2018, BGH-2019, BGH-2020, BGH-2021, BGH-2026, BGH-2027, BGH-2029, BGH-2032, BGH-2033, BGH-2034, BGH-2035, BGH-2038, BGH-2039 Amarelo, BGH-2039 Vermelho, BGH-2041, BGH-2046, BGH-2052, BGH-2054, BGH-2055, BGH-2057, BGH-2060, BGH-2062, BGH-2064, BGH-2065, BGH-2068, BGH-2069, BGH-2071, BGH-2072, BGH-2073, BGH-2074, BGH-2075, BGH-2076, BGH-2077, BGH-2078, BGH-2080, BGH-2081, BGH-2082, BGH-2083, and BGH-2086. Besides, the cultivars Débora and Fanny were used as controls and Santa Clara as susceptibility standard (Tófoli and Kurozawa 1993). All accessions, provided by Purdue University (USA), were of the *Solanum lycopersicon* species and included in the UFV genebank in November 1966 (data of color, fruit size and shape, plant production and soluble solids content of each accession in Table 1).

The experiment was established in a randomized block design with two replications and five plants per plot, with three plants. The seedlings were grown in polystyrene trays of 128 cells containing a commercial substrate. When the plants had four leaves, 25 days after sowing, they were transplanted to an area previously used for tomato cultivation. The soil was plowed, disked and limed according to recommendations of Ribeiro et al. (1999).

Plants were spaced 0.60 m and rows 1.00 m apart. Technical-cultural practices were applied weekly, as well as topdressings. The crop was sprinkler-irrigated, to increase the local moisture and boost the epidemiological disease process.

To obtain the inoculation solution, diseased leaves were collected in different planting areas and *A.solani* propagules isolated in the plant pathology laboratory of UFV. After isolation and identification, the pathogen was cultured as described by Foolad et al. (2000) and the pathogenicity of detached leaflets of 45-day-old tomato plants evaluated. The five isolates used in this study were selected according to the pathogen aggressiveness (Table 2).

These five isolates were cultured separately on PDA medium (25 ± 2°C, 12-h photoperiod). On the seventh day of incubation, 15 mL of distilled water was added to each dish and the fungus was bruised and mycelium removed with a brush. Sporulation on the dishes without lids was stimulated (25 ± 2°C, 12-h black light photoperiod) for 60h after mycelium removal. Thereafter, the conidia were removed with 10 mL of distilled water added to each dish, by scraping the surface with a soft toothbrush. Then the suspension was filtered through a double layer of sterile gauze.

**Table 12.1 Color, fruit size and shape, yield per plant and content of soluble solids of the accessions used in this experiment**

| Accession | Fruit color | Fruit size | Fruit shape | Yield Plant–1 (g) | SS* (Brix) | Accession | Fruit color | Fruit size | Fruit shape | Yield Plant4 (g) | SS* (Brix) |
|---|---|---|---|---|---|---|---|---|---|---|---|
| BGH-700 | ND | ND | ND | ND | ND | BGH-2041 | Red | Intermediate | Slightly flattened | 1,733.35 | 3.53 |
| BGH-2000 | Red | Intermediate | Strongly rounded | 3,005.00 | 4.23 | BGH-2046 | Red | Intermediate | Slightly flattened | 1,733.35 | 3.53 |
| BGH-2002 | Red | Small | Heart-shaped | 1,443.30 | 2.96 | BGH-2052 | Red | Intermediate | Pyramid-shaped | 3,201.60 | 3.23 |
| BGH-2003 | Red | Intermediate | Flattened | 2,145.00 | 3.26 | BGH-2054 | Orange | Intermediate | Flattened | 3,251.10 | 4.00 |
| BGH-2004 | Red | Intermediate | Flattened | 1,918.30 | 3.63 | BGH-2055 | Orange | Small | Flattened | 508.8 | 2.86 |
| BGH-2006 | Red | Intermediate | Heart-shaped | 1,412.22 | 3.16 | BGH-2057 | Red | Intermediate | Slightly flattened | 4,231.60 | 2.96 |
| BGH-2008 | Red | Intermediate | Flattened | 1,927.51 | 4.46 | BGH-2060 | Red | Intermediate | Pyramid-shaped | 4,231.60 | 2.96 |
| BGH-2013 | Red | Intermediate | Flattened | 3,033.60 | 4.73 | BGH-2062 | Red | Small | Cylindric | 2,358.30 | 5.10 |
| BGH-2014 | Red | Intermediate | Slightly flattened | 1,448.88 | 4.83 | BGH-2064 | Red | Intermediate | Flattened | 6,353.30 | 3.23 |
| BGH-2016 | Red | Intermediate | Flattened | 2,683.80 | 3.96 | BGH-2065 | Red | Intermediate | Strongly rounded | 3,300.50 | 3.46 |
| BGH-2017 | Red | Intermediate | Flattened | 2,822.77 | 4.46 | BGH-2068 | Red | Intermediate | Rounded | 3,460.50 | 4.30 |
| BGH-2018 | Red | Small | Flattened | 1,647.80 | 3.16 | BGH-2069 | Red | Intermediate | Slightly flattened | 5,122.20 | 3.50 |
| BGH-2019 | Red | Intermediate | Flattened | 1,208.90 | 3.33 | BGH-2071 | Red | Large | Slightly flattened | 4,450.80 | 3.60 |
| BGH-2020 | Red | Intermediate | Flattened | 1,996.90 | 3.46 | BGH-2072 | Red | Intermediate | Flattened | 3,573.30 | 3.23 |
| BGH-2021 | Red | Intermediate | Slightly flattened | 2,731.95 | 3.60 | BGH-2073 | Red | Intermediate | Slightly flattened | 4,210.50 | 4.10 |

| | | | | | | | | | | | |
|---|---|---|---|---|---|---|---|---|---|---|---|
| BGH-2026 | Red | Large | Slightly flattened | 2,391.65 | 3.33 | BGH-2074 | Red | Small | Rounded | 2,710.50 | 5.03 |
| BGH-2027 | Red | Large | Flattened | 3,181.94 | 3.50 | BGH-2075 | Red | Intermediate | Flattened | 3,937.70 | 4.53 |
| BGH-2029 | Red | Intermediate | Slightly flatened | 1,448.90 | 3.23 | BGH=2076 | Red | Intermediate | Flattened | 3,937.70 | 3.43 |
| BGH-2032 | Red | Small | Strongly rounded | 2,153.35 | 4.23 | BGH=2077 | Orange | Intermediate | Slightly flattened | 2,363.30 | 3.06 |
| BGH-2033 | Red | Intermediate | Slightly flattened | 1,585.55 | 4.13 | BGH=2078 | Orange | Large | Flateened | 3,721.10 | 3.43 |
| BGH-2034 | Red | Intermediate | Pyramid-shaped | 1,957.50 | 3.63 | BGH-2080 | Red | Interemdiate | Rounded | 1,974.40 | 3.13 |
| BGH-2035 | Red | Intermediate | Slightly flattened | 2,736.70 | 3.50 | BGH=2081 | Red | Large | Flattened | 3,430.50 | 3.40 |
| BGH-2038 | Red | Intermediate | Slightly flattened | 1,728.23 | 3.46 | BGH=2082 | ND | ND | ND | ND | ND |
| BGH-2039-A** | Yellow | Large | Flattened | 1,866.11 | 2.73 | BGH=2083 | Red | Large | Flattened | 3,706.60 | 3.63 |
| BGH=2039-V*** | Red | ND | ND | ND | ND | BGH-2086 | Red | Intermediate | Rounded | 2.346.10 | 3.16 |

*Soluble solids.
**Yellow.
***Red.
(ND) no data.

**Table 12.2 Origin and sampling date of A. solani isolates used in this experiment**

| Isolate | Host | Origin | Sampling date |
|---|---|---|---|
| AS 086 | Tomato | Ponta Grossa-PR | 04/2000 |
| As 207 | Tomato | Bueno Brandao-MG | 01/2006 |
| AS 242 | Tomato | Conselheiro Lafaiete-MG | 05/2005 |
| AS 272 | Tomato | Domingos Martins-ES | 01/2005 |
| AS 339 | Tomato | Colmeia-TO | 11/2005 |

**Table 12.3 Means of the area under the disease progression curve (AUDPC) for 50 tomato accessions of the UFV genebank, evaluated for resistance to Alternaria solani**

| Accession | AUDPC | Accession | AUDPC |
|---|---|---|---|
| BGH-2002 | 44.47 A | BGH-2071 | 23.01 D |
| BGH-2055 | 42.16 A | Santa Clara | 22.53 D |
| BGH-2004 | 39.82 A | BGH-2060 | 22.23 D |
| BGH-2003 | 37.26 B | BGH-2029 | 21.10D |
| BGH-2046 | 37.01 B | BGH-2000 | 20.97 D |
| BGH-2052 | 34.19 B | BGH-2076 | 20.70 D |
| BGH-2038 | 33.99 B | BGH-2069 | 19.56D |
| BGH-2068 | 32.54 B | BGH-2021 | 19.24D |
| BGH-2041 | 30.56 C | BGH-2006 | 18.90D |
| BGH-2082 | 29.90 C | BGH-2083 | 18.71 D |
| BGH-2072 | 28.83 C | BGH-2026 | 18.56 D |
| BGH-2080 | 28.47 C | BGH-2020 | 18.33 D |
| BGH-2027 | 28.23 C | BGH-2016 | 18.05D |
| BGH-2039-Red | 27.33 C | BGH-2062 | 17.66 D |
| BGH-2064 | 27.28 C | BGH-2033 | 17.38 D |
| BGH-2086 | 26.84 C | BGH-2014 | 16.61 D |
| BGH-2077 | 26.80 C | BGH-2081 | 15.29E |
| BGH-2039-Yellow | 26.76 C | BGH-2034 | 15.19E |
| Fanny | 26.03 C | BGH-700 | 14.86 E |
| Debora | 25.83 C | BGH-2057 | 14.26 E |
| BGH-2013 | 25.66 C | BGH-2035 | 13.53 E |
| BGH-2019 | 25.59 C | BGH-2054 | 12.07E |
| BGH-2075 | 24.47 C | BGH-2018 | 11.50 E |
| BGH-2073 | 24.06 C | BGH-2065 | 11.21 E |

| | | | |
|---|---|---|---|
| BGH-2017 | 24.00 C | BGH-2008 | 9.48 E |
| BGH-2078 | 23.82 C | BGH-2032 | 8.S7E |
| BGH-2074 | 23.74 C | | |

Means followed by the same letter in the column did not differ from each other at 5 % probability, by the Scott-Knott test.

Coefficient of variation = 14.04 %; Mean standard error = 2.350; Standard deviation = 3.324.

All plants were inoculated 45 days after transplanting with a manual backpack sprayer (5 L). A suspension of $10^4$ conidia $mL^{-1}$ was applied, consisting of a mixture of the above isolates. No fungicide was used after inoculation. There were five assessments, the first 48 hours after inoculation and the others every three days.

The disease severity was assessed on all leaves. The diseased leaf area was considered in percent according to Horsfall and Barrat (1945) (0 means 0 % of diseased leaf area and 100 simply means 100 % leaf area damaged by the pathogen). This criterion is based on the size and number of lesions; the two components are independent of each other in the disease progress (Boff et al. 1991). Therefore, the percentage of defoliation and number of infected leaves can be analyzed as a direct result of the higher or lower susceptibility of a plant.

The assessments were carried out by three raters, trained according to the program Severity Pro 1.0 (Nutter and Litwiller 1998), and three previously labeled plants of each plot were evaluated. All leaves of each plant were evaluated and the grades of each leaf of the same plant given by the three evaluators averaged. The disease severity on each plant was determined according to the average of all leaves of a plant. These severity values were used to calculate the area under the disease progress curve (AUDPC), based on the model proposed by Campbell and Madden (1990).

$$AACPD = \sum_{1}^{n-1} \frac{(Yi + Yi + 1)}{2} (ti + 1 - ti)$$

where $n$ is the number of reviews, $y$ percentage of disease severity and $t$ is the time spent with the evaluations, in days.

Analysis of variance was performed with the AUDPC data and means of genotypes were grouped by the Scott-Knott test at 5% probability, using software Genes (Cruz 1997).

## Results and Discussion

The data of the disease reaction represented by the AUDPC showed that the difference between the tomato accessions from the UFV genebank (Table 3) was significant, demonstrating genetic variability among genotypes. The AUDPC values of the sub-samples BGH-2081, BGH-2034, BGH-700, BGH-2057, BGH-2035, BGH-2054, BGH-2018, BGH-2065, BGH-2008, and BGH-2032 were lower than the susceptibility standard Santa Clara.

According to Paula and Oliveira (2003), the AUDPC represents epidemics best. According to these authors, this curve can also be helpful in the evaluation of control strategies and prediction of future disease levels.

The use of severity to evaluate the intensity of leaf spot - diseases is probably more appropriate (Kranz 1988). Moreover, according to this author, the severity criterion can be used as a differentiating characteristic of resistance or susceptibility of accessions.

In the experimental period, temperatures were high in the early crop development, and milder in the later stages (Table 4). After inoculation, temperatures were mostly around 20 °C on average, the leaves were exposed to wetness for nine hours per week. In a similar study, Paula and Oliveira (2003) observed an AUDPC of 484.33 for Santa Clara, while in this study the AUDPC of the same cultivar was 22.43. This difference may be due to environmental conditions, which were not ideal for the pathogen development in the test period.

Maiero et al. 1989). Therefore, evaluations of plant resistance in the field, as in the present study, are more appropriate since the reliability of the results is greater (Foolad et al. 2000).

The AUDPC values for early blight on the accessions were lower than of the susceptibility standard Santa Clara. The resistance level of cultivars on the market is insufficient to be recommended as a control method of early blight (Foolad et al. 2000, Martin and Hepperly 1987). Some studies show that tomato sub-samples with higher resistance levels than of those on the market are being used in breeding programs, leading to the development of cultivars

**Table 12.4 Mean monthly rainfall and maximum, minimum and mean temperatures in Viçosa-MG in the test period**

| Month | Rain (mm) | Maximum Temperature (°C) | Minimum Temperature (°C) | Mean Temperature (°C) |
|---|---|---|---|---|
| February | 149 | 30.36 | 18.73 | 22.30 |
| March | 122 | 29.99 | 17.99 | 22.00 |
| April | 53 | 27.66 | 17.26 | 20.00 |
| May | 27 | 26.75 | 13.30 | 17.60 |

Reports in the literature about the climate effect on the development of tomato early blight suggest that severe epidemics occur most frequently at temperatures > 25°C, coupled with high humidity (Maffia et al. 1980, Rotem 1994). In addition, moisture favors *A. solani* sporulation, further increasing the disease severity in the test (Sherf and Macnab 1986).

The assessments after inoculation showed that the disease symptoms were expressed in the plant, aggravating gradually in some accessions. The resistance of most genotypes characterized under laboratory conditions was not confirmed under field conditions (Foolad et al. 2000, with high pathogen resistance levels (Barksdale and Stoner 1973, Gardner 1988, Nash and Gardner 1988, Gardner and Shoemaker 1999). Thus, the sub-samples BGH-700, BGH-2008, BGH-2018, BGH-2032, BGH-2034, BGH-2035, BGH-2054, BGH-2057, BGH-2065, and BGH-2081 can be used as resistance sources in breeding programs.

**Acknowledgements**

The authors are indebted to the Research Foundation of the State of Minas Gerais – F APEMIG for the undergraduate students' research scholarship and to the UFV for providing the necessary infrastructure.

## Caracterização de subamostras de tomateiro quanto à resistência à pinta preta

**RESUMO:** *O objetivo deste trabalho foi caracterizar 50 subamostras de tomateiro do Banco de Germoplasma de Hortaliças da Universidade Federal de Viçosa (BGH-UFV). Foram avaliadas juntamente com as testemunhas Débora, Fanny e Santa Clara, em experimento em blocos ao acaso, com duas repetições. O experimento ocor reu na Horta de Pesquisas da UFV, no período de fevereiro a maio de 2007. Avaliou-se a severidade da doença, que é a porcentagem da área foliar lesionada. Os valores de severidade foram transformados em área abaixo da curva de progresso da doença (AACPD), possibilitando uma melhor visualização dos resultados. Foi realizada a análise de variância, seguido do agrupamento das médias de AACPD pelo teste de Scott-Knott, a 5% de significância. As subamostras BGH-2081, BGH-2034, BGH-700, BGH-2057, BGH-2035, BGH-2054, BGH-2018, BGH-2065, BGH-2008 e BGH-2032 apresentaram menor média de AACPD em relação às testemunhas, podendo ser utilizadas em futuros programas de melhoramento.*

**Palavras-chave:** Alternaria solani; Solanum lycopersicon; *banco de germoplasma; estresse biótico; r ecursos genéticos; pré-melhoramento.*

## REFERENCES

Balbi-Peña MI, Becker A, Stangarlin JR, Franzener G, Lopes MC and Schwan-Estrada KRF (2006) Controle de *Alternaria solani* em tomateiro por extratos de *Curcuma longa* e curcumina-II avalicao *in vivo.* **Fitopatologia Brasileira 31:** 401-404.

Barksdale TH (1971) Field evaluation for tomato early blight resistance. **Plant Disease Report 55:** 807-809.

Barksdale TH and Stoner AK (1973) Segregation for horizontal resistance to tomato early blight. **Plant Disease Report 57**: 964-964.

Barratt RW and Richards MC (1944) Physiological maturity in relation to Alternaria blight in tomato. **Phytopathology 34:** 997.

Basu PK (1974) Measuring early blight, its progress and influence on fruit losses in nine tomato cultivars. **Canadian Plant Disease Survey 54:** 45-51.

Batista DC, Lima MA, Haddad F, Maffia LA and Mizubuti ESG (2006) Validation of decision support systems for tomato early blight and potato late blight, under Brazilian conditions. **Crop Protection 25:** 664-670.

Boff P, Zambolim L and Vale FXR (1991) Escalas para avaliação de severidade da mancha-de-estenfílio (*Stemphylium solani*) e da pinta preta (*Alternaria solani*) em tomateiro. **Fitopatologia Brasileira 16:** 280-283.

Campbell CL and Madden LV (1990) **Introduction to plant disease epidemiology.** John Wiley & Sons, New York, 532p.

Castro MEA, Zambolim L, Chaves GM, Cruz CD and Matsuoka K (2000) Variabilidade patogênica deAlternaria solani, agente causal da pinta-preta do tomateiro. **Summa Phytopatologica 8:** 24-28.

Chaerani R, Groenwold R, Stam P and Voorrips RE (2007) Assessment of early blight (*Alternaria solani*) resistance in tomato using a drop inoculation method. **Journal of General Plant Pathology 73:** 96-103.

Cruz CD (1997) **Programa Genes - aplicativo computacional em genética e estatística.** Editora UFV, Viçosa, 442p.

Datar VV and Mayee CD (1982) Conidial dispersal of Alternaria solani in tomato. **Indian Phytopathology 35:** 68-70.

Foolad MR, Ntahimpera N, Christ BJ and Lin JY (2000) Comparison of field, green-house, and detached-leaflet evaluations of tomato germ plasm for early blight resistance. **Plant Disease 84**: 967-972.

Foolad MR, Zhang M, Khan AA, Niño-Liu D and Lin G (2002) Identification of QTLs for early blight (*Alternaria solani*) resistance in tomato using backcross populations of a *Lycopersicon esculentum x L. hirsutum* cross. **Theoretical and Applied Genetics 104:** 945-958.

Gardner RG (1988) NC EBR-1 and NC EBR-2 early blight resistant tomato breeding lines. **HortScience 23:** 779-781.

Gardner RG and Shoemaker PB (1999) 'Mountain Supreme' early blight resistant hybrid tomato and its parents, NC EBR-3 and NC EBR-4. **HortScience 34**: 745-746.

Hallauer AR and Miranda Filho JB (1988) **Quantitative genetics in maize breeding**. Iowa State University Press, Ames, 468p.

Holm AL, Rivera VV, Secor GA and Gudmestad NC (2003) Temporal sensitivity of Alternaria solani to foliar fungicides. **American Journal of Potato Research 80:** 33-40.

Horsfall JG and Barratt RQ (1945) An improved grading system for measuring plant diseases. **Phytopathology 35:** 655.

Jones JB, Jones JP, Stall RE and Zitter TA (1991) Infectious antifungal. **Plant Physiology 108:** 17-27.

Kranz J (1988) Measuring plant disease. In Kranz J and Rotem J (eds.) **Experimental techniques in plant disease epidemiology**. Springer-Verlag, Heidelberg, p.35-50.

Lopes CA and Santos JRM (1994) **Doenças do tomateiro** . Embrapa/CNPH, Brasília, 67p.

Maffia LA, Martins MCP and Matsuoka K (1980) Doenças do tomateiro. **Informe Agropecuário 6:** 42-60.

Maiero M, Ng TJ and Barksdale TH (1989) Combining ability estimates for early blight resistance in tomato. **Journal of the American Society for Horticultural Science 114:** 118-121.

Maiero M, Ng TJ and Barksdale TH (1990) Genetic resistance to early blight in tomato breeding lines. **HortScience 25:** 344-346.

Martin FW and Hepperly P (1987) Sources of resistance to early blight, Alternaria solani, and transfer to tomato, Lycopersicon esculentum. **Journal of Agriculture of the University of Puerto Rico 71:** 85-95.

Morales EAV, Valois ACC and Nass LL (1997) **Recursos genéticos vegetales**. SPI, Brasília, 79p.

Nash AF and Gardner RG (1988) Tomato early blight resistance in a breeding line derived from *Lycopersicon esculentum* PI 126445. **Plant Disease 72**: 206-209.

Nutter FW and Litwiller D (1998) **Programa severity pro 1.0.** Iowa State University.

Patterson JM and Nokes SE (2000) Incorporation of chlorothalonil persistence on processing tomato into TOM-CAST. **Agricultural Systems 64:** 171-187.

Paula RS and Oliveira WR (2003) Resistência de tomateiro (*Lycopersicon esculentum*) ao patógeno *Alternaria solani*. **Pesquisa AgropecuáriaTropical 33:** 89-95.

Ribeiro AC, Guimarães PTG and AlvarezV VH (1999) **Recomendações para o uso de corretivos e fertilizantes em Minas Gerais: 5ª Aproximação** . Editora UFV, Viçosa, 359p.

Rotem J (1994) **The genus Alternaria: biology, epidemiology, and pathogenicity.** APS Press, St Paul, 326p.

Schuelter AR, Marochio J, Souza CS, Philippsen CCO, Heck MC, Lannes SD, Schuster I, Finger FL and Souza IRP (2006) Genetic control of modified genomic region in a firm ripening tomato (Lycopersicon esculentum Mill.) mutant. **Crop Breeding and Applied Biotechnology 6:** 261-268.

Sherf AF and Macnab AA (1986) Tomato. In Sherf AF and Macnab AA (eds.) **Vegetable diseases and their control**. John Wiley & Sons, New York, p. 599-696.

Silva DJH, Moura MC and Casali VWD (2001) Banco de germoplama de Hortaliças – UFV : histórico e conteúdo. **Horticultura Brasileira 19:** 108-114.

Tambarussi EV, Melotto-Passarin DM, Gonzalez SG, Brigati JB, Jesus FA, Barbosa AL, Dressano K and Carrer H (2009) In silico analysis of Simple Sequence Repeats from chloroplast genomes of Solanaceae species. **Crop Breeding and Applied Biotechnology 9:** 344-352.

Tófoli JG and Kurozawa C (1993) Avaliação da resistência de cultivares e híbridos de tomateiro à pinta preta ( Alternaria solani). **Summa Phytopathologica 19:** 39-40.

Vale FXR, Zambolim L and Chaves GM (1992) Avaliação fitossanitária da cultura do tomateiro em regiões produtoras de Minas Gerais e Espírito Santo. **Fitopatologia Brasileira 17:** 211.

Vallois ACC, Salomão AN and Allem AC (1996) **Glossário de recursos genéticos vegetais**. SPI, Brasília, 62p.

**Early Blight Disease of Tomato**
***Edited by:*** **Virendra Kumar**
**ISBN: 978-93-5056-879-8**
***Edition:*** **2017**
***Published by:*** **Discovery Publishing House Pvt. Ltd., New Delhi (India)**

# Morphological and Physiological Characterization of *Alternaria solani* Isolated from Tomato in Jordan Valley

[1]Khalaf M. Alhussaen

## ABSTRACT

*Alternaria solani* is known economically important and the casual agent of early blight on potato and tomato. Identification of plant pathogens is very important in helping to find effective disease control or management methods. Morphology and physiology characteristics of *Alternaria solani* were investigated for identification and variability. The optimum pH levels of Alternaria solani grow *in vitro* were 6-7 and the optimum growing temperatures of the isolates recovery in this study was 25 and 30°C. The mycelial width between 0.8-1.5 urn and the conidia are 35-75 μm in length and 10-20 um in width and 2-7 transverse septa and 1 -4 longitudinal septa. This study pointed that there Was a variation in the population of *Alternaria solani* isolated from Jordan valley based on morphology and physiology characteristics.

**Keywords:** *Alternaria solani*, early blight, morphology and physiology characteristics, tomato, Jordan valley, disease control.

The species *of Alternaria solani* (Ellis and G. Martin) Jones and Grout was first recorded in 1882 in New Jersey, USA on potato plants (Bose and Som, 1986). The genus of *Alternaria* is indigenous to soil and many of their species are pathogenic to plants including *Alternaria solani* which is known economically important and the casual agent of early blight on potato and tomato.

Early blight of tomato is an important and widely distributed disease throughout the world resulting economic yield losses. Symptoms of early blight on tomato plant start on lower, old and mature leaves which become chlorotic and abscise prematurely spots. These spots may enlarge until they are one-half inch in diameter. Spots have concentric rings or ridges that form a target-like pattern and are often surrounded by a yellow halo. Moreover, these symptoms affect stem and fruits as well (Barksdale and Stoner, 1977; Agrios, 2005).

---

[1] Department of Plant Production and Protection, Faculty of Agriculture, Jerash University, Jerash, Jordan

The classification *of Alternaria solani* is belong to the phylum Ascomycota, class Othideomycetes, order Pleosporales and to family Pleosporaceae (Simmons, 2007). According to morphological characters and phylogenetic analyses, *Alternaria solani* belong to larg, long-beaked and noncatenated spores group of the genus *Alternaria* (Simmons, 2000). The mycelium consisted of septate, branched, light brown hyphae which turned darker with age. The conidiophores were short, 50-90 um and dark coloured. Conidia were 120-296x12-20 urn in size, beaked, muriform dark coloured and borne singly. However in culture, they formed short chains. Singh (1987a, b) report that the conidia contained 5-10 transverse septa and 1-5 longitudinal septa.

In most pathogens, there is a variation between the populations from different areas. Moreover, it is well known that the variation in populations of plant pathogens directly affects disease control, especially when the method related to the development of resistant cultivars and fungicide usage. *Alternaria solani* found to be a highly variable pathogen (Castro *et al.,* 2000; Pryor and Michailides, 2002).

Various researches have been characterized *Alternaria solani* in different part of the word (Petrunak and Christ, 1992; Martinez *et al.,* 2004; Lourenco *et al.,* 2009). However in Jordan, a few researches have been investigated *Alternaria solani* and most of them about control the disease (Al-Mughrabi, 2004; Goussous *et al.,* 2010; Abu-El-Samen and Al-Shudifat, 2011). This study is designed to characterize the fungus of *Alternaria solani* isolated from tomato plants grown in Jordan valley based on morphology and physiology features.

## Materials and Methods

**Isolation:** Tomato leaves showing typical early blight symptoms were collected from different farms in the Jordan valley in early 2012. The infected leaves were cut into small bits measuring about 5 mm and surface sterilized in 1 % sodium hypochlorite solution for 1 min, rinsed with sterile distilled water. Pieces were then placed on Potato Dextrose Agar (PDA) and incubated under 12 h light and 12 h dark at 25±1°C according to Naik *et al.* (2010). Pure culture of the fungus was obtained by Hyphal Tip Isolation Method.

## Physiological studies

**Effect of pH levels:** Four isolates were selected based on colony to study the effect of pH on growth *in vitro* for *A. solani* and examined on PDA. The pH of the medium was adjusted to various levels 4, 4.5, 5, 5.5, 6, 6.5, 7, 7.5 and 8 by adding 0.1 N sodium hydroxide and 0.1 N hydrochloric acid. About 5 mm discs taken from 7 days old culture were inoculated and incubated under 12 h light and 12 h dark at 25±1°C for 7 days. Three replications were used for each isolate and treatment. The diametefof the colony growth was measured and recorded after 7 days. General Linear Model (GLM) ANO VA was used to differences (p = 0.05) between treatments mean (SPSS Ver. 10).

**Effect of temperature:** Eight temperatures from 5-40°C (5°C intervals) were used to incubate PDA Petri dish cultures of the four *Alternaria solani* isolates selected to find out the optimum temperature as well as the lowest and the highest temperatures at which fungal and growth occurred All incubation was carried out under 12 h light and 12 h dark for 7 days at 25 ± 1°C. Three replicates were used for each isolate at each temperature. Growth was measured after 7 days using two diameter measurements perpendicular to each other. General Linear Model (GLM) ANOVA was used to differences ($p \leq 0.05$) between treatments mean (SPSS Ver. 10).

**Morphological characterization:** The morphological characters of representative isolates of the four *Alternaria solani* isolates including conidia size (length and width), length of beak and hyphal width and number of septa in conidia were measured under power objective 40X using light microscope. The *Alternaria solani* cultures were 7 days old grown on PDA.

## Results

**Isolation:** All isolates recovery from tomato leaves showing typical early blight symptoms collected from Jordan valley area were identified as *Alternaria solani* based on the morphological characteristics according to Alternaria identification manual (Simmons, 2007).

### Physiological studies

**Effect of pH levels:** The optimum pH level of the four isolates *of Alternaria solani* tested was 7. Moreover, all isolate tested grew very well at pH levels of 6 and 6.5. At pH levels of 4.5, 5, 5.5 and 7.5, all four isolates were grew well. However, slightly growth was appeared at pH levels of 4 and 8 for all isolates tested (Table 1).

There were significant differences in colony growth between the four *Alternaria solani* isolates tested at each pH levels ($p = 0.01$). Moreover, there were significant differences between the colony growth at different pH levels for each isolate ($p = 0.00$). However, there were no significant differences in colony growth for each isolate between pH levels of 6, 6.5 and 7 (Table 1).

**Effect of temperature:** Isolates *of Alternaria solani* have an optimum growth temperature of 30°C. They also grew well at temperature of 30°C. At temperature 20°C, *Alternaria solani* grew slightly (mean). Limited growth was occurred at temperatures of 10 and 40°C but no growth was appeared at temperature of 5°C (Table 2).

There were significant differences in colony growth between the four *Alternaria solani* isolates tested at each temperature ($p = 0.01$). Moreover, there were significant differences between the colony growth at different temperatures for each isolate ($p = 0.00$). Nevertheless, there were no significant differences in colony growth for each isolate between temperatures of 25 and 30°C (Table 2).

**Table 13.1 Mean growth (mm) of 4 isolates *of Alternaria solani* incubated on PDA with nine pH levels (4, 4.5, 5, 5.5, 6, 6.5, 7, 7.5 and 8) in 12 h light and 12 h dark. Growth was measured after 7 days Mycelial diameter growth (mm) of different isolates**

| pH level | Isolate 1 | Isolate 2 | Isolate 3 | Isolate4 |
|---|---|---|---|---|
| 4.0 | $3.9^b$ | $3.3^b$ | $3.5^b$ | $3.3^b$ |
| 4.5 | $5.3^c$ | $5.1^c$ | $5.4^c$ | $5.0^c$ |
| 5.0 | $6.8^d$ | $7.0^d$ | $6.9^d$ | $6.6^d$ |
| 5.5 | $6.7^d$ | $6.6^d$ | $6.8^d$ | $6.8^d$ |
| 6.0 | $8.1^e$ | $7.9^e$ | $8.3^e$ | $8.1^e$ |
| 6.5 | $8.6^e$ | $8.7^e$ | $8.5^e$ | $8.5^e$ |
| 7.0 | $8.8^e$ | $8.9^e$ | $8.6^e$ | $8.7^e$ |
| 7.5 | $5.4^c$ | $5.0^c$ | $5.2^c$ | $5.3^c$ |
| 8.0 | $2.1^g$ | $2.0^g$ | $2.1^g$ | $2.0^g$ |

Means followed by the same letter are not significantly different from each other at *p* £ 0.05; *n* = 3 for each isolate at each pH level.

**Table 13.2 Mean growth (mm) of 4 isolates of *Alternaria solani* incubated at right different temperatures from 5-40°C on PDA in 12 h light and 12 h dark. Growth was measured after 7 days**

| Temperature (°C) | Mycelial diameter growth (mm) of different isolates | | | |
|---|---|---|---|---|
| | Isolate 1 | Isolate 2 | Isolate 3 | Isolate 4 |
| 05 | $0.0^g$ | $0.0^g$ | $0.0^g$ | $0.0^g$ |
| 10 | $0.1^b$ | $0.2^b$ | $0.2^b$ | $0.1^b$ |
| 15 | $1.1^c$ | $1.9^c$ | $1.2^c$ | $I.0^c$ |
| 20 | $2.1^d$ | $2.8^d$ | $2.4^d$ | $2.8^d$ |
| 25 | $8.6^e$ | $8.8^e$ | $8.8^e$ | $8.5^e$ |
| 30 | $8.8^e$ | $8.7^e$ | $8.9^e$ | $8.3^e$ |
| 35 | $2.9^d$ | $3.5^d$ | $3.1^d$ | $3.5^d$ |
| 40 | $0.2^b$ | $0.1^b$ | $0.1^b$ | $O.I^b$ |

Means followed by the same letter are not significantly different from each other at *p* £ 0.01; *n* = 3 for each isolate at each temperature.

**Morphological characterization:** The morphology characterization of the selective four isolates of *Alternaria solani* recovery from Jordan valley area, indicated the conidiophores were formed singly or in groups or flexuous brown to olivaceous brown. The conidia were solitary straight or slightly flexuous or muriform or ellipsoidal tapering to beak, pale and sometimes branched The conidia were 35-75 um in length and 10-20 um in width (Table 3). There were 2-7 transverse septa and 1 -4 longitudinal septa. The mycelial width was 0.8-1.5 um.

## Discussion

This is the first study to characterize *Alternaria solani,* the casual agent of early blight on tomato isolated from Jordan valley. A scarcity of studies in Jordan on *Alternaria solani* on disease management were done and fungicides sensitivity (Al-Mughrabi, 2004; Abu-El-Samen and Al-Shudifat, 2011). Variation in populations of plant pathogens is important to control strategies. This study demonstrates that there was a variation in the population *of Alternaria solani* isolated from Jordan valley based on morphology and physiology characteristics.

*Alternaria solani* isolated in this study was identified based on morphology and physiology characteristics according to the *Alternaria* identification manual (Simmons, 2007). Four isolates were selected to represent all recovery isolates based on colony characteristics in this study for the morphology and physiology characteristics. The results of this study pointed that the optimum pH level of *Alternaria solani* grow *in vitro* were 6-7. Moreover, the optimum growing temperature of the isolates recovery in this study was 25 and 30°C. These results are contestant with Ibrahim *et al.* (2009) who found that the optimum conditions *for Alternaria solani* isolated from North of Jordan were 25°C and pH 7 when they study the ability of *Atternaria solani* to utilize the polyester-polyurethane. Moreover, Naik *et al.* (2010) reported that the optimum growth and the maximum sporulation temperatures were 25 and 30°C. Furthermore, other research found that *Alternaria solani* has an optimum growth temperature of 25°C and pH level of 6.5 (Tatiana *et al,* 2010).

**Table 13.3: Morphological characteristics of Alternaria solani isolated from tomato**

| Isolates | Mycelial width (μm) | Conidia size (mm) | | Length of beak (μm) | Septa in conidia | |
|---|---|---|---|---|---|---|
| | | Length | Width | | Horizontal | Vertical |
| 1 | 0.8-1.2 | 25-50 | 10-15 | 8-10 | 3-5 | 1-4 |
| 2 | 1.1-1.5 | 35-65 | 10-20 | 10-14 | 2-5 | 1-3 |
| 3 | 0.9-1.3 | 45-75 | 15-20 | 12-17 | 4-7 | 1-3 |
| 4 | 1.0-1.4 | 40-65 | 10-15 | 11-15 | 3-6 | 2-4 |

Morphology features *of Alternaria solani* described in this study were found to have mycelial width between 0.8-1.5 um. Moreover, the conidia are 35-75 um in length and 10-20 um in width and 2-7 transverse septa and 1-4 longitudinal septa. Naik *et al.* (2010) describe *Alternaria solani* isolated from tomato plants and those results were agreed with the results presented in this study. However, other research found that the conidia were solitary straight or slightly flexuous, oblong or ellipsoidal tapering to a beak, smooth, 150-300 um in length, 13-20 um thick in the broadest part with 8-10 transverse and 1-4 longitudinal s'epta (Arunakumara, 2006). Furthermore, Kumar *et al.* (2008) reported that the width of conidiogenous hyphae were 1.17-9.56 micro.

## Conclusion

The results of this research found that there were variations in the population of *Alternaria solani* isolated from Jordan valley based on morphology and physiology characterization. In Jordan, there was no study look into the population *of Alternaria solani* based on morphology and physiology characterization. However, there were a few study look into the variation *of Alternaria solani of* fungicides sensitivity (Al-Mughrabi, 2004; Abu-El-Samen and Al-Shudifat, 2011). In the world, various studies look into the population of *Alternaria solani* based on both morphology and molecular characteristics (Petrunak and Christ, 1992; Weir *et al.*, 1998; Van der Waals *et al.*, 2004; Lourenco *et al.*, 2009 ). Other studies found there were a variation in the population *of Alternaria solani* based on the pathogenicity (Kumar *et al.*, 2008; Naik *et al.*, 2010). Further studies should investigate the population of *Alternaria solani* in Jordan based on genetic variation.

## REFERENCES

Abu-El-Samen, P.M. and A.M. Al-Shudifat, 2011. Sensitivity of tomato early blight isolates *(Alternaria solani)* from Jordan to mancozeb, chlorothalonil and azoxystrobin fungicides. Proceedings of the APS, IPPC Joint Meeting, Honolulu, Hawaii, August 6-10, 2011, The American Phytopathological Society.

Agrios, G.N., 2005. Plant Pathology. 5th Edn., Academic Press, New York, USA., ISBN-13: 9780120445653, Pages 922.

Al-Mughrabi, K.I., 2004. Sensitivity of Jordanian isolates of *Alternaria solani* to mancothane. Phytopathol. Mediterraneans: 14-19.

Arunakumara, K.T., 2006. Studies on *Alternaria solani* (Ellis and Martin) Jones and Grout causing early blilght of tomato. M.Sc. Thesis, University of Agricultural Sciences. Dharwad.

Barksdale, T.H. and A.K. Stoner, 1977. study of the inheritance of tomato early blight resistance. Plant Dis. Rptr., 61: 63-65.

Bose, K. and G. Som, 1986. Vegetable Crops in India. Nayaprakash Publishing, Calcutta, Pages: 773.

Castro, ME.A., L. Zambolim, G.M. Chanes, C.D. Cruz and K. Matsuoka, 2000. Pathogenic variability of *Alternaria solani,* the causal agent of tomato early blight. Summa-Phytopathologica, 26: 24-28.

Goussous, S.J., P.M. Abu-El-Samen and R.A. Tahhan, 2010. Antifungal activity of several medicinal plants extracts against the early blight pathogen *(Alternaria solani).* Arch. Phytopathol. Plant Protec., 43. 1746-1758.

Ibrahim, I.N., A. Maraqa, K.M. Hameed, I.M. Saadoun, H.M. Maswadeh and T. Nakajima-Kambe, 2009. Polyester-polyurethane Biodegradation by *Alternaria Solani,* Isolated from Northern Jordan. Adv. Environ. Biol., 3:162-170.

Kumar, V., S. Haldar,K. Pandey, R. Singh, A. SinghandP. Singh, 2008. Cultural, morphological, pathogenic and molecular variability amongst tomato isolates of *Alternaria solani* in India. World J. Microbiol. Biotechnol., 24: 1003-1009.

Lourenco, Jr. V., A. Moya, F. Gonzalez-Candelas, I. Carbone, L.A. Maffia and E.S.G. Mizubuti, 2009. Molecular diversity and evolutionary processes of *Alternaria solani* in Brazil inferred using genealogical and coalescent approaches. Phytopathology, 99: 765-774.

Martinez, S.P., R. Snowdon and J. Pons-Kuhnemann, 2004. Variability of Cuban and international populations *of Alternaria solani* from different hosts and localities: AFLP genetic analysis. Eur. J. Plant Pathol, 110: 399-409.

Naik, M.K., Y. Prasad, K.V. Bhat and G.S.D. Rani, 2010. Morphological, Physiological, Pathogenic and molecular variability among isolates of *Alternaria solani* from tomato. IndianPhytopthol., 63: 168-173.

Petrunak, D.M. and B.J. Christ, 1992. Isozyme variability in *Alternaria solani* and *A. alternate.* Phytopathology, 82: 1343-1347.

Pryor, B.M. and T.J. Michailides, 2002. Morphological, pathogenic and molecular characterization of *Alternaria* isolates associated with Alternaria late blight of pistachio. Phytopathology, 92: 406-416.

Simmons, E., 2000. Alternaria themes and variations (244-286) species on Solanaceae. Mycotaxon, 75: 1-115.

Simmons, E., 2007. *Alternaria:* AnIdentification Manual. CBS Fungal Biodiversity Centre, Utrecht, Netherlands.

Singh, S., 1987a. Diseases of Vegetable Crops. Oxford and IBH Pub. Co. Pvt. Ltd., New Delhi, India.

Singh, S.N., 1987b. Response of chilli cultivars to *Alternaria alternate* and losses under field conditions. Farm Sci. J., 2: 96-97.

Tatiana, T.M.S. Rodrigues, L.A. Maffia, O.D. Dhingra and E.S.G. Mizubuti, 2010. *In vitro* production of conidia *of Alternaria solani.* Trop. Plant Pathol., 35: 203-212.

Van der Waals, J.E., L. Korsten and B. Slippers, 2004. Genetic diversity among *Alternaria solani* Isolates from Potatoes in South Africa. Plant Dis., 88: 959-964.

Weir, T.L., D.R. Huff, B.J. Christ and C.P. Romaine, 1998. RAPD-PCR analysis of genetic variation among isolates of *Alternaria solani* and *Alternaria alternate* from potato and tomato. Mycologia, 99:813-821.

**Early Blight Disease of Tomato**
***Edited by:*** **Virendra Kumar**
**ISBN: 978-93-5056-879-8**
***Edition:*** **2017**
***Published by:*** **Discovery Publishing House Pvt. Ltd., New Delhi (India)**

# Tomato Early Blight (*Alternaria solani*): The Pathogen, Genetics and Breeding for Resistance

[1]Reni Chaerani, [2]Roeland E. Voorrips

## ABSTRACT

Alternaria solani causes diseases on foliage (early blight), basal stems of seedlings (collar rot), stems of adult plants (stem lesions), and fruits (fruit rot) of tomato. Early blight is the most destructive of these diseases and hence receives considerable attention in breeding. For over 60 years, breeding for early blight resistance has been practiced, but the development of cultivars with high levels of resistance has been hampered by the lack of sources of strong resistance in the cultivated tomato and by the quantitative expression and polygenic inheritance of the resistance. In some accessions of wild species, high levels of early blight resistance have been found, but breeding lines still have unfavorable horticultural traits from the donor parent. Recently, the first linkage maps with loci controlling early blight resistance have been developed based on interspecific crosses. These maps may facilitate marker-assisted selection. This overview presents the current knowledge about the A. solani–tomato complex with respect to its biology, genetics, and breeding.

**Keywords:** Early blight · Tomato · Alternaria solani · Resistance · Genetics · Breeding.

## Introduction

Early blight is the major disease symptom caused by the fungus *Alternaria solani* (Ellis & Martin) Sorauer. This disease, which in severe cases can lead to complete defoliation, is most damaging on tomato [*Solanum lycopersicum* L. (Peralta et al. 2005, syn. *Lycopersicon esculentum* Mill.)] in regions with heavy rainfall, high humidity, and fairly high temperatures (24°–29°C). Epidemics can also occur in semi-arid climates where frequent and prolonged nightly dews occur (Rotem and Reichert 1964). Apart from the leaf symptoms that are known as early blight (EB), *A. solani* can cause less economically important symptoms on tomato, including collar rot (basal stem lesions at the seedling stage), stem lesions on the adult plant, and fruit rot (Walker 1952). Yield losses up to 79% from EB damage have been reported from Canada, India, the United States, and Nigeria (Basu 1974b; Datar and Mayee 1981; Sherf and MacNab 1986; Gwary

[1] Plant Research International, PO Box, 16, 6700 AA Wageningen, The Netherlands.

and Nahunnaro 1998). Collar rot can cause seedling losses of 20% to 40% in the field (Sherf and MacNab 1986).

Control measures for these diseases include a 3- to 5-year crop rotation, routine applications of fungicides, and the use of disease-free transplants (Madden et al. 1978; Sherf and MacNab 1986). Fungicide treatments are generally the most effective control measures, but are not economically feasible in all areas of the world and may not be effective under weather conditions favorable for epidemics (Herriot et al. 1986). Resistant cultivars are potentially the most economical control measure because they can extend the intervals between fungicide sprays while maintaining control of the disease (Madden et al. 1978; Shtienberg et al. 1995; Keinath et al. 1996).

Progress in breeding for EB resistance has been limited by the lack of effective resistance genes in cultivated tomato (Vakalounakis 1983; Poysa and Tu 1996; Banerjee et al. 1998; Vloutoglou 1999) and by the quantitative expression and polygenic inheritance of the resistance (Barksdale and Stoner 1977; Maiero et al. 1989; Nash and Gardner 1988a; Maiero et al. 1990a; Thirthamallappa and Lohithaswa 2000). Sources for EB resistance have been identified in wild relatives of tomato. Some of these have been utilized through traditional breeding approaches, but an increased level of resistance is negatively correlated with earliness (Nash and Gardner 1988a; Maiero et al. 1989; Foolad and Lin 2001; Foolad et al. 2002a) and yield (Barrat and Richards 1944). The most resistant breeding lines and hybrid cultivars with acceptable horticultural characteristics that are currently available have moderate resistance to EB and mature slightly later (Gardner 1988; Gardner and Shoemaker 1999; Gardner 2000). Hence, resistant cultivars with better horticultural traits are still needed.

Classical quantitative genetic analyses have provided estimates of the number of quantitative trait loci (QTLs) for EB resistance, of the average gene action and of the heritabilities from which the prospects for progress in breeding programs based on phenotypic selection can be estimated (Nash and Gardner 1988a; Maiero et al. 1990a, b). However, with such studies, the effects of individual genes and their locations on the tomato genome cannot be deter-mined. More recent genetic studies on EB resistance have been directed to the use of molecular marker maps for mapping and characterizing the QTLs that determine the resistance (Foolad et al. 2002b; Zhang et al. 2003; Chaerani et al. submitted). Markers closely linked to QTLs can be used to select individual plants with the most desirable QTLs. By fine mapping, we can also resolve whether the unfavorable traits associated with EB resistance are due to pleiotropic effects of resistance genes or to closely linked genes. If they are linked, marker-based selection might fa-cilitate breaking of the linkage.

In this article we review the literature pertaining to as-pects of resistance to EB, and, to a lesser extent, also to collar rot and stem lesions. The article describes:

- The biology of *A. solani* and the symptoms caused by the fungus, and methods for selecting resistance to EB and collar rot.
- The known sources of resistance followed by classical genetic studies of EB, resistance to collar rot and stem lesions, and the genetic interrelationship among the diseases.
- The mapping of resistance genes.
- Physiological aspects affecting EB resistance and characterization of EB resistance.
- Perspectives for EB resistance breeding.

## The pathogen

Since the first description by Ellis and Martin in 1882 (cited in Sherf and MacNab 1986), *Alternaria solani*, previously known as *A. porri* f. sp. *solani* (Neergaard 1945), has been the object of intensive studies (Strandberg 1992; Rotem 1994). *A. solani* belongs to the Fungi Imperfecti (Deuteromycotina) in the class Hyphomycetes and order Hyphales (Agrios 2005). An ascomycete fungus, *Pleospora solani*, has been claimed by Esquivel (1984) as the teleomorph stage of *A. solani*, but this has not been confirmed by others. *A. solani* belongs to the large-spored group, characterized by separate conidia borne singly on simple conidiophore, within the genus *Alternaria* (Neergaard 1945). The conidia of *A. solani* are muriform and beaked (Neergaard 1945; Ellis and Gibson 1975). Like other members of the genus *Alternaria*, *A. solani* has transverse and longitudinal septate conidia, multinucleate cells, and dark-colored (melanized) cells (Rotem 1994). The melanins protect against adverse environmental conditions including resistance to microbes and hydrolytic enzymes (Rotem 1994).

## Disease cycle

Under free moisture or near-saturated humidity at a wide range of temperatures (8°–32°C), conidia germinate to produce one or more germ tubes. These subsequently penetrate the host epidermal cells directly by means of appressoria or they enter through stomata or wounds by hyphal growth (Sherf and MacNab 1986; Perez and Martinez 1999; Agrios 2005; Fig. 14.1). Penetration can occur at temperatures between 10° and 25°C (Sherf and MacNab 1986). Host colonization is facilitated by enzymes (cellulases, pectin methyl galacturonase) that degrade the host cell wall and by a number of toxins that kill host cells and enable the pathogen to derive nutrients from the dead cells (Rotem 1994). Lesions become visible 2–3 days after infection, and spore production occurs 3–5 days later (Sherf and MacNab 1986). This relatively short disease cycle allows for polycyclic infection (Sherf and MacNab 1986). The fungus survives between crops as mycelia or conidia in soil, plant debris, and seed (Sherf and MacNab 1986; Fig. 1). Chlamydospores can also serve as survival structures (Basu 1974a; Patterson 1991). Therefore, the life cycle of *A. solani* includes soil- and seed- as well as air-borne stages, making the pathogen difficult to control by means of rotation

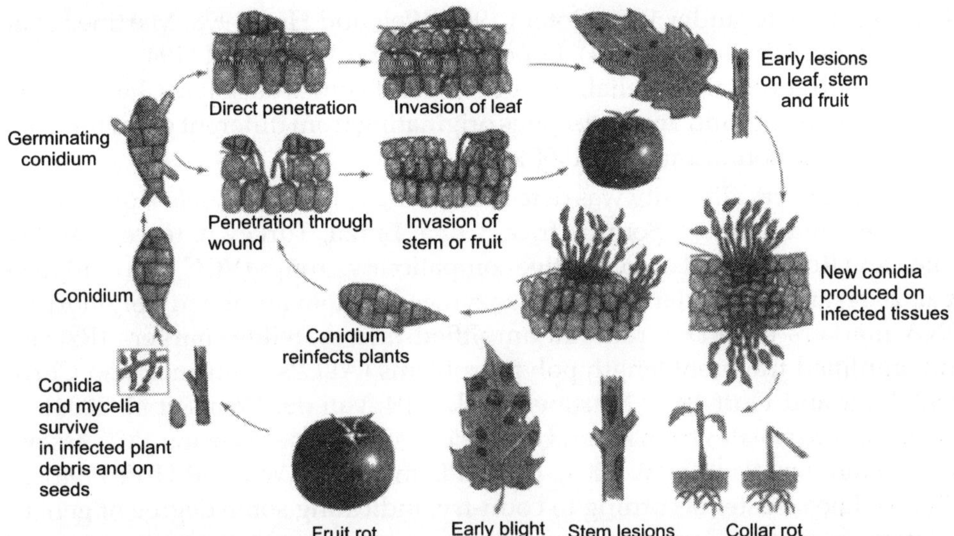


**Fig. 14.1 Infection process, development and symptoms of diseases caused by *Alternaria solani*. Adapted from Agrios (2005, p 455), with permission from Elsevier**

and sanitation. The main hosts of *A. solani* are solanaceous crops including tomato, potato, eggplant, and pepper (Neergaard 1945; Ellis and Gibson 1975).

## Toxin production

Eleven toxins have been identified in culture filtrates of *A. solani* (Montemurro and Visconti 1992). Among these, alternaric acid and solanapyrone A, B, and C are able to induce necrotic symptoms similar to EB symptoms (Montemurro and Visconti 1992). Alternaric acid is one of the major metabolites in the filtrates (Brian et al. 1952) and is probably the main metabolite responsible for the development of necrotic and chlorotic symptoms (Pound and Stahmann 1951). Alternaric acid is already present in dormant spores and is produced and released by germinating spores (Langsdorf et al. 1990). Alternaric acid is not phytotoxic when sprayed alone on tomato leaves, but it enhances the infection process and the development of necrotic symptoms when added to spore suspensions of *A. solani* (Langsdorf et al. 1990). Another factor in *A. solani* spores was required for infection. This substance, referred to as S1, is nontoxic and is present in a water-soluble fraction from chloroform extracts of spore-germination fluid. This factor allowed the spores of a nonpathogenic strain of *A. alternata* to cause necrotic symptoms on tomato and potato (Langsdorf et al. 1990).

## Variability among isolates

Although *A. solani* appears to have only a nonsexual life cycle, it has a relatively high variation in morphology in vivo and in vitro, physiology, genetic makeup, and pathogenicity among isolates (Bonde 1929; Wellman 1943; Neergaard 1945;

Henning and Alexander 1959; Rotem 1966; Weir and Huff 1998; Martinez et al. 2004; van der Waals et al. 2004). Bonde (1929) and Neergaard (1945) classified *A. solani* into conidial, mycelial, and intermediate types of isolates. Patho-genic differences were found among isolates originating from different germ tube tips from the same conidium (Stall 1958).

A high genetic diversity was detected among isolates of *A. solani* originating from the United States, South Africa, Cuba, Brazil, Turkey, Greece, Canada, China and Russia based on vegetative compatibility groups (VCG, van der Waals et al. 2004) and molecular markers [isozymes, random amplified polymorphic DNA markers (RAPDs), random amplified microsatellite markers (RAMs), and amplified fragment length polymorphisms (AFLPs); Petrunak and Christ 1992; Weir and Huff 1998; Martinez et al. 2004; van der Waals et al. 2004]. In studies where isolates from several countries were compared using VCG assays, RAMs (van der Waals et al. 2004), or RAPD markers (Weir and Huff 1998), *A. solani* isolates cluster according to coun-try, indicating some degree of genetic isolation. In contrast, isolates from the same country are not distinctly separated by geographical origin (Petrunak and Christ 1992; Weir and Huff 1998; Martinez et al. 2004; van der Waals et al. 2004). This can be ascribed to short- or medium-distance dispersal of the airborne spores and movement of plant material within the countries (Weir and Huff 1998; van der Waals et al. 2004). In many cases, isolates originating from tomato and potato clustered according to their hosts based on RAPD (Weir and Huff 1998) and AFLP markers (Martinez et al. 2004), suggesting host specialization. Organ specificity was reported to occur among Bulgarian isolates by Stancheva (1990), but has not been described by other authors. Associations of molecular markers with variability in physiology, morphology, and virulence are not known.

So far, conclusive evidence for the existence of physiological races is lacking. Physiological races are defined based on differential host specificity (Mehrotra and Areja 1990; Schlegel 2003). Therefore, the report of the presence of physiological races of *A. solani* (Bonde 1929) is not correct according to the current definition because it described them in terms of variability in physiological, morphological, and ecological characters in in vitro culture. Henning and Alexander (1959) characterized isolates on tomato and related species with quantitative variation in resistance. Some of these isolates, which showed cultural differences, appeared to be host specific, but the pattern of infection was not consistent between experiments. This was attributed to heterogeneity of the host lines and the unstable nature of the isolate cultures (Henning and Alexander 1959). Similarly, Castro et al. (2000) could not demonstrate consistent host-specific reactions of isolates.

Heterokaryosis could be the driving force for genetic variation in *A. solani* (Stall 1958). Heterokaryosis is the occurrence of genetically different nuclei in the same cells. This can be the result of hyphal anastomosis, a process observed in *A. solani* (Stall and Alexander 1957; Stall 1958). After establishment of heterokaryosis, this state may be maintained or lost during further cell divisions. Also nuclear migration is possible through septal pores between cells of conidia, conidiophores, mycelia, and cells connecting these structures, allowing dissociation of unlike nuclei leading to homokaryosis, and, conversely, also to the reestablishment of heterokaryosis (Stall 1958). Therefore, even isolates obtained from single conidia and hyphal tips are genetically unstable. In their studies, Stall and Alexander (1957) observed frequent occurrence of anastomoses but failed to obtain heterokaryosis as indicated by the absence of segregation of cultural types.

The ability of *A. solani* to maintain high genetic variability allows it to react quickly to changing environments. For example, a recent study demonstrated that isolates in the midwestern United States have become less sensitive to a fungicide resulting in significant losses of disease in glass-house cultures (Pasche et al. 2004). The high genetic diver-sity and high degree of gene flow within countries could break down genetic resistance in the host; this possibility has been advanced as one of the reasons for the absence of potato cultivars with complete resistance to *A. solani* in South Africa (van der Waals et al. 2004).

**Disease symptoms**

All aboveground parts of plants can be infected by *Alternaria solani*, and various names have been given for the different symptoms, which often leads to confusion (Sherf and MacNab 1986). In this article, we refer to symptoms on foliage as early blight (EB), to symptoms on fruits as fruit rot, to symptoms on stems of seedlings as collar rot, and those on stems of adult plants as stem lesions (Walker 1952).

The first symptoms of EB are small, dark, necrotic le-sions that usually appear on the older leaves and spread upward as the plants become older (Sherf and MacNab 1986). As lesions enlarge, they commonly have concentric rings with a target-like appearance, and they are often surrounded by a yellowing zone. In severe epidemics, *A. solani* can cause premature defoliation, which weakens the plants and exposes the fruit to injury from sunscald (Sherf and MacNab 1986).

Large, dark, and sunken lesions may appear on the stems of seedlings at the ground line, causing partial girdling known as collar rot (Sherf and MacNab 1986). Seedlings are weakened and can die when the stem is completely girdled by the lesion. On the main stem and side branches of adult plants, the fungus causes small, dark, slightly sunken areas that enlarge to form dark brown, elongated spots, which occasionally have concentric rings like those on the leaves. These spots are scattered along the stem and branches (Walker 1952). Some authors make no distinction between collar rot and stem lesions (Gardner 1990). In older literature, collar rot and stem lesions are sometimes referred to as stem cankers (Barksdale and Stoner 1977), a term that is currently reserved for the disease caused by *A. alternata* (Sherf and MacNab 1986).

On green or ripe fruits, dark, velvety, sunken spots may occur at the stem end. These spots occasionally develop from mycelia extending from stem lesions and can reach a considerable size and also develop distinct concentric markings (Sherf and MacNab 1986). Semi-ripe fruits are more susceptible than ripe ones (Mehta et al. 1975). Heavily infected fruits frequently drop before they mature. On susceptible genotypes, the calyx and blossom may also be infected (Pandey et al. 2003).

## Screening methods

Reliable and repeatable techniques for large-scale screening are necessary to identify host plant resistance. Techniques have been developed for EB and collar rot resistance screening under field, glasshouse, and laboratory conditions. In the laboratory, both fungal inocula (spores and mycelia) and fungal toxins have been used in screening for resistance.

### Inoculum production

*Alternaria solani* can be artificially grown in various culture media, but it does not readily sporulate in vitro. Spore production requires special conditions such as mycelial wounding or the transfer of culture pieces onto a minimal medium or filter paper followed by exposure to harsh conditions (Lukens and Horsfall 1968; Barksdale 1969; Shahin and Shepard 1979). Efficient sporulation can be induced by exposing cultures under diurnal light in a partially opened culture dish, after removal of aerial mycelia (Barksdale 1969). For maintenance of a wild-type culture, Barksdale (1969) suggested mass transfer of sections of culture that have "normal appearing areas" because variants in culture are often obtained even though the culture was started from single spores. When spores derived from cultures are difficult to obtain, mixed inocula of spores and mycelia from dried, infected leaves are sometimes used in field experiments (Thirthamallappa and Lohithaswa 2000).

### Field screening

In field tests, large populations can be assessed under nor-mal growing conditions during the whole life cycle of the plants. Artificial inoculation by (repeated) spraying of inoculum and/or the use of spreader rows is required to enhance natural infection and to obtain uniform disease pressure. Prior to inoculation, it is often necessary to pre-vent or eradicate foliar diseases with scheduled fungicide sprays (Nash and Gardner 1988a).

EB severity in the field is assessed in terms of percentage defoliation and the average fraction of necrotic leaf area on the plant (Horsfall and Barrat 1945). Symptoms on the upper leaves can be disregarded because the necrotic areas on these leaves are less than 2% of the total damage during the growing season

(Basu 1974b). Therefore, counting the number of leaves with 75%–100% necrosis in the lower half of the plants (Basu 1974b) or estimating the percentage of necrotic area in the middle third of the plant canopy (Christ 1991) are reliable indicators for EB severity.

EB epidemics initially progress slowly but accelerate as plants mature, resulting in a typical sigmoidal disease progress curve (Nash and Gardner 1988b). Occasionally the disease curve is bimodal, which could be due to the emer-gence of new healthy leaves after the first cycle of infection (Pandey et al. 2003). Therefore, a once-only evaluation can underestimate or overestimate the actual level of resistance of a particular host, and field assessments must be based on several observations over time that are used to calculate the area under the disease progress curve (AUDPC). The AUDPC integrates the host, pathogen, and environmental effects during the epidemic (Pandey et al. 2003).

In spite of their advantages, field tests also have their problems: they are slow, labor intensive, highly affected by the presence of other pathogens, not suitable for evaluation of single plants in a large-scale experiment, and they are sensitive to environmental conditions that are difficult to control.

**Glasshouse screening**

Assays in a glasshouse or controlled-environment chamber with seedlings or small plants provide uniform, favorable, repeatable environmental conditions and permit several cycles of screening per year, thus offering more reliable results. Glasshouse and field test results correspond well (Banerjee et al. 1998; Foolad et al. 2000). Glasshouse or controlled-environment chamber evaluations of young plants were mainly used for preliminary selection of material resistant to *A. solani* from large germplasm collections (Barksdale 1969; Vakalounakis 1983; Poysa and Tu 1996; Vloutoglou 1999) and to study the inheritance of resistance to collar rot. Glasshouse evaluation of EB resistance is rarely performed for genetic studies (Chaerani et al. submitted).

The current glasshouse screening methods for *A. solani* resistance are based on the method established by Barksdale (1969). Generally, seedlings are spray-inoculated with spores at an age of 4–6 weeks (Barksdale 1969; Marcinkowska 1982; Nash and Gardner 1988b; Banerjee et al. 1998; Vloutoglou 1999; Foolad et al. 2000). Leaves can be injured prior to spraying by rubbing the leaf between thumb and forefingers (Poysa and Tu 1996). Plants are incubated for 24h under 100% relative humidity (RH) followed by 12–16h of 100% RH during the night for 5–7 days in a mist chamber, mimicking the repeated nightly dew in nature. During the day, plants are exposed to ambient RH to allow the development of disease symptoms. A leaf wetness period of at least 4h after inoculation was required for infection (Moore 1942; Vloutoglou and Kalogerakis 2000). Increasing this period up to 24h induced progressively higher EB severity, but longer periods of humidity did not increase severity further (Vloutoglou 1999).

EB severity is usually estimated 7 days after spray inocu-lation as the percentage necrotic area on leaves that were present at the time of inoculation (leaves emerging after inoculation are not affected, Barksdale 1969; Vloutoglou 1999). In the case of a low incidence of necrotic spots, EB severity is expressed as the number of lesions (Barksdale 1969).

Disease severity can be determined more precisely and objectively by measuring lesion sizes when the inoculum is applied as single drops on leaflets (Nash and Gardner 1988b; Chaerani et al. in press).

Glasshouse tests have also been used for assessing resistance to collar rot and stem lesions (Gardner 1990; Maiero et al. 1990b). The basal stem of seedlings is sprayed with spores and covered with soil (Maiero et al. 1990b) or seedlings are placed in a humidity chamber (Gardner 1990). Collar rot is usually rated in three to five symptom grades (Reynard and Andrus 1945; Gardner 1990; Maeiro et al. 1990b). Screening for collar rot and stem lesions in the glasshouse is fast and can be used instead of field screening for EB resistance, provided that the resistance to these disease symptoms is closely associated with EB resistance in the materials used, such as in C1943 and derived lines (Gardner 1990).

Glasshouse tests have the advantages over field tests that conditions are more reproducible, the duration of the test is shorter, and, especially after droplet inoculation, the test is more objective and precise data can be obtained. However, conditions in the glasshouse cannot be fully controlled, and some genotypes are not well adapted to glasshouse conditions.

**Laboratory assays**

Locke (1948) used detached leaflet assays for evaluation of EB resistance as a means to circumvent the influence of growth habit, which may affect the reaction of plants in the field or glasshouse. The method involved the application of inoculum droplets on either punctured (Locke 1948) or nonpunctured (Foolad et al. 2000), young, fully expanded leaflets. Locke (1948) claimed the method to be reliable; Lynch et al. (1991) and Foolad et al. (2000), however, concluded that detached leaflet assays did not correlate well with field and glasshouse screenings. These results might imply that a whole plant is required for the expression of EB resistance, which is known to be influenced by physiological characters of the plant such as earliness, determin-ism (Nash and Gardner 1988a; Maiero et al. 1989; Foolad and Lin 2001; Foolad et al. 2002a), and potential yield (Barrat and Richards 1944), as well as by plant age and nutritional status (Rotem 1994).

To circumvent the problem of apparent resistance in late-maturing cultivars, Bussey and Stevenson (1991) in-duced early senescence in juvenile potato leaf tissue by floating excised disks on a solution containing auxins [1-naphthaleneacetic acid (NAA), 2,4-dichlorophenoxyacetic acid (2,4-D)]. A very late-maturing cultivar that was highly resistant in the field was more susceptible when tested using the leaf disk assay, suggesting that the assay may be less influenced by cultivar maturity than the field test (Bussey and Stevenson 1991). The results of the other tested cultivars agreed with those obtained in the field (Bussey and Stevenson 1991).

Laboratory assays on detached leaflets therefore show promise for studying particular aspects of resistance and for eliminating confounding influences of whole-plant physiology. However, these methods need to be carefully adapted to the research question in hand and cannot be relied on as a replacement for field or glasshouse tests.

### Toxin assays

Several authors reported that culture filtrate of *A. solani* could be used to distinguish EB-resistant genotypes from susceptible genotypes, at least in progenies of some sources of resistance (Lodha 1977; Stancheva 1988; Maiero et al. 1991). Genotypes with collar rot resistance were more tolerant to culture filtrate than those with only EB resistance (Maiero et al. 1991). In contrast, Lynch et al. (1991) found that the result of culture filtrate assays using detached leaflets did not correspond with the result from glasshouse or field tests.

Darakov (1995) proposed a new approach of selecting EB resistance by means of gametophytic selection in the presence of an unidentified toxin obtained from culture filtrate of *A. solani*. Pollen tube elongation correlated well with the level of EB resistance of the mother plant. Female gametophytes were selected by treating styles of emasculated flowers with drops of toxin, and, after pollination, collecting seeds from plants that yielded the most seeds. After two rounds of selection with toxin, selected plants with enhanced seed-bearing capacity were assessed in the field for EB resistance. Plant selections from toxin-treated plants had enhanced EB resistance compared with those derived from plants selected with a water treatment.

Laboratory assays using *A. solani* toxins can help to elu-cidate specific aspects of the pathogenesis process. However, the effects of *A. solani* toxins do not seem to correlate with the pathogenicity of isolates and do not have a role in the establishment of the pathogen in the host (Langsdorf et al. 1990). This is in contrast to toxins produced by formae speciales of *Alternaria alternata,* which do elicit most symptoms of the disease on susceptible plants and have the same differential host specificity as the fungal isolates and can therefore be used reliably to screen for resistance (Gilchrist and Grogan 1975).

### Sources of resistance

In the cultivated tomato, high levels of resistance to EB are rare. Two old breeding lines, 71B2 and C1943, probably bred from *Solanum lycopersicum* sources, have been de-scribed as highly and moderately resistant to EB, respec-tively (Table 1). Some moderately resistant hybrids and breeding lines have been developed from these sources, such as "Plum Dandy," NC EBR-5 and -6 (71B2), "Mountain Supreme," and NC-EBR-2 (C1943). Poysa and Tu (1996) identified only 11 moderately resistant lines from more than 500 tomato cultivars and breeding lines for EB resistance.

Some accessions of the wild species *Solanum habrochaites* (syn. *Lycopersicon hirsutum*), *Solanum peruvianum* (syn. *Lycopersicon peruvianum*), and *Solanum pimpinellifolium* (syn. *Lycopersicon pimpinellifolium*) are resistant to EB (Table 1). Success in incorporating resis-tance is limited because most breeding lines, e.g., NC EBR-1, NC EBR-2 (Gardner 1988), NC EBR-4 (Gardner and Shoemaker 1999), and HRC90.303 and HRC91.341 (Poysa and Tu 1996) are still late maturing, indeterminate, and relatively low yielding. These lines are derived from *L. hirsutum* accessions.

A high level of collar rot resistance has been found in the cultivated tomato such as in the old cultivar Devon Surprise and breeding line C1943. Additionally, Stancheva et al. (1991) reported sources of resistance to collar rot and stem lesions in several wild species (Table 1).

**Classical studies of genetics of resistance**

Most genetic studies on the inheritance of EB resistance using different sources of resistance (*Solanum lycopersicum, Solanum habrochaites*, and *Solanum pimpinellifolium*) arrived at the same conclusion that the resistance is a quantitative trait that is controlled polygenically (Table 2). The estimated minimum number of controlling factors is two (Barksdale 1977) or three (Nash and Gardner 1988a). Analysis using quantitative genetic methods (generation mean analysis and scaling tests) and several sources of resistance (C1943, NC EBR-2, IHR 1939, and IHR 1816) revealed additive and dominant genetic control with the presence of epistatic effects (Maiero et al. 1990a; Nash and Gardner 1988a; Thirthamallappa and Lohithaswa 2000).

The EB resistance genes in C1943 and 71B2 are recessive and not allelic (Barksdale and Stoner 1977; Maiero et al. 1989). However, in crosses of these two resistance sources with another susceptible genotype, the F1 hybrids were in-termediate, indicating additive genetic control or partial dominance (Maiero et al. 1989). Recessive genes have been reported in *S. lycopersicum* 83602029 (Stancheva 1991), IHR1939, and IHR1816 by Thirthamallappa and Lohithaswa (2000). Partially dominant inheritance has been found in *S. pimpinellifolium* and *S. habrochaites* (Martin and Hepperly 1987).

The line 87B187, derived from *S. habrochaites* PI 390662, shared common resistance genes with NC EBR-2, although this line was developed via C1943 from a *S. lycopersicum* source (Maiero et al. 1990a). Also, Thirthamallappa and Lohithaswa (2000) reported independent genes in IHR 1939 (*S. pimpinellifolium* L4394) and IHR 1816 (derived from NC EBR-1, developed from *S. habrochaites* PI 126445).

In contrast to the studies just described, one study reported a monogenic, dominant inheritance in *S. habrochaites* PI 134417 (Datar and Lonkar 1985). Their conclusion is arguable because a highly resistant F1 does not necessarily indicate complete dominance of EB resistance as was observed by Foolad and Lin (2001). The resistance phenotypes in the F2 population derived from *S. habrochaites* PI 134417 were grouped into resistant, intermediate, and susceptible, and a 3:1 segregation was observed, leading to the conclusion of monogenic inheritance (Datar and Lonkar 1985). However, EB resistance is a quantitatively expressed character, and the assignment of three phenotypic classes is therefore arbitrary and may have led by chance to the 3:1 segregation (Foolad and Lin 2001).

**Table 14.1 Genetic sources of resistance to early blight, collar rot, and stem lesion**

| Original source | Resistant line or variety resistance | Test(s) used to confirm | References |
|---|---|---|---|
| Early blight resistance | | | |
| *Solanum lycopersicum* (syn. *Lycopersicon esculentum*)[a] | | | |
| Unknown source | C1943 | F | Barksdale 1971 |
| 68B134 | 71B2 | F | Barksdale 1969 |
| Syn. *Lycopersicon esculentum* f. sp. *cerasiforme*[b] PI 406758 | – | F | Martin and Hepperly 1987 |
| C1943 | NC EBR-2 | F, G | Gardner 1988 |
| Unknown accessions | HRC90.145, HRC | G | Poysa and Tu 1996 |
| | 90.158, HRC 90.159 | | |
| NC EBR-1 | NC EBR-4 | F | Gardner and Shoemaker 1999 |
| NC EBR-1 | IHR1816 | F | Thirthamallappa and |
| | Lohithaswa 2000 | | |
| NC EBR-1 and -2 | NC EBR-3 | F | Gardner and Shoemaker 1999 |
| NC EBR-3 and -4 | Mountain Supreme | F | Gardner and Shoemaker 1999 |
| NC EBR-5 and -6 | Plum Dandy | F | Gardner 2000 |
| 71B2 | NC EBR-5 | F | Gardner 2000 |
| 71B2 | NC EBR-6 | F | Gardner 2000 |
| *Solanum habrochaites* (syn. *Lycopersicon* | | | |
| PI 127827 | – | L | Locke 1949 |

| | | | |
|---|---|---|---|
| PI 390514, PI 390662 | – | F | Martin and Hepperly 1987 |
| PI 126445 | NC EBR-1 | F | Gardner 1988 |
| PI 1390662 | 87B187 | F | Maiero et al. 1990a |
| B 6013 | H-7, H-22, H-25 | F | Kallo and Banerjee 1993 |
| Unknown accessions | HRC90.303, HRC 91.279, HRC 91.341 | G | Poysa and Tu 1996 |
| LA2100, LA2124, LA2204 | – | G | Poysa and Tu 1996 |
| PI 126445 | NC39E | F | Foolad et al. 2002a |
| *Solanum peruvianum* (*Lycopersicon* | | | |
| PE33 | *pimpinellifolium*) [a] | G | Poysa and Tu 1996 |
| *Solanum pimpinellifolium* (syn. *Lycopersicon* | | | |
| PI 365912, PI 390519 | – | F | Martin and Hepperly 1987 |
| A 1921 | P-1 | F | Kallo and Banerjee 1993 |
| L4394 (IHR1939) | – | F | Thirthamallappa and Lohithaswa 2000 |
| Collar rot resistance | | | |
| Unknown source | Devon Surprise | F | Reynard and Andrus 1945 |
| Unknown source | C1943 | G | Maiero et al. 1990b |
| *Solanum pimpinellifolium* (syn. *Lycopersicon* | – | ? | Stancheva et al. 1991 |
| *Solanum lycopersicum* (syn. *Lycopersicon* | *humboldtii*)[b] 87610003 | ? | Stancheva et al. 1991 |
| *Solanum chilense* (syn. *Lycopersicon* | *chilense*)[a] 87610011 | ? | Stancheva et al. 1991 |
| Stem lesion resistance | | | |
| *Solanum lycopersicum* 83602029 | *cheesmanii* f. *typicum*)[b] 15 | ? | Stancheva et al. 1991 |

| | | | |
|---|---|---|---|
| *Solanum cheesmaniae* (syn. *Lycopersicon chaeesmanii f. typicum)*[b] | – | ? | Stancheva et al. 1991 |
| *Solanum neorickii* (syn. *Lycopersicon minutum*)[b] 87610006 | | ? | Stancheva et al. 1991 |

F, Field; G, greenhouse; L, laboratory

[a]Peralta et al. (2005)

[b]Peralta, Knapp, and Spooner (personal communication)

There have been only a few genetic studies published on resistance to the other disease symptoms caused by *Alternaria solani*, a fact that may be caused by the less damaging effect of these two disease symptoms (Table 2). One study on collar rot resistance reported a monogenic inheritance (Reynard and Andrus 1945), whereas Maiero et al. (1990b) showed quantitative expression of resistance. Analysis by Maiero et al. (1990b) using a joint scaling test showed that both additive and dominance effects controlled collar rot resistance in C1943 and NC EBR-2 sources, although the dominance effect of susceptibility appeared to be more important.

Only one study on stem lesion resistance has been published that reported that the resistance is a quantitative trait controlled by dominant genes in *S. lycopersicum* source (Stancheva 1991; Table 2). Both additive and dominant genetic components conferred resistance, which was complicated by epistatic effects.

Fruit rot has escaped attention in genetic studies even though it may cause substantial direct losses (Datar and Mayee 1981). Resistance to fruit rot may be controlled inde-pendently from EB resistance because fruit rot incidence is not necessarily associated with EB severity (Barksdale 1971).

Little is known about the genetic relationships among the resistances to EB, collar rot, and stem lesions. Maiero et al. (1990b) postulated that the collar rot resistance gene in C1943 and its derived line, NC EBR-2, is one of the genes that confer EB resistance or is closely linked with EB resis-tance genes because these lines have both EB and collar rot resistance.

**Table 14.2 Classical genetic studies of early blight, collar rot, and stem lesion resistance in tomato**

| Resistant parent[a] | Population type | Tests | Analysis method | Genetic control | Reference |
|---|---|---|---|---|---|
| **Early blight** | | | | | |
| *Solanum lycopersicum* 71B2 | F1 | F | Diallel, midparent–hybrid comparison | Recessive polygenic | Maiero et al. (1989) |
| *Solanum lycopersicum* C1943 | F1 | F | Diallel, midparent–hybrid comparison | Recessive polygenic | Maiero et al. (1989) |

| | | | | | |
|---|---|---|---|---|---|
| *Solanum lycopersicum* C1943 | F1, F2, BC1, BC2 | F | Diallel, midparent–hybrid comparison, generation means, joint scaling tests | Recessive polygenic with additive and epistatic (dom × dom) effects | Maiero et al. (1990a) |
| *Solanum lycopersicum* NCEBR-1 | F1, F2, BC1, BC2 | F | Generation means, joint scaling tests | At least 3 genes with additive, dominance, and epistatic (add × add, add × dom, dom × dom) effects | Nash and Gardner (1988b) |
| *Solanum lycopersicum* NCEBR-2 | F1 | F | Diallel, midparent–hybrid comparison | Polygenic, partial dominant | Maiero et al. (1990a) |
| *Solanum lycopersicum* 87B187 | F1 | F | Diallel, midparent–hybrid comparison | Polygenic, partial dominant | Maiero et al. (1990) |
| *Solanum lycopersicum* 83602029 | F1, F2, BC1, BC2 | ? | Diallel, generation means | Quantitative, dominant genes with additive, dominance, and epistatic effects | Stancheva (1991) |
| IHR 1816 (= *Solanum lycopersicum* NCEBR-1) | F1, F2, BC1, BC2 | F | Joint scaling tests | Recessive polygenic with additive and epistatic (add × dom) effects at seedling stage; with additive, dominance and epistatic (add × add) effects at adult stage | Thirthamallappa and Lohithaswa (2000) |
| IHR 1939 (= *Solanum* | F1, F2, BC1, BC2 | F | Joint scaling tests | Recessive polygenic with additive and epistatic (add × dom) effects at seedling stage; with additive, dominance and epistatic (add × add) effects at adult stage | Thirthamallappa and Lohithaswa (2000) |

| | | | | | |
|---|---|---|---|---|---|
| *Solanum lycopersicum* NC39E Collar rot | F2, F3 | F | Midparent-segregating population means comparison | Polygenic, partial dominant | Foolad et al. (2002a) |
| *Solanum lycopersicum* C1943, NCEBR-2 Stem lesion | F1, F2, BC1, BC2 | G | Diallel, midparent–hybrid comparison, generation means, joint scaling tests | Recessive polygenic with additive and dominant effects | Maiero et al. (1990b) |
| *Solanum lycopersicum* 83602029 | F1, F2, BC1, BC2 | ? | Generation means | Recessive polygenic with additive, dominance, and epistatic effects | Stancheva (1991) |

[a]New nomenclature based on Peralta et al. (2005); see Table 1 for synonyms.

In addition, stem lesion resistance may be independent of EB resistance. Barksdale and Stoner (1973, 1977), based on field observations but unsupported by a genetic analysis, assumed that stem lesion resistance segregated independently from EB resistance. Recently, several QTLs that affected both EB severity and stem lesions have been re-ported (Chaerani et al. submitted).

Heritability of EB resistance has been estimated in crosses involving *S. habrochaites* PI 126445 (Foolad and Lin 2001) and derived lines NC EBR-1 and NC39E (Nash and Gardner 1988a; Foolad et al. 2002a). Depending on the calculation method, heritability estimates were low to moderate in two crosses involving NC EBR-1 (Nash and Gardner 1988a). Based on parent–offspring (PO) regression, narrow-sense heritability ($h^2$) for AUDPC was estimated as 0.26 and 0.38 (Nash and Gardner 1988a). Higher $h^2$ estimates were obtained from a cross with *S. habrochaites* PI126445 (0.70, Foolad and Lin 2001) and from a cross with *S. lycopersicum* NC39E (0.65, Foolad et al. 2002a), also based on PO regression.

Those studies showed that additive genetic components play a small to moderate role in the quantitative expression of resistance. The low to moderate heritability estimates indicate that progress based on phenotypic evaluations only is likely to be slow. Furthermore, these classical genetic studies give general indications on the likely progress in selection of resistant material but do not provide informa-tion on the effects of individual resistance genes and their location on the tomato genome.

## Mapping resistance genes

Given the low to moderate heritability estimates, a marker-aided selection approach is potentially useful to accelerate the transfer of EB resistance genes into new tomato cultivars. Foolad et al. (2002b) were the first to map QTLs for EB resistance. They used backcross progenies of a cross between *Solanum habrochaites* PI 126445 and a susceptible tomato line. Mapping was done in the BC1 generation and validated in the BC1S. Fourteen QTLs were identified, which together explained 57% of the total phenotypic varia-tion. For all QTLs, the positive allele originated from the resistant parent. In a subsequent study, Zhang et al. (2003) used a selective genotyping approach on a different part of the same BC1 population. Seven QTLs were detected, in-cluding one previously mapped major and three minor QTLs. One of the QTLs in this study inherited the resis-tance allele from the susceptible parent.

Chaerani et al. (submitted) identified six QTLs for EB resistance in F2 and F3 populations from a cross between the resistant *Solanum arcanum* LA2157 and a susceptible tomato. Different environments and phenotypic scoring methods were used in this study, in contrast to the previous mapping studies, which used one type of environment and disease measure. In addition, resistance to stem lesions was also assessed in the F3 population. Interestingly, EB QTLs detected in the F2 population were not always detected in the F3 population, and vice versa. This indicates the presence of environment-specific or plant age-specific QTLs. Three QTL regions for stem lesion resistance coincided with EB resistance QTLs, which allows simultaneous selection for resistance to both types of disease symptoms. The explained phenotypic variation per EB resistance QTL, 7% to 16%, was in the same range as that of Foolad et al. (2002b). One QTL for stem lesion resistance, however, had a large effect, explaining 31% of the total variation. For two of the six QTLs, the susceptible parent contributed the resistance alleles. Several of the QTLs found in the cross of *S. habrochaites* PI 126445 (Foolad et al. 2002b; Zhang et al. 2003) overlapped with those found in the *S. arcanum* LA1257.

Although many EB resistance QTLs have been identified, many of them have relatively small effects. Not all QTLs need to be incorporated to achieve a significant increase in resistance. Foolad et al. (2002b) and Zhang et al. (2003) recommended a combination of four to six QTLs, which explained more than 40% of total phenotypic varia-tion for use in marker-assisted breeding, and Chaerani et al. (submitted) suggested two QTLs that had prominent effects under different environments and gave both EB and stem lesion resistance. It still needs to be determined, however, whether the level of resistance contributed by these QTLs would be of sufficient practical importance. The EB mapping studies have not yet reached the stage at which QTLs can be mapped precisely enough to be included in a breeding program.

### Association of early blight resistance with plant maturity, potential yield, and determinism

The strong correlation between EB resistance and late maturity, low yield, and indeterminate plant type (Nash and Gardner 1988; Foolad and Lin 2001, Foolad et al. 2002a, b) has limited the development of lines or cultivars with a high level of resistance. The QTL study of Foolad et al. (2002b) just described aimed to identify QTLs for resistance without altering the agronomic traits. Therefore, they removed plants with poor characteristics from their population be-fore attempting to map the QTLs. However, none of the plants in the ensuing generations had a resistance level equal to that of the donor parent or the F1 hybrid (Foolad et al. 2002b).

The association of late maturity with EB resistance has also been documented for potato EB (e.g., Johanson and Thurston 1990). As in tomato, it is not yet clear whether this correlation is caused by closely linked genes or by pleiotropic effects of genes. A mapping study for EB and maturity in potato identified five EB resistance QTLs, explaining 62% of the total phenotypic variation for resistance (Zhang 2004). Three of these five QTLs explained 98% of the total phenotypic variation for maturity. The other two EB resis-tance QTLs, which did not have an effect on (foliage) maturity, explained 33% of the total phenotypic variation for resistance (Zhang 2004). In potato therefore about half the genotypic variation for EB resistance is also linked to maturity; still, this may be due to either close linkage or to pleiotropic effects. A very similar situation occurs in the potato–late blight (*Phytophthora infestans*) interaction (Visker et al. 2003).

Even on susceptible plants, the younger, topmost leaves are usually free of EB symptoms, while the older, lower leaves may be necrotized by the fungus (Johanson and Thurston 1990). Attempts have been made to clarify the physiological mechanisms for this apparent resistance in young tissues and plants. Low sugar content has been suggested as the cause of higher EB susceptibility in older or weakened leaves and plants (Rotem 1994): late in the season, leaves of maturing plants might be susceptible due to translocation of sugars to the ripening fruit. An in vitro study by Sands and Lukens (1974) provided indirect evidence that abundant glucose in the medium inhibited the production of cell-degrading enzymes by *Alternaria solani*. The low sugar content hypothesis might explain the increased susceptibility of physiologically old plants or those that have a high fruit to foliage ratio (Barrat and Richards 1944). Another explanation of the relative resistance of young tissues is that the concentrations of three glycoalkaloids (solanine, chaconine, and solanidine), which are capable of inhibiting growth of *A. solani* in vitro, are higher in young tomato leaves, and then steadily decline as leaves and plant mature (Sinden et al. 1972).

The higher resistance of late-maturing cultivars can similarly be explained in terms of sugar and alkaloid contents. Late-maturing cultivars generally have an indeterminate, vine-type growth habit and continue producing new foliage (Johanson and Thurston 1990). In contrast, early maturing types have a determinate growth habit and do not continue producing new foliage throughout the season. Therefore, late-maturing cultivars might appear resistant compared with the early maturing types just because fruit initiation is delayed and more young leaves are present throughout the season.

If physiological mechanisms are the only cause of EB resistance, then it might be impossible to find recombinants with a high resistance level and highly desirable horticultural characteristics in a segregating population. In that case, tomato breeders can only expect to obtain acceptable EB resistance levels in varieties with midseason or late season maturity. However, variation in the resistance of potato occurs between cultivars of the same maturity class, indicating that differences in resistance are not always or exclusively an artifact of maturity effects (Holley et al. 1983; Christ 1991). So far, EB resistance screening in tomato, in contrast to potato, has not taken into account maturity classes or yield potential (Douglas and Pavek 1972).

**Characterization of resistance**

Several epidemiological parameters have been identified in *Alternaria solani*–tomato and *A. solani*–potato interactions, including infection efficiency (IE), lesion expansion rate (LER), latency period (LP), incubation period (IP), sporulation rate (SR), and sporulation capacity (SC). Tomato lines with a higher level of resistance typically had a lower IE, slower LER, slower SR, and lower SC, but LP did not differ significantly compared with susceptible lines (O'Leary and Shoemaker 1983). IP was most important in determining cultivar ranking in potato; resistant cultivars had a longer IP (Pelletier and Fry 1989). SC was found to correspond linearly with lesion size (Pelletier and Fry 1989; Johnson and Teng 1990).

Secondary plant metabolites correlated to EB resistance include a higher total phenolic content (tannin, flavonol, and phenol) in leaves and stems of EB-resistant varieties (Bhatia et al. 1972). The tannin content in all varieties fluctuated as the plant matured but reached a maximum content by the 14th week in leaves and by the 10th week in stems. In addition, the fruits of resistant varieties contained a higher amount of phenolic compounds than those of susceptible varieties (Bhatia et al. 1972). The constitutive ex-pression of phenols, which are thought to function as preformed inhibitors, has been associated with nonhost resistance (Nicholson and Hammerschmidt 1992).

At the cellular level, events during the infection by *A. solani* involve general defense responses that are also found in other plant–pathogen interactions involving quantitative resistance. These responses are basically similar to those after hypersensitive responses in monogenic resistance, but they are expressed more slowly and at a lower level (Agrios 2005). In EB-resistant lines, a stronger, more rapid induc-tion of the pathogenesis-related (PR) proteins chitinase and β-1,3-glucanase (Lawrence et al. 1996, 2000), peroxidase (PO, Fernandez et al. 1996), and phenyalalanine ammonium lyase (PAL; Solorzano et al. 1996) were observed during the early infection process compared with those in susceptible lines (Lawrence et al. 1996, 2000). Chitinases and glucanases probably slow fungal ingress in the plant as indicated by their inhibition of the in vitro growth of *A. solani* (Lawrence et al. 1996). Enzyme preparations from resistant lines also induced the in vitro release of elicitors of the hypersensitive response (HR) from *A. solani*, whereas enzymes from susceptible lines did not (Lawrence et al. 2000).

PO is involved in the production of reactive oxygen species, which are directly toxic to the pathogen or indirectly reduce the spread of the pathogen by increasing the cross-linkage and lignification of the plant cell walls (Hammond-Kosack and Jones 1996). PAL is the key enzyme in the synthesis of the secondary, endogenous signaling molecule salicylic acid (SA), which in turn activates the expression of a variety of PR genes (Mauch-Mani and Slusarenko 1996).

Polyphenol oxidase (PPO) F is systemically upregulated in response to *A. solani* infection and is detected in leaves of upper nodes but not in lower nodes (Thipyapong and Steffens 1997). This induction pattern coincides with the observation of temporary resistance of young leaves to *A. solani* infection (Johanson and Thurston 1990). PPOs catalyze the oxidation of phenols to quinines, reactive molecules that induce cell death and barriers to secondary infection (Thipyapong and Steffens 1997). PPO F is induced within lesions but not around the lesions during early infection and necrotic lesion development. Other defense-related responses to infection with *A. solani* in-volve the elevated expression of the PR-1B gene after exog-enous application of SA on tomato roots (Spletzer and Enyedi 1999), the PR-1-like protein after leaf treatment of tomato with arachidonic acid (Coquoz et al. 1995), and the sequential expression of two ACC synthase genes (*ST-ACS4* and *ST-ACS5*) in potato (Schlagnhaufer et al. 1997).

The biological effects of the genes underlying the identified EB-resistance QTLs remain unclear. A candidate gene approach, either using genes involved in the pathogen recognition process [resistance genes (R genes) or R gene analogs (RGAs), Foolad et al. 2002b] or those involved in the defense response process [defense response genes (DR genes), Faris et al. 1999] as molecular markers for QTL analysis, is potentially useful for analyzing EB resistance. Because resistance to *A. solani* does not seem to be race specific and is not mediated by genes with a major effect, R genes are unlikely to be involved in this resistance. There-fore, DR genes are more likely candidate genes for the QTLs involved in EB resistance. Faris et al. (1999) provided a convincing example. They mapped DR genes on a wheat linkage map where QTLs for several diseases had previ-ously been identified. These DR genes were shown to be more significantly associated with disease resistance and explained more of the phenotypic variation than did the original markers used for QTL detection. Mapping at a higher resolution is also needed, however, before establish-ing any functional relationship.

## Concluding remarks

A wealth of information on the tomato–*Alternaria solani* interaction is available. However, some important aspects need further attention.

No conclusive evidence is available so far concerning the existence of physiological races. This should be studied using homozygous tester lines and isolates that are as homogeneous as possible.

The strong association of negative horticultural traits with the expression of EB resistance seems to be a general rule, for which no conclusive genetic explanation has yet been offered. Meanwhile, breeders should be aware that selection for resistance will only produce useful results if the plant material is comparable in terms of earliness and yield.

QTLs for EB resistance have been identified in populations from interspecific crosses. Before these can be used in a marker-assisted breeding program, fine mapping is needed to avoid introgressing large parts of donor genome along with the resistance gene. Also, before QTLs are used in a breeding program, their pleiotropic effects on other traits should be investigated.

## Acknowledgments

The comments of Dr. P. Lindhout and Prof. P. Stam are gratefully acknowledged. Financial support was provided by the Royal Netherlands Academy of Arts and Sciences in the frame-work of the Scientific Programme Indonesia–Netherlands.

## REFERENCES

Agrios GN (2005) Plant pathology, 5th edn. Elsevier, London

Banerjee MK, Chhabra ML, Saini PS (1998) Responses of tomato cultivars to *Alternaria* blight. Tests Agrochem Cultiv 19:50–51 Barksdale TH (1969) Resistance of tomato seedlings to early blight. Phytopathology 59:443–446

Barksdale TH (1971) Field evaluation for tomato early blight resis-tance. Plant Dis Rep 55:807–809

Barksdale TH, Stoner AK (1973) Segregation for horizontal resistance to tomato early blight. Plant Dis Rep 57:964–965

Barksdale TH, Stoner AK (1977) A study of the inheritance of tomato early blight resistance. Plant Dis Rep 61:63–65

Barrat RW, Richards MC (1944) Physiological maturity in relation to Alternaria blight in tomato. Phytopathology 34:997

Basu PK (1974a) Existence of chlamydospores of *Alternaria porri* f. sp. *solani* as overwintering propagules in soil. Phytopathology 61:1347– 1350

Basu PK (1974b) Measuring early blight, its progress and influence on fruit losses in nine tomato cultivars. Can Plant Dis Surv 54:45– 51

Bhatia IS, Uppal DS, Bajaj KL (1972) Study of phenolic contents of resistant and susceptible varieties of tomato (*Lycopersicum esculentum*) in relation to early blight disease. Indian Phytopath 25:231–235

Bonde R (1929) Physiological strains of *Alternaria solani*. Phytopathol-ogy 19:533–548

Brian PW, Elson GW, Hemming HG, Wright JM (1952) The phyto-toxic properties of alternaric acid in relation to the etiology of plant disease caused by *Alternaria solani* (Ell. & Mart.) Jones & Grout. Ann Appl Biol 39:308–321

Bussey MJ, Stevenson WR (1991) A leaf disk assay for detecting resistance to early blight caused by *Alternaria solani* in juvenile potato plants. Plant Dis 75:385–390

Castro MEA, Zambolim L, Chavez GM, Cruz CD, Matsuoka K (2000) Pathogenic variability of *Alternaria solani*, the causal agent of to-mato early blight. Summa Phytopathologica 26:24–28

Chaerani R, Groenwold R, Stam P, Voorrips RE Assessment of early blight (*Alternaria solani*) resistance in tomato using a droplet inocu-lation method. J Gen Plant Pathol (in press)

Christ BJ (1991) Effect of disease assessment method on ranking po-tato cultivars for resistance to early blight. Plant Dis 75:353–356 Coquoz JL, Buchala AJ, Meuwly PH, Métraux JP (1995) Arachidonic acid induces local but not systemic synthesis of salicylic acid and confers systemic resistance in potato plants to *Phytophthora infestans* and *Alternaria solani*. Phytopathology 85:1219–1224

Darakov OB (1995) Gametophytic selection of tomatoes for resistance to early blight disease. Sex Plant Reprod 8:95–98

Datar VV, Lonkar SG (1985) Inheritance of resistance in tomato early blight. J Mah Agric Univ 10:357–358

Datar VV, Mayee CD (1981) Assessment of losses in tomato yield due to early blight. Indian Phytopath 34:191–195

Douglas DR, Pavek JJ (1972) Screening potatos for field resistance to early blight. Am Potato J 49:1–7

Ellis MB, Gibson IAS (1975) *Alternaria solani* no. 45 set 48. Common-wealth Mycological Institute, Kew, Surrey, UK

Esquivel EA (1984) *Pleospora solani* sp. nov, teleomorphosis of *Alter-naria solani* (Ell. & Mart.) Jones & Grout. Phytopathology 74:1014 Faris JD, Li WL, Liu DJ, Chen PD, Gill BS (1999) Candidate gene analysis of quantitative disease resistance in wheat. Theor Appl

Genet 98:219–225

Fernandez A, Solorzano E, Peteira B, Fernandez E (1996) Peroxidase induction in tomato leaves with different degrees of susceptibility to *Alternaria solani*. Revista de Protección Vegetal 11:79–83

Foolad MR, Lin GY (2001) Heritability of early blight resistance in a *Lycopersicon esculentum* × *Lycopersicon hirsutum* cross estimated by correlation between parent and progeny. Plant Breed 120:173– 177

Foolad MR, Ntahimpera N, Christ BJ, Lin GY (2000) Comparison of field, greenhouse, and detached-leaflet evaluations of tomato germ plasm for early blight resistance. Plant Dis 84:967–972

Foolad MR, Subbiah P, Ghangas GS (2002a) Parent–offspring correla-tion estimate of heritability for early blight resistance in tomato, *Lycopersicon esculentum* Mill. Euphytica 126:291–297

Foolad MR, Zhang LP, Khan AA, Niño-Liu D, Lin GY (2002b) Identification of QTLs for early blight (*Alternaria solani*) resistance in tomato using backcross populations of a *Lycopersicon esculentum* × *Lycopersicon hirsutum* cross. Theor Appl Genet 104:945–958

Gardner RG (1988) NC EBR-1 and NC EBR-2 early blight resistant tomato breeding lines. HortScience 23:779–781

Gardner RG (1990) Greenhouse disease screen facilitates breeding resistance to tomato early blight. HortScience 25:222–223

Gardner RG (2000) "Plum Dandy", a hybrid tomato, and its parents, NC EBR-5 and NC EBR-6. HortScience 35:962–963

Gardner RG, Shoemaker PB (1999) "Mountain Supreme" early blight-resistant hybrid tomato and its parents, NC EBR-3 and NC EBR-4. HortScience 34:745–746

Gilchrist DG, Grogan RG (1975) Production and nature of a host-specific toxin from *Alternaria alternata* f.sp. *lycopersici*. Phytopathology 66:165–171

Gwary DM, Nahunnaro H (1998) Epiphytotics of early blight of tomatoes in Northeastern Nigeria. Crop Protection 17:619–624

Hammond-Kosack KE, Jones JDG (1996) Resistance gene-dependent plant defense responses. Plant Cell 8:1773–1791

Henning RG, Alexander LJ (1959) Evidence of existence of physiologic races of *Alternaria solani*. Plant Dis Rep 43:298–308

Herriot AB, Haynes FL Jr, Shoemaker PB (1986) The heritability of resistance to early blight in diploid potatoes (*Solanum tuberosum* subsp. *phureja* and *stenotonum*). Am Potato J 63:229–232

Holley JD, Hall R, Hofstra G (1983) Identification of rate-reducing resistance to early blight in potato. Can J Plant Pathol 5:111–114 Horsfall JG, Barrat RW (1945) An improved grading system for measuring plant diseases. Phytopathology 35:655

Johanson A, Thurston HD (1990) The effect of cultivar maturity on the resistance of potato to early blight caused by *Alternaria solani*. Am Potato J 67:615–623

Johnson KB, Teng PS (1990) Coupling a disease progress model for early blight to a model of potato growth. Phytopathology 80:416– 425

Kallo G, Banerjee MK (1993) Early blight resistance in *Lycopersicon esculentum* Mill. transferred from *L. pimpinellifolium* (L.) Mill. and *L. hirsutum f. glabratum* Mull. Gartenbauwiss 58:238–240

Keinath A, DuBose VB, Rathwell PJ (1996) Efficacy and economics of three fungicide application schedules for early blight control and yield of fresh-market tomato. Plant Dis 80:1277–1282

Langsdorf G, Furuichi N, Doke N, Nishimura S (1990) Investigations of *Alternaria solani* infections: detection of alternaric acid and a susceptibility-inducing factor in the spore-germination fluid of *A. solani*. J Phytopathol 128:271–282

Lawrence CB, Joosten MHAJ, Tuzun S (1996) Differential induction of pathogenesis related proteins in tomato by *Alternaria solani* and the association of a basic chitinase isozyme with resistance. Physiol Mol Plant Pathol 43:361–377

Lawrence CB, Singh NP, Qiu J, Gardner RG, Tuzun S (2000) Consti-tutive hydrolytic enzymes are associated with polygenic resistance of tomato to *Alternaria solani* and may function as an elicitor release mechanism. Physiol Mol Plant Pathol 57:211–220

Locke SB (1948) A method for measuring resistance to defoliation diseases in tomato and other *Lycopersicon* species. Phytopathology 38:937–942

Locke SB (1949) Resistance to early blight and Septoria leaf spot in the genus *Lycopersicon*. Phytopathology 39:829–836

Lodha PC (1977) Reaction of some tomato cultivars to culture filtrate of *Alternaria solani* (Ell. et Mart.) Jones et Grout. Phytopathologia Mediterranea 16:36–37

Lukens RJ, Horsfall JG (1968) Glycolate oxidase, a target for antisporulants. Phytopathology 58:1671–1673

Lynch DR, Wastie RL, Stewart HE, MacKay GR, Lyon GD, Nachmias A (1991) Screening for resistance to early blight (*Alternaria solani*) in potato (*Solanum tuberosum* L.) using toxic metabolites produced by the fungus. Potato Res 34:297–304

Madden L, Pennypacker SP, MacNab AA (1978) FAST, a forecast system for *Alternaria solani* on tomato. Phytopathology 68:1354– 1358

Maiero M, Ng TJ, Barksdale TH (1989) Combining ability estimates for early blight resistance in tomato. J Am Soc Hort Sci 114:118–121 Maiero M, Ng TJ, Barksdale TH (1990a) Genetic resistance to early blight in tomato breeding lines. HortScience 25:344–346

Maiero M, Ng TJ, Barksdale TH (1990b) Inheritance of collar rot resistance in the tomato breeding lines C1943 and NC EBR-2. Phy-topathology 80:1365–1368

Maiero M, Bean GA, Ng TJ (1991) Toxin production by *Alternaria solani* and its related phytotoxicity to tomato breeding lines. Phyto-pathology 81:1030–1033

Marcinkowska J (1982) Fungi of the genus *Alternaria* occurring on tomato. Acta Agrobotanica 34:261–276

Martin FW, Hepperly P (1987) Sources of resistance to early blight, *Alternaria solani*, and transfer to tomato, *Lycopersicon esculentum*. J Agric Univ Puerto Rico 71:85–95

Martinez SP, Snowdon R, Pons-Kuhnemann J (2004) Variability of Cuban and international populations of *Alternaria solani* from dif-ferent hosts and localities: AFLP genetic analysis. Eur J Plant Pathol 110:399–409

Mauch-Mani B, Slusarenko AJ (1996) Production of salicylic acid pre-cursors is a major function of phenylalanine ammonium lyase en-zymes in the resistance of Arabidopsis to *Peronospora parasitica*. Plant Cell 8:203–212

Mehrotra RS, Areja KR (1990) An introduction to mycology. New Age International Publishers, New Delhi, p 648

Mehta P, Vyas KM, Saksena SB (1975) Pathological studies on fruit rot of tomato caused by *Alternaria solani* and *A. tenuis*. Indian Phytopath 28:247–252

Montemurro N, Visconti A (1992) *Alternaria* metabolites – chemical and biological data. In: Chelkowski J, Visconti A (eds) *Alternaria* biology, plant disease and metabolites. Elsevier, Amsterdam, pp 449–558

Moore WD (1942) Some factors affecting the infection of tomato seed-lings by *Alternaria solani*. Phtyopathology 32:399–403

Nash AF, Gardner RG (1988a) Heritability of tomato early blight resistance derived from *Lycopersicon hirsutum* PI 126445. J Am Soc Hort Sci 113:264–268

Nash AF, Gardner RG (1988b) Tomato early blight resistance in a breeding line derived from *Lycopersicon hirsutum* PI 126445. Plant Dis 72:206–209

Neergaard P (1945) Danish species of *Alternaria* and *Stemphylium*: taxonomy, parasitism, economic significance. Oxford University Press, London, pp 260–287

Nicholson RL, Hammerschmidt R (1992) Phenolic compounds and their role in disease resistance. Annu Rev Phytopathol 30:369– 389

O'Leary DJ, Shoemaker PB (1983) Components of resistance for to-mato early blight. Phytopathology 73:803

Pandey KK, Pandey PK, Kallo G, Banerjee MK (2003) Resistance to early blight of tomato with respect to various parameters of disease epidemics. J Gen Plant Pathol 69:364–371

Pasche JS, Wharam CM, Gudmestad NC (2004) Shift in sensitivity of *Alternaria solani* to $Q_o$I fungicides. Plant Dis 88:181–187

Patterson CL B (1991) Importance of chlamydospores as primary in-oculum of *Alternaria solani*, incitant of collar rot and early blight on tomato. Plant Dis 75:274–278

Pelletier JR, Fry WE (1989) Characterization of resistance to early blight in three potato cultivars: incubation period, lesion ex-pansion rate, and spore production. Phytopathology 79:511–517

Peralta IE, Knapp S, Spooner DM (2005) New species of wild tomatoes (*Solanum* section *Lycopersicon*: Solanaceae) from northern Peru. Syst Bot 30:424–434

Peréz S, Martinéz B (1999) Infection of tomato cultivars by *Alternaria solani* (E & M) J & G. Revista de Protección Vegetal 14:1–5

Petrunak DM, Christ BJ (1992) Isozyme variability in *Alternaria solani* and *A. alternata*. Phytopathology 82:1343–1347

Pound GS, Stahmann MA (1951) The production of a toxic material by *Alternaria solani* and its relation to the early blight disease of tomato. Phytopathology 41:1104–1114

Poysa V, Tu JC (1996) Response of cultivars and breeding lines of *Lycopersicon* spp. to *Alternaria solani*. Can Plant Dis Surv 76:5–8 Reynard GB, Andrus CF (1945) Inheritance of resistance to the collar-rot phase of *Alternaria solani* on tomato. Phytopathology 35:25–36 Rotem J (1966) Variability in *Alternaria porri* f. sp. *solani*. Israel J Bot 15:48–57

Rotem J (1994) The genus *Alternaria* biology, epidemiology, and pathogenicity, 1st edn. APS, St. Paul, MN, pp 48–203

Rotem J, Reichert I (1964) Dew – a principal moisture factor enabling early blight epidemics in a semiarid region of Israel. Plant Dis Rep 48:211–215

Sands DC, Lukens RJ (1974) Effect of glucose and adenosine phos-phates on production of extracellular carbohydrases of *Alternaria solani*. Plant Physiol 54:666–669

Schlagnhaufer CD, Arteca RN, Pell EJ (1997) Sequential expression of two 1-aminocyclopropane-1-carboxylate synthase genes in response to biotic and abiotic stresses in potato (*Solanum tuberosum* L.) leaves. Plant Mol Biol 35:683–688

Schlegel RHJ (2003) Encyclopedic dictionary of plant breeding and related subjects, 1st edn. Food Product, New York, p 320

Shahin EA, Shepard JF (1979) An efficient technique for inducing profuse sporulation of *Alternaria* species. Phytopathology 69:618– 620

Sherf AF, MacNab AA (1986) Vegetable diseases and their control. Wiley, New York

Shtienberg D, Blachinsky D, Kremer Y, Ben-Hador G, Dinoor A (1995) Integration of genotype and age-related resistance to reduce fungicide use in management of *Alternaria* diseases of cotton and potato. Phytopathology 85:995–1002

Sinden SL, Goth RW, O'Brien MJ (1972) Effect of potato alkaloids on the growth of *Alternaria solani* and their possible role as resistance factors in potatoes. Phytopathology 63:303–307

Solorzano E, Fernandez A, Peteira B, Fernandez E (1996) Polyphenol oxidases and phenylalanine ammonium lyases induction in tomato leaves infected with *Alternaria solani*. Revista de Protección Vegetal 11:153–157

Spletzer ME, Enyedi AJ (1999) Salicylic acid induces resistance to *Alternaria solani* in hydroponically grown tomato. Phytopathology 89:722–727

Stall RE (1958) An investigation of nuclear number in *Alternaria solani*. Am J Bot 45:657–659

Stall RE, Alexander LJ (1957) Heterocaryotic variation in *Alternaria solani*. Phytopathology 47:34

Stancheva I (1988) Evaluating the susceptibility of tomato to *Alternaria solani* by using the cultural filtrate of the pathogen. Rasteniev'dni-Nauki 25:71–76

Stancheva I (1990) Intraspecies differentiation of *Alternaria solani* according to aggressiveness degree. Genetika-i-Selektsiya 27:60– 64

Stancheva I (1991) Inheritance of the resistance to injuries on the growth mass caused by *Alternaria solani* in the tomato. Genetika-i-Selektsiya 24:232–236

Stancheva I, Lozanov I, Achkova Z (1991) Sources of resistance to *Alternaria solani* in the tomato in wild growing species of the genus *Lycopersicon*. Genetika-i-Selektsiya 24:126–130

Strandberg JO (1992) *Alternaria* species that attack vegetable crops: biology and options for disease management: In: Chelkowski J, Visconti A (eds) *Alternaria* biology, plant disease and metabolites. Elsevier, Amsterdam, pp 175–208

Thipyapong P, Steffens JC (1997) Tomato polyphenol oxidase: differ-ential response of the polyphenol oxidase F promoter to injuries and wound signals. Plant Physiol 115:409–418

Thirthamallappa, Lohithaswa HC (2000) Genetics of resistance to early blight (*Alternaria solani* Sorauer) in tomato (*Lycopersicum esculentum* L.) Euphytica 113:187–193

Vakalounakis DJ (1983) Evaluation of tomato cultivars for resistance to *Alternaria* blight. Ann Appl Biol 102:138–139

Van der Waals JE, Korsten L, Slippers B (2004) Genetic diversity among *Alternaria solani* isolates from potatoes in South Africa. Plant Dis 88:959–964

Visker MHPW, Keizer LCP, van Eck HJ, Jacobsen E, Colon LT, Struik PC (2003) Can the QTL for late blight resistance on potato chromosome 5 be attributed to foliage maturity type? Theor Appl Genet 106:317–325

Vloutoglou I (1999) Evaluation of tomato cultivars and hybrids for resistance to *Alternaria solani* infection. Tests Agrochem Cultiv 20:48–49

Vloutoglou I, Kalogerakis SN (2000) Effects of inoculum concentra-tions, wetness duration and plant age on development of early blight (*Alternaria solani*) and on shedding of leaves in tomato plants. Plant Pathol 49:339–345

Walker JC (1952) Diseases of vegetable crops, 1st edn. MacGraw-Hill, New York

Weir TL, Huff DR (1998) RAPD-PCR analysis of genetic variation among isolates of *Alternaria solani* and *Alternaria alternata* from potato and tomato. Mycologia 90:813–821

Wellman FL (1943) A technique to compare virulence of isolates of *Alernaria solani* on tomato leaflets. Phytopathology 41:698–706

Zhang LP, Lin GY, Niño-Liu D, Foolad MR (2003) Mapping QTLs conferring early blight (*Alernaria solani*) resistance in a *Lycoper-sicon esculentum* × *L. hirsutum* cross by selective genotyping. Mol Breed 12:3–19

*Zhang R (2004) Genetic characterization and mapping of partial resis-tance to early blight in diploid potato. Ph.D. dissertation, Pennsylva-nia State University, University Park, PA*

**Early Blight Disease of Tomato**
***Edited by:*** **Virendra Kumar**
**ISBN: 978-93-5056-879-8**
***Edition:*** **2017**
***Published by:*** **Discovery Publishing House Pvt. Ltd., New Delhi (India)**

# Management of Early Blight Disease of Tomato C.V. 'Kashi Amrit' through Fungicides, Bioagents and Cultural Practices In India

[1]Virendra Kumar, RC Gupta, PC Singh, KK Pandey, Rajesh Kumar, AB Rai and Mathura Rai

Early blight is most important disease of tomato in India and caused by two pathogen i.e. alternaria solani and Alternaria alternata f. sp. lycopersici. Symptoms of early blight appear on all above ground parts of plants. Mostly disease appears in vegetative phase of plant growth before flowering and is more prevalent between flowering to fruit ripening and continue till the crop completely senescent.

Tomato crop is damaged due to sever infection of A. *solani* every year in India. The disease severity was recorded up to 90% in Varanasi region by Pandey *et al.*, 2002 it is also one of the commonest cause of seedling blight or damping off in tomato causing dark lesion in rootlets (Bose *et al.*, 2002). Regarding the management of early blight of tomato many workers had done lot of works based on the chemical control. Most of the new generation fungicides are highly specific and single site in mode of action. These fungicides affects only one or perhaps two steps in a genetically control events into the metabolism of the fungus. The present study confined to develop integrated mimagement Gchedule with safe and effective fungicides.

The experiment was conducted at Indian Institute of Vegetable Research during 2003-04 and 2004-05 in randomized block design with three replications using 'Kashi Amrit' variety. Eight different treatments VIZ., Mancozeb (0.25%), copper oxychloride (0.3%), hexaconazole (0.05%), azoxystrobin (0.2%), .4.. niger V (0.4%), A. niger-V + sticker (0.4% + 0.1 %), removal of lower infected leaves and control treatment. The plot size was 4.5 × 3.6 m and spacing was 60 × 45 cm. SOWing was done in September. All the fungicides was sprayed at 10 days interval starting from 90 days of planting. In the treatment of removal of lower infected leaves, only all lower infected leaves were hand picked and burnt to reduce the concentration of inoculum. The scoring of disease intensity (early blight) was recorded as described by Pandey et al. (2003) which is as under.

[1] Indian Institute of Vegetable Research, Varanasi-227305

| Rating Number | Reaction description |
|---|---|
| 0 | Free from infection |
| 1 | < 10% surface area covering leaf, stem, and fruit infected by early blight |
| 2 | 11-25% foliage of plant covered with a few isolated spot. |
| 3 | Many spot coalesced on the leaves, covering 26-30% surface area of plant. |
| 4 | 51-75% area of the plants, infected, fruit also infected at apical end defoliation, and blightening started. Sunken lesions with prominent concentric ring on stem, petioles and fruit |
| 5 | < 75% area of plant part blighted, severe lesion on stem, and fruit rotting on apical end. |

First observation on disease severity was recorded before the beginning of first spray of fungicides, and subsequent observations before each spray, and finally disease severity was recorded 10 days after last spray. Data recorded in percentage were transformed to arc sin values before analysis.

It was observed that azoxystrobin was very effective in managing the *Alternana* leaf spot problem because in Azoxystrobin treatment leaf blight treatment were recordedl1.56 and 10.24 in two successive years respectively (Table 1) Another systemic fungicide namely hexaconazole resulted almost similar performance as broad spectrum fungicide like copper oxychloride, and mancozeb. Among the bioagents, A. niger along with sticker have given

**Table 15.1 Effect of different treatment on disease incidence and yield during 2003-04 & 2004-05**

| Treatments | Doses (%) | 2003-04 | | | 2004-05 | | |
|---|---|---|---|---|---|---|---|
| | | Leaf blight incidence (%) | Alternaria infected fruit (g/ plot) | Total yield (g/plot) | Leaf blight incidence (%) | Alternana infected fruit g/ spot) | Total yield (g/ plot) |
| $T_1$ - Mdncozeb | 0.25% | 17.50 | 4915.00 | 39943.33 | 23.23 | 833.33 | 8166.66 |
| $T_2$ - Copper oxychloride | 0.2% | 18.56 | 4539.66 | 37946.00 | 22.13 | 900.00 | 7600.00 |
| $T_3$ - HexaconazoJe | 0.05% | 18.23 | 3952.66 | 47563.66 | 21.33 | 60813 | 8508.33 |
| $T_4$ - Azoxystrobin | 0.2% | 1.56 | 1551.66 | 42024.33 | 10.24 | 333.33 | 7850.00 |
| $T_5$ - *A. niger* | 0.4% | 14.45 | 529366 | 40978.66 | 15.16 | 133333 | 7950.00 |
| $T_6$ - *A. niger* + sticker | 0.4% + 0.1% | 10.20 | 4408.13 | 37144.33 | 18.2 | 1816.66 | 7450.00 |
| $T_7$ - Removal of lower infected leaves | — | 12.96 | 1660.66 | 4147266 | 10.53 | 345.13 | 7650.00 |
| $T_8$ - Control | — | 24.00 | 7137.33 | 35419.0 | 292 | 1466.66 | 703333 |
| LSD at 5% | | 1.02 | 80.48 | 601.7 | 0.76 | 488.58 | 315042 |
| CV | | 3.22 | 1.10 | 0.96 | 2. 12 | 9.98 | 21.93 |

satisfactory result in reducing the disease. Data presented in table-l, indicate that among the all fungicides hexaconazole followed by azoxystrobin was found best for maximum healthy fruit yield. In present study the efficacy of hexaconazole, and azoxystrobin as compared to mancozeb, and copper oxychloride was found very high in both years. It was found that maximum fruit yield observed in treatment hexaconazolc (47563.66 g/plot), followed by azoxystrobin (42024.33 g/plot) in removal of lower infected leaves treatment (41472.66 g/plot) during the year 2003-04 as compared to control (35419.0 g/plot). A nigher + sticker recorded second lowest yield of 37144.33 g/plot in 2003-04, while in treatment of hexaconazole (8508.33 g/plot), followed by azoystrobin (7850.00 g/plot) in removal of lower infected leaves treatment (7650.00 g/plot) in 2004 05 as compared to control (7033.33 g/plot).

Minimum diseased fruit was observed by two fungicides *i.e.* azoxystrobin, hexaconazole and removal of lower infected leaves treatments in both successive year. Although the maximum disease reduction was in azoxystrobin in terms of leaf blight, and fruit rot.

Chaulwar (1992) reported that mancozeb was most effective in reducing the disease intensity and increase the yield 'Pusa Ruby'. Patil pi *al* (2003) reported that crbendazim was best fungicides to minimize the disease II1cidencc and highest fruit yield while according to Datar and Mayee (1985), Fentin hydroxide and mancozeb were superior for the controlling the disease. Many other workers viz., Maheshari *el al* (1991), Bassler, and Hausladen (2003) reported mancozeb as most effective fungicide for the management of early blight, and maximum fruit yield. In our finding mancozeb was controlling the disease significantly, and increasing yield but it was found 3'; best fungicide among the tested fungicides.

Hexaconazole (0.05%) and azoxystrobin (0.2%) can be recommended to the farmers for the management of early blight disease of tomato be more beneficial and economic to the farmers.

## REFERENCES

Basseler AK and Hausladen SP (2003). Effect of some fungicides on infection of tomato with leaf mold, and early blight. Arab J. Pl. Prot. 7(2): 126-132.

Bose TK, KJvir j, Maithy TK, Parthasarathy VA and Sam MG (2002). "Vegetable Crops" Valume-I, pp. 69 (t 154).

Choulwar AB and Datar VV (19941. Tolerance of *Alternaria* solarll to fungicides. I Maharastra Agril. Univ. 19(1): 133-134.

Maheshwari SK, Gupta PC and Gandhi SK (1991). Evaluation of different fungitoxicants dgainst edrly blight of tomato *(Lycopersicon eseu/enwm* Mill.). Agricultural Science Digest Karnal, 11(4) 201-202.

Pandey KK, Pandey PK, and Satpathy S (2002). Integrated management of disease, and insects of tomato, chilli, and cole crops. Tech. Bull. 9: 7.

Pandey KK, Pandey PK, Kalloa G and Benerjee MK (2003). Resistance to eddy blight of tomato with respect to various parameters of disease epidemics. J. General Pl. Path. 69(6): 364-371.

Patil MJ, U key SP and Raut BT (2003). Evaluation of fungicides, and botanicals for the management of early blight *(A. solani)* of tomato. PKV Res. J. 25(1): 49-51.

**Early Blight Disease of Tomato**
*Edited by:* Virendra Kumar
**ISBN:** 978-93-5056-879-8
*Edition:* 2017
*Published by:* Discovery Publishing House Pvt. Ltd., New Delhi (India)

# Identification of Resistant Sources against Early Blight Disease of Tomato

[1]Prabhash C. Singh, Rajesh Kumar*, [1]Major Singh,
[1]Ashutosh Rai, M.C. Singh** and Mathura Rai

## ABSTRACT

One hundred forty two tomato genotypes including wild and cultivated lines were screened for resistance against early blight disease caused by Alternaria solani. Evaluations were conducted in vivo and in vitro for disease severity and host resistance of the plants. Eight lines (EC-520057, EC-520058, EC-520059, EC-520061, EC-508765, EC-538394, H-88-78-1 and EC-501583) showed highly resistant reaction against the fungus; three lines were found resistant, 5 lines moderately resistant whereas 33 lines showed moderately susceptible besides 57 susceptible and 36 highly susceptible lines against the disease under natural epiphytotic condition. Screening under in vitro, revealed that eight genotypes were highly resistant, 3 resistant and 7 as moderately resistant. It was found that the accessions of wild relatives of tomato were highly resistant which may be utilized for the development of pre-bred lines or recombinant inbred lines or in other molecular research activities for the improvement of tomato. Some of the cultivated genotypes as resistant/moderately resistant under in-vivo and in-vitro like H-86, VRT-2, NC EBR-4 and RCMT-1 may directly be promoted for growing in disease prone areas.

**Keywords:** *Alternaria solani*, Early blight resistance, tomato genotypes.

## Introduction

Early blight is the major disease of tomato [*Solanum lycopersicum* L. (Peralta *et al.*, 13) syn. *Lycopersicon esculentum* Mill.)] caused by the fungus *Alternaria solani* (Ellis & Martin) Sorauer. The disease in severe cases can lead to complete defoliation and is most damaging on tomato in regions with heavy dew, rainfall, high humidity, and fairly high temperatures (24-29°C). Epidemics can also take place in semi-arid climates where frequent and prolonged nocturnal dews occur (Rotem and Reichert, 16). Early blight causes considerable yield loss to the tomato crop especially in northern plains and peninsular parts of India. It

[1] Division of Crop Improvement, Indian Institute of Vegetable Research, Post Box 5002, Varanasi, Uttar Pradesh

* Corresponding author's E-mail: rajes74@gmail.com

** Ex-Reader, Department of Horticulture, UP Autonomous College, Varanasi

is increasingly becoming a limiting factor for successful cultivation of tomato in these regions. Apart from the leaf symptoms of circular concentric rings with yellow halo, known as early blight (EB), *A. solani* can also cause symptoms as collar rot (basal stem lesions at the seedling stage), stem lesions on the adult plant, and fruit rot (Walker, 20). Yield losses up to 79% from early blight damage have been reported from India, Canada, United States and Nigeria (Basu *et al.*, 2). Collar rot can cause seedling losses of 20 to 40 per cent in the field (Sherf and MacNab, 17). *A. solani* has the capability to grow over a wide range of temperatures, i.e. 4 – 36°C (Pound, 14).

Application of several fungicides has been recommended to control the disease, however, non-judicial use of the fungicides adds up to the human and environmental hazards. As the disease severity is more during fruiting stage, the toxic effects of fungicides also restrict the applicability of these chemicals. Thus the availability of resistant to moderately resistant genotypes may reduce the dependency on fungicides and can also be an effective component of integrated disease management strategy. The available sources of resistance are mostly confined to the weedy relatives, like *Lycopersicon hirsutum* (Barksdale and Stoner, 1), *L. pimpinellifolium* (Kalloo and Banerjee, 10), *L. esculentum* var. *cerasiforme* (Fageria, 6), which are not in practical or commercial use due to several unacceptable linked traits. However, cultivars with moderate degree of resistance have been evolved, *e.g.* Meltive and Nemato (Vakalounakis, 19), NC EBR-1, 2, and NC EBR-4 (Gardner, 7,8). The genetics of resistance to early blight has been reported as both, monogenic dominant (Datar and Lonkar, 5) as well as polygenic recessive at both seedling and adult plant stage (Thirthammallappa and Lohithaswa, 18). This manuscript reports the results of an experiment planned to identify resistant sources in tomato through screening under natural as well as artificial condition with the objective to identify genotype which may be used for commercial cultivation in disease prone areas and/or could be utilized in development of population for genetical/molecular studies.

## Materials and Methods

A total of 142 genotypes including cultivars, pre-bred lines and weedy relatives of tomato were selected for this study; twenty plants of each genotype were planted on the raised beds at the 60 cm × 45 cm spacing after 25 days of seed sowing in three replications. The investigation was carried out at the experimental farm of Indian Institute of Vegetable Research (IIVR), Varanasi during the main cropping seasons of (Rabi) 2007-08 & 2008-09. All the recommended package of practices for cultivation of tomato was followed in order to raise a good crop, except fungicide application. The plant materials and facilities used herein were obtained from tomato breeding unit of the Vegetable Improvement Division.

Field screening of 142 tomato genotypes was done against early blight resistance during the cropping season of 2007-08 and 2008-09 in the month of

February-March under natural epiphytotic conditions. Average disease severity of early blight was recorded at 90 and 120 days after transplanting. Ten plants from each genotype were randomly selected and scored individually using 0-5 rating scale (Table 1) based on leaf area, stem and fruit covered by blight symptoms following the rating scale described by Pandey *et al.* (12). Disease incidence was calculated on the basis of per cent of infected leaves and stem.

Percentage disease index (PDI) was calculated as follows:

$$\text{PDI} = \frac{\text{Sum of all rating} \times 100}{\text{Total no. of observations} \times \text{Maximum rating grade}}$$

**Table 16.1 Scale for rating of early blight disease in tomato**

| Rating | Reaction description |
|---|---|
| 0 | Free from infection |
| 1 | < 10% surface area covering leaf, stem and fruit infected by early blight |
| 2 | 11-25% foliage of plant covered with a few isolated spot |
| 3 | Many spot coalesced on the leaves, covering 26-50% surface area of plant |
| 4 | 51-75% area of the plants infected, fruits also infected at peduncle end defoliation and blightening started. Sunken lesions with prominent concentric ring on stem, petioles and fruits |
| 5 | < 75% area of plant part blighted, severe lesion on stem and fruit rotting on peduncle end |

The mean value of the PDI from ten individual plants was calculated for each of the observations at 90 and 120 days after transplanting and averaged. Host plant reaction was classified based on the mean PDI value as highly resistant (0-5) resistant (5.1-12), moderately resistant (12.1-25), moderately susceptible (25.1-50), susceptible (50.1-75) highly susceptible (> 75).

Early blight of tomato is more prevalent during the month of January to April in northern India when it receives congenial condition for its perpetuation. Diseased samples were collected from tomato plots at IIVR, Varanasi. Pathogen was isolated from leaves, twigs, and fruit of tomato, and was purified by hyphal tip method. Circular margin, dark brown and smooth velvety zonation was recorded in the Varanasi isolate (Va). The isolate were maintained in the media containing potato dextrose agar (PDA). The entire culture slant were sealed and preserved at 4°C.

Artificial screening was done in order to confirm the field screening during 2007-08. Genotypes were tested against the most virulent isolate of *A. solani*, *Va-6* (Kumar *et al.*, 11). under artificial condition on healthy stem pieces (bits) of tomato. Thirty six genotypes were selected for artificial screening on the basis of their reaction under field condition ranging from highly resistant to susceptible. An inoculation technique developed by Pandey *et al.* (11) was followed to test the genotypes with pure mycelial culture of *A. solani*. Ten-day-old cultures of

Varanasi (Va-6) isolate was taken for inoculation. Culture bits of 20 mm size was ground in 50 ml of sterilized distilled water with sterilized pestle and mortar and filtered with sterilized muslin cloth in a clean test tube aseptically. The culture suspension was maintained up to 150 colonies per ml and was transferred in conical flask. Young and healthy stem pieces of tomato were washed thoroughly with sterilized distilled water and then surface sterilized with 0.1% $HgCl_2$ solution followed by rinsing with sterilized distilled water for three times. The surface-sterilized stems were then placed over sterilized moist blotting sheets in a plastic tray. The stems were place in two rows, one row of stem pieces were inoculated with sterilized needle, and the other was used as control. Each stem was inoculated with 5 µl of freshly prepared fungal suspension. Plastic trays were incubated at 25 ± 2°C and 95 per cent humidity for 9 days and observations were recorded twice after 6$^{th}$ and 9$^{th}$ day of incubation. The lesion size was measured for each observation as length of the lesion multiplied by its width and the mean was calculated. The genotypes were categorized on the basis of the average size of the lesions (mm$^2$) as 0 or no lesion development (highly resistant), 1-15 mm$^2$ (resistant), 16-30 (moderately resistant), 31 -40 (moderately susceptible), 41-50 (susceptible) and > 51 mm$^2$ (highly susceptible) following Chaerani *et al*. (4) with slight modifications.

**Results and Discussion**

A total of 142 genotypes/lines of diverse origin were transplanted and screened against early blight disease under natural epiphytotic condition. Out of 142

**Table 16.1 Screening of tomato genotypes against early blight disease under natural epiphytotic condition.**

| Reaction | PDI | Genotype(s) |
|---|---|---|
| HR | 0-5 | EC-520057, EC-520058, EC-538394, EC-508765, EC-520059, EC-520061, EC-501583, H-88-78-1 (8) |
| R | 5.1-12 | EC-538404 (NC EBR-4), VRT-2, EC-538393 (3) |
| MR | 12.1-25 | KS-118, LA-4040-1, H-88-78-2, H-88-78-3, RCMT-1 (5) |
| MS | 25.1-50 | Arka Saurabh, IST-7, JTP-02-7, DT-2, F-6050-1, DARL-63, LA-4044-2, LA-4012-1, IIVR-SEL-1, Shalimar, BT-120, ATL-97-44, VLT-34, H-86-3, DARL-64, Pant-T-7, Punjab Chhuhara, DVRT -2, F-4036-1, F-5013-3, NDTS-2002-3, F-7001-1, F-7025-1, F-6102-1, LA-17-1, BT-136, VTG-87, LA-7421, Neptune, CHRT-4, F-7045-1, F-6012-1, SKAUT-2 (33) |
| S | 50.1-75 | F-6021-1, VRT-35-1, VRT-35-2, VRT-41-1, 126-PD-1, VRT-5-1, VRT-40-2, VRT-43-1, VRT-2-1, TLH-30-1, TMT-415, LA-3940-1, LA-3947-1, NDTS-2002-2, NDTVR-60-1, Punjab Upma, PS-1, PDT-3-1, PDT-3-1-1, Pant-T-3, RCMT-2, IIVR-Sel-3, Improved Shalimar-1, H-86, H-86-2, KTDS-171, KS-16, LA-3941-1, LA-3951-1, LA-3997-1, LA-4055-1, F-4002-1, F-5055-1, F-5025-1, F-6061-1, F-7028-1, F-6109-1, F-5010-1, Arka Vikas, Co-3, CH-3, DARL-62, DT-10, DVRT-1, DVRT-1-1, EC-519785-1, F-4036-2, F-5013-1, F-5013-2, F-5013-4, F-4049-1, F-5070-2, F-7011-1, F-6004-1, F-6010-1, F-6010-2, F-6016-1 (57) |

| | | |
|---|---|---|
| HS | >75 | DVRT-1-2, EC-519769-1, EC-519731-1, EC-519730-1, F-6024-1, F-5020-1, F-4012-1, F-6022-1, F-7012-1, F-4047-1, F-6059-1, EC-538401(NC EBR-1), FEB-2-1, FEB-2-2, FEB-4-1, FEB-4-2, FLB-4-1, H-88-1, H-86, HAT-118-1, HAT-122-1, LA-3971-1, LA-4059-1, LA-3772-1, LA-3772-2, LA-3959-1, VFN-8, TLH-17-1, VRT-32-1, SEL-7, TH-806, TLH-27-1, VRT-40-1, VRT-4-1, VRT-1-1, VRT-31-1 (36) |

HR = Highly resistant, R = Resistant, MR = Moderately resistant, MS = Moderately susceptible, S = Susceptible, HS = Highly susceptible, PDI = Percent disease incidence

lines, eight (EC-520057, EC-520058, EC-520059, EC-520061, EC-508765, EC-538394, H-88-78-1 and EC-501583) were found as highly resistant, three lines (EC-538404 (NC EBR-4), VRT-2 and EC-538393) resistant, five lines (KS-118, LA-4040-1, H-88-78-2, H-88-78-3 and RCMT-1) moderately resistant, 33 lines showed moderately susceptible, 57 lines susceptible and 36 lines showed the highly susceptible reaction against early blight disease caused by *Alternaria solani* (Table 1). Among the highly resistant category, except EC-501583, all the four accessions belong to the wild relative (*L. hirsutum* syn. *Solanum habrochaites*) of tomato. All other lines were of *L. esculentum* species. It was observed that the genotypes with indeterminate growth habit showed either highly resistant, resistant or moderately resistant reaction as has been reported by Pandey *et al.* (12).

During screening, it was observed that symptoms of early blight appeared on all parts of the plant above ground. Leaf spot symptoms were scattered, brown to dark brown with concentric rings. As the natural inoculum's pressure increased, the spots coalesced and enlarged during the month of March every year. Chlorotic halo was also observed around the spot in most of the genotypes.. The stem lesions were usually restricted to one side of the stem and become elongated and sunken. Mature stem lesion clearly showed concentric rings. Fruit symptoms gradually progressed on apical portion of fruit as dark brown, depressed, firm with distinct continuous rings on fruits. The disease was more prevalent at fruit ripening stage and continued till the crop completely reached to senescence. Generally early blight of tomato was common during January to April (when average temperature varied from 15 to 30°C).

Confirmation of field screening was done through artificial screening on 36 selected genotypes. Although, the concentration of the inoculum was constant for all the genotypes during the inoculation process, the differential reactions of the genotypes against *A. solani* isolate suggests variable potential of genotypes against Va-6 isolate of *A. solani*. Among 36 genotypes, eight (EC-520057, EC-520059, EC-501583, EC-508765, EC-520058, EC-538394, EC-520061, H-88-78-1 ) were found highly resistant, three (NC EBR-4, VRT-2 and H-86) as resistant and seven (DVRT-2, EC-538393, DARL-63, H-88-78-2, LA-4040-1, RCMT-1 and KS-118) as moderately resistant while, eight lines were found moderately susceptible and seven lines as susceptible (Table 2). The earliest and most severe infection was observed in three genotypes; VRT-32-1, F-4012-1 and Co-3, indicating that these three genotypes are the most susceptible among the lot.

**Table 16.2 Artificial screening of tomato genotypes using 'stem bits' against Va6 isolate of A. solani**

| Sl.No. | Genotype | Source | Species | Lesion size ($mm^2$) | Reaction |
|---|---|---|---|---|---|
| 1 | EC-520057 | AVRDC, Taiwan | *L. hirsutum* | 0 | HR |
| 2 | EC-520059 | AVRDC, Taiwan | *L. hirsutum* | 0 | HR |
| 3 | EC-501583 | AVRDC, Taiwan | *L. esculentum* | 0 | HR |
| 4 | EC-508765 | AVRDC, Taiwan | *L. esculentum* | 0 | HR |
| 5 | EC-520058 | AVRDC, Taiwan | *L. hirsutum* | 0 | HR |
| 6 | EC-538394 | AVRDC, Taiwan | *L. esculentum* | 0 | HR |
| 7 | EC-520061 | AVRDC, Taiwan | *L. hirsutum* | 0 | HR |
| 8 | H-88-78-1 | IIVR, Varanasi | *L. esculentum* | 0 | HR |
| 9 | NC EBR-4 | NCSU, USA | *L. esculentum* | 2 | R |
| 10 | VRT-2 | IIVR, Varanasi | *L. esculentum* | 3 | R |
| 11 | H-86 | IIVR, Varanasi | *L. esculentum* | 6 | R |
| 12 | DVRT-2 | IIVR, Varanasi | *L. esculentum* | 12 | MR |
| 13 | EC-538393 | AVRDC, Taiwan | *L. esculentum* | 12 | MR |
| 14 | DARL-63 | Pithoragarh | *L. esculentum* | 12 | MR |
| 15 | H-88-78-2 | IIVR, Varanasi | *L. esculentum* | 12 | MR |
| 16 | LA-4041 | TGRC, USA | *L. esculentum* | 15 | MR |
| 17 | RCMT-1 | Shillong, Meghalaya | *L. esculentum* | 24 | MR |
| 18 | KS-118 | Kalyanpur, UP | *L. esculentum* | 24 | MR |
| 19 | BT-136 | OUAT, Orissa | *L. esculentum* | 30 | MS |
| 20 | FEB-2 | IIVR, Varanasi | *L. esculentum* | 35 | MS |
| 21 | H-88-78-3 | IIVR, Varanasi | *L. esculentum* | 32 | MS |
| 22 | EC-538401 | AVRDC, Taiwan | *L. esculentum* | 36 | MS |
| 23 | F-5013-4 | IIVR, Varanasi | *L. esculentum* | 30 | MS |
| 24 | Sel-7 | HAU, Haryana | *L. esculentum* | 30 | MS |
| 25 | Arka Vikas | IIHR, Bangalore | *L. esculentum* | 36 | MS |
| 26 | VRT-43 | IIVR, Varanasi | *L. esculentum* | 36 | MS |
| 27 | CH-3 | HARP, Ranchi | *L. esculentum* | 49 | S |
| 28 | F-6050-1 | IIVR, Varanasi | *L. esculentum* | 48 | S |
| 29 | EC-519769 | AVRDC, Taiwan | *L. esculentum* | 42 | S |
| 30 | EC-519785 | AVRDC, Taiwan | *L. esculentum* | 49 | S |
| 31 | FEB-4-1 | IIVR, Varanasi | *L. esculentum* | 48 | S |

| 32 | VFN-8 | USA | *L. esculentum* | 42 | S |
|---|---|---|---|---|---|
| 33 | H-88-1 | IIVR, Varanasi | *L. esculentum* | 49 | S |
| 34 | VRT-32-1 | IIVR, Varanasi | *L. esculentum* | 50 | HS |
| 35 | F-4012-1 | IIVR, Varanasi | *L. esculentum* | 60 | HS |
| 36 | Co-3 | TNAU, Coimbatore | *L. esculentum* | 66 | HS |

[a] Av. of three stem bits of each genotype.

In this study, eight genotypes were found as highly resistant under natural field screening as well as under artificially inoculated condition. The disease severity increased with growth of the plants. It has been observed that even on susceptible plants, the topmost younger leaves are usually free from early blight symptoms, whereas the older and lower leaves may be greatly affected and necrotized by the fungus (Johanson and Thurston, 9). Physiological mechanism controlling this apparent resistance in foliage has been clarified and Rotem (15) suggested that low sugar content as the cause of higher susceptibility in older or weakened leaves and plants. During later stages, leaves of maturing plant might be susceptible due to translocation of sugars to the ripening fruits. The genotypes exhibiting similar type of reaction under both natural and field conditions gives more reliable state for selecting the resistant or tolerant genotypes as there may be cases of disease escape under natural field condition due to environmental or some other reasons. The suggestion of Chaerani and Voorrips (3) is worth mentioning who opined that the carefully adapted laboratory assays on explants, like stem bits, however, show greater promise for studying particular aspects of resistance/susceptibility and for eliminating the confounding influences of whole-pant physiology under the natural conditions.

The results indicated that the accessions of wild species were highly resistant and may be utilized as sources for the development of pre-bred lines or recombinant inbred lines or in other molecular works for the improvement of tomato against early blight disease. Some of the cultivated genotypes as resistant/moderately resistant like H-86, VRT-2, NC EBR-4 and RCMT-1 may also be promoted for growing in disease prone areas besides using them in development of resistant/tolerant varieties.

## REFERENCES

Barksdale, T.H. and Stoner, A.K. 1977. A study of the inheritance of tomato early blight resistance. *Plant Dis. Rep.* **61**: 63-65.

Basu, P.K. 1974. Measuring early blight, its progress and influence on fruit losses in nine tomato cultivars. *Canadian Pl. Dis. Survey*, **54**: 45-51.

Chaerani, R. and Voorrips, R.E. 2006. Tomato early blight (*Alternaria solani*): the pathogen, genetics and breeding for resistance. *J. Gen. Plant. Pathol.* **72**: 335-47.

Chaerani, R., Groenwold, R., Stam, P. and Voorrips, R.E. 2007. Assessment of early blight (*Alternaria solani*) resistance in tomato using a droplet inoculation method. *J. Gen. Plant. Pathol.* **73**: 96-103.

Datar, V.V. and Lonkar, S.G. 1985. Inheritance of resistance in tomato early blight. *J. Maharashtra Agric. Univ.* **10**: 357-58.

Fageria, M.S. 1997. Genetic analysis of resistance to *Alternaria* leaf spot in tomato. *J. Mycol. Pl. Pathol.* **27**: 286-89.

Gardner, R.G. 1988. NC EBR-1 and NC EBR-2 early blight resistant tomato breeding lines. *HortSci.* **23**: 779-81.

Gardner, R.G. and Shoemaker, P.B. 1999. "Mountain Supreme" early blight resistance hybrid and its parents, NC EBR-3 and NC EBR-4. *HortSci.* **34**: 745-46.

Johanson, A. and Thurston, H.D. 1990. The effect of cultivar maturity on the resistance of potato to early blight caused by *Alternaria solani*. *American Potato J.* **67**: 615-23.

Kalloo, G. and Banerjee, M.K. 1993. Early blight resistance in *Lycopersicon esculentum* transferred from *L. pimpinellifolium* and *L. hirsutum* f. *glabratum*. *Gartenbauuissenschaft*, **58**: 238-39.

Kumar, V., Haldar, S., Pandey, K.K., Singh, R.P., Singh, A.K. and Singh, P.C. 2008. Cultural morphological, pathogenic and molecular variability amongst tomato isolates of *Alternaria solani* in India. *World J. Microbiol. Biotech.* **24**: 1003-9.

Pandey, K.K., Pandey, P.K., Kalloo, G. and Banerjee, M.K. 2003. Resistance to early blight of tomato with respect to various parameters of disease epidemics. *J. Gen. Pl. Pathol.* **69**: 364-71.

Peralta, I.E., Knapp, S. and Spooner, D. M. 2005. New species of wild tomatoes (*Solanum* section *Lycopersicon*: Solanaceae) from Northern Peru. *Syst. Bot.* **30**: 424-34.

Pound, G.S. 1951. Effect of air temperature on incidence and development of early blight disease of tomato. *Phytopathol.* **41**: 127-35.

Rotem, J. 1994. *The genus Alternaria: Biology, Epidemiology, and Pathogenicity* (1st edn.) APS, St. Paul, MN, pp. 48-203. *Identification of Resistant Sources against Early Blight Disease of Tomato*

Rotem, J., and Reichert, I. 1964. Dew - a principal moisture factor enabling early blight epidemics in a semiarid region of Israel. *Plant Dis. Rep.* **48**: 211-15.

Sherf, A.F. and MacNab, A.A. 1986. *Vegetable Diseases and their Control*. John Wiley and Sons, New York, pp. 634-640.

Thirthammallappa and Lohithaswa, H.C. 2000. Genetics of resistance to early blight (*Alternaria solani Sorauer*) in tomato (*Lycopersicon esculentum* L.). *Euphytica*, **113**: 187-93.

**Early Blight Disease of Tomato**
***Edited by:* Virendra Kumar**
**ISBN: 978-93-5056-879-8**
***Edition:* 2017**
***Published by:* Discovery Publishing House Pvt. Ltd., New Delhi (India)**

# QTL Identification for Early Blight Resistance (*Alternaria solani*) in a *Solanum lycopersicum* × *S. arcanum*

[1]R. Chaerani, [2]M.J.M. Smulders, [3]C.G. van der Linden, [4]B. Vosman, [5]P. Stam, [6]R.E. Voorrips

## ABSTRACT

Alternaria solani (Ellis and Martin) Sor-auer, the causal agent of early blight (EB) disease, infects aerial parts of tomato at both seedling and adult plant stages. Resistant cultivars would facilitate a sustainable EB management. EB resistance is a quantitatively expressed character, a fact that has hampered effective breeding. In order to identify and estimate the effect of genes conditioning resistance to EB, a quantitative trait loci (QTL) mapping study was performed in F2 and F3 populations derived from the cross between the susceptible Solanum lycopersicum (syn. Lycopersicon esculentum) cv. 'Solentos' and the resistant Solanum arcanum (syn. Lycopersicon peru-vianum) LA2157 and genotyped with AFLP, micro-satellite and SNP markers. Two evaluation criteria of resistance were used: measurements of EB lesion growth on the F2 plants in glasshouse tests and visual ratings of EB severity on foliage of the F3 lines in a field test. A total of six QTL regions were mapped on chromosomes 1, 2, 5–7, and 9 with LOD scores ranging from 3.4 to 17.5. Three EB QTL also confer resistance to stem lesions in the field, which has not been reported before. All QTL displayed significant additive gene action; in some cases a dominance effect was found. Additive × additive epistatic interactions were detected between one pair of QTL. For two QTL, the susceptible parent contributed resistance alleles to both EB and stem lesion resistance. Three of the QTL showed an effect in all tests despite methodological and environmental differences.

**Keywords:** *Alternaria solani*, Early blight resistance, tomato genotypes.

## Introduction

Early blight (EB), incited by Alternaria solani (Ellis and Martin) Sorauer, is one of the most damaging diseases in many tomato production areas worldwide (Sherf and MacNab 1986). Symptoms caused by A. solani include collar rot on

[1] Indonesian Center for Agricultural biotechnology and Genetic Resources Research and Development (ICABIOGRAD), Jln. Tentara Pelajar no. 3A, Bogor 16111, Indonesia.
[2] Plant Research Internationa, P.O. Box 386, 6700 AJ Wageningen, The Netherlands.
[3] Laboratory of Plant Breeding, Department of Plant Sciences, Wageningen University, P.O. Box 386, 6700 AJ Wageningen, The Netherlands.
[4] Division of Crop Improvement, Indian Institute of Vegetable Research, Post Box 5002, Varanasi, Uttar Pradesh.

seedlings, leaf blight, stem lesions, and fruit rot. The disease is characterized by formation of dark, necrotic lesions with concentric rings giving a target-like appearance. Leaf blight, commonly referred to as EB, is the most devastating of these symptoms. EB lesions first appear on the oldest leaves and spread upwards as the plants grow. Lesions enlarge and merge, resulting in early senescence and gradual defoliation. Complete defoliation may occur and leave fruits exposed to sun-scalding.

Early blight is prevalent in Indonesia and can cause yield losses as high as 23% (Manohara 1971; Bos and Kartapradja 1977). Frequent applications of fungicides are necessary to control the disease; however, the incidence and severity of EB remain high due to heavy and frequent rainfall in the region. Even partial resis-tance would be an important improvement, because in combination with fungicides it could extend the intervals of fungicidal spray and therefore increase the net return of the growers.

Recently, a strong source of resistance to an Indo-nesian isolate of A. solani was identified in Solanum arcanum LA2157 (syn. Lycopersicon peruvianum LA2157) (R. Chaerani et al. submitted). In glasshouse tests, the average lesion size (LS) was only 1.4 $mm^2$ compared to 23.0–108.0 $mm^2$ on susceptible tomato accessions. S. arcanum LA2157 is known as resistance source to other pathogens, including bacterial canker (Sandbrink et al. 1995; Van Heusden et al. 1999), and root knot nematode (Veremis et al. 1999). The cross with Solanum lycopersicum (syn. L. esculentum) is difficult but possible through in vitro embryo rescue (Bru¨ggemann et al. 1996).

Resistance may be difficult to transfer from wild species to cultivated tomato since it is accompanied by unacceptable horticultural traits including inferior fruit quality, late maturity, low-yielding ability, and inde-terminate growth habit. Moreover, the quantitative expression and polygenic inheritance of EB resistance has limited the development of EB resistant cultivars using traditional breeding approaches.

Classical genetic studies revealed at least two genes with additive and dominance effects and epistatic interactions that confer resistance to EB symptoms (Barksdale and Stoner 1977; Nash and Gardner 1988; Maiero et al. 1990; Thirthamalappa and Lohithaswa 2000). According to Stancheva (1991) resistance to stem lesions was a quantitative trait conferred by additive and dominant genes with epistatic effects but the correlation with EB resistance was not investi-gated.

The identification of markers closely linked to resistance genes is of great benefit for breeding for two reasons. First, these markers allow selection based on marker genotype rather than resistant phenotype and secondly they enable minimizing unfavorable linkage drag. With the aid of a genetic linkage map, Foolad and co-workers (Foolad et al. 2002; Zhang et al. 2003) have identified and estimated the magnitude of quantitative trait loci (QTL) effects in a Solanum habrochaites (syn. L. hirsutum) resistance source using backcross populations. Using interval mapping and selective genotyping approaches, they identified fourteen QTL dispersed over 11 tomato chromosomes. Four QTL were potentially useful in marker assisted-breeding programs since they were stable across environments. It should be realized that such genes may not be effective in other regions of the world, where different A. solani populations may occur and other growth conditions prevail.

The current study is aimed at identification of QTL for EB resistance effective in Indonesia. Using F2 and F3 populations derived from a cross with S. arcanum LA2157 as the donor parent we have located EB resistance QTL, some of which also confer resistance to stem lesions. To our knowledge this is the first report of QTL for stem lesion resistance.

## Materials and Methods

### *Plant material*

The mapping population was composed of 176 F2 individuals obtained from one embryo-rescued F1 plant of a cross between EB susceptible S. lycopersicum cv. 'Solentos' (De Ruiter Seeds) and an EB resistant S. arcanum LA2157 (Bru¨ggemann et al. 1996). To allow replicated tests the F2 individuals were clonally propagated in vitro. Seeds were germinated on MS medium containing 1.0% sucrose and 0.8% agar (Murashige and Skoog 1962) at 25LC. After 2–3 weeks shoots were cut and transferred to MS medium sup-plemented with 2.0% sucrose and 0.4% agar. Clones were multiplied by transferring nodes to a fresh med-ium and cultured for 3–4 weeks. Prior to transfer to the glasshouse, shoots with two leaves were cut and root formation was induced on MS medium containing 1.5% sucrose, 0.8% agar, and 0.25 mg $l^{-1}$ filter-sterilized IBA for 10–14 days. Rooted shoots were transferred to rock wool blocks in a glasshouse (18–20LC) and allowed to acclimatize for 2 weeks. Plants were further grown for 4–5 weeks before inoculation with A. solani and received standard fertilization. Both 'Solentos' and LA2157, a moderately EB resistant (HRC86.329) and a susceptible (HRC90.145) genotype (Poysa and Tu 1996; Chaerani et al. 2006), which served as controls in resistance tests, were also clonally propagated in vitro. One set of F2 clones was allowed to self-pollinate to produce F3 seeds for use in a field test.

## Early blight resistance evaluation

### *F2 glasshouse test*

The complete evaluation of the F2 population (176 different genotypes) consisted of two series of four tests; each test was considered a block in the statistical analyses. In each test, one plant of 44 of the F2 clones, and two plants of each parent and control genotype were tested. Leaflets on intact plants were inoculated with A. solani isolate 60, which was cultured and applied using the droplet test method (R. Chaerani et al. submitted). Abaxial surfaces of 12 terminal leaflets of four leaves were inoculated with spore droplets. Two droplets of 10 μl of 4 × $10^3$ spores $ml^{-1}$ agar 0.1% were applied on each leaflet, making up a total of 24 inoculation sites on each plant. EB LS (length × width) was measured with a ruler on 4, 7, 10, and 14 days after inoculation.

The area under the lesion expansion curve (AU-LEC) was calculated using the following formula:

$$AULEC = \sum_{i=-1}^{n-1} \{([R_{i+1} + R_i]/2) \times (t_{i+1} - t_i)\}$$

where $R_i$ is the LS at the ith observation, $t_i$ is time (days after planting) at the ith observation, and n is the total number of observations. The AULEC values were then converted to the relative AULEC (RAULEC) by dividing each value by the period from the date of the first appearance of appreciable EB lesions, which was 2 days after inoculation, to the date of disease evalu-ation, and by the maximum LS recorded up to the final evaluation date. The theoretical maximum RAULEC value therefore is 100%.

Lesions that did not grow beyond 1 $mm^2$ were counted at 7 DPI. The percentage of these small lesions (PS mL) was strongly correlated with LS ($r^2$ = 0.82).

### F3 field test

Seeds were obtained from 156 F2 plants. Eight-week-old seedlings were transplanted in a field in Wana-yasa (600 m altitude), West Java, Indonesia at a within-row distance of 0.35 m and a between-row distance of 0.9 m on raised beds (30 cm high, 30 cm wide). The field test consisted of two blocks. Each block contained an 8-plant plot of each F3 family and the P1 ('Solentos'), and six 8-plant plots of each P2 (LA2157), HRC 90.145 and HRC 86.329. The field was bordered with cv. Ratna (East-West Seed Indo-nesia), a susceptible S. lycopersicum cultivar. Beds were covered with black polyethylene mulch to prevent the growth of weeds and watered with sub-surface irrigation. Standard recommendations of fertilizer and growth regulator were applied. Insecti-cidal spray was done as necessary and a fungicide was applied once to prevent damping-off disease (Pythium spp.).

Each plant was artificially inoculated six times on December 13 and 20, 2004, January 3, 17, and 24, and February 7, 2005. Inocula were obtained from infected leaves, which were fragmented in a blender, sieved through cheesecloth and diluted ten times. At each inoculation about 30–60 l of inoculum was sprayed to the field.

Plants were individually rated for EB severity seven times at weekly interval from December 30, 2004 until February 9, 2005, on a scale of 0–7, where 0 =

no symptoms, 1 = trace to 1%, 2 = 2–5%, 3 = 6–10%, 4 = 11–25%, 5 = 26–50%, 6 = 51–75%, and 7 = 76– 100% of total foliage on middle third of canopy in-fected (Christ 1991). Stem infection was rated once on February 7 using a scale of 0–4, where 0 = no infection, 1 = minute (up to 1 mm in diameter) and few lesions, 2 = minute, scattered lesions, 3 = slightly larger (>1– 3 mm in diameter) and scattered lesions, and 4 = many sunken, well-developed lesions, covering >50% stem surface. Percentage of EB index (PEBI) and percent-age of stem lesion index (PStLI) for each plot were calculated using the following formula:

$$\text{Percentage of disease index} = \frac{\text{sum of all ratings}}{\text{number of plants} \times \text{maximum rating grade}} \times 100$$

The percentage of EB indices were used to calculate the area under the disease progress curve (AUDPC) analogous to the AULEC calculation and converted to the relative AUDPC (RAUDPC) using a similar method as for AULEC.

**DNA isolation and marker analysis**

For the SSR and SNP analysis, DNA was isolated from freeze-dried leaves using cell lysis and protein/polysaccharide precipitation methods according to Fulton et al. (1995) followed by DNA binding and elution using the DNAeasy Plant Mini Kit column (Qiagen, Venlo, The Netherlands). DNA for AFLP analysis was prepared by Keygene N.V. from fresh, young leaves.

Thirty-six SSR markers were used in this population, including SSR11, SSR14, SSR22, SSR27, SSR32, SSR38, SSR40, SSR45, SSR52, SSR74, SSR86, SSR115, SSR135, SSR248, SSR320, SSR356 (Sol Genomics Network at www.sgn.cornell.edu; Table 1); LE20592, LECAB9, LECHI3, LECHSOD, LEHMG2A, LEILV1B, LESODB, LESSF, LEWIPIG (Smulders et al. 1997), LED10, LEE102 (Bredemeijer et al. 1998); TMS22, TMS48 (Areshchenkova and Ganal 1999); STRBCS1b (Sandbrink et al. 2000); EST245053, EST253712, EST259379 (Areshchenkova and Ganal 2002) and three new SSRs: LEB147, LED6, and S75487 (Table 1). PCR were done in 20-ll volumes containing 10 ng of genomic DNA, 0.2 lM each of forward and reverse primers, 2 ll of 10· Goldstar reaction buffer, 2.5 mM $MgCl_2$, 0.1 mM each of dNTP, and 0.4 U of GoldstarTaq DNA polymerase (Euro-gentec, Maastricht, The Netherlands). DNA amplifi-cation was performed in a PTC-100 or PTC-200 thermocycler (MJ Research Inc., Waltham, MA, USA) using a profile of 3-min pre-denaturation at 94LC fol-lowed by 35–40 cycles of 30 s at 94LC, 30 s at 50 or 55LC, 45 s at 72LC, and finalized by a 10-min extension at 72LC. The PCR products were separated on 2.5– 3.5% agarose gel (w/w) and visualized by ethidium bromide staining or separated on a 6% polyacrylamide gel and stained as described in the Promega Silver Staining Kit (Promega, Madison, WI, USA).

## Table 17.1 Primer sequences for amplification of SSR and SNP markers

| SSR markers[a] | | | SNP markers | | |
|---|---|---|---|---|---|
| Name | | Sequence (5′–3′) | Name | | Sequence (5′–3′) |
| LEB147 | F: | CAAAAAAGAGTGAGGTAGTAGACA | Aco1 | F: | TGTTTGTTTCAATTTATCAGTCATACT |
| | R: | GAACGAGGAAGTGCAGTAAC | | R: | CCGTTTCATTTTACGTGTCTTAGT |
| LED6 | F: | GGAAGAACCCATAGATGATTA | ASR1 | F: | CATTCGTTTCAAAATAAGTGTTGTTG |
| | R: | ACCTATATAAAGTATAATAAACCCT | | R: | CAGCTGCTGCTATCTCTTCCTC |
| S75487 | F: | TTTGTAAACATTACTTAAGAACACG | ASR3 | F: | CATGTCCTAAATTTTTGTGTCTAGTTAT |
| | R: | TTTTGCTAATCCCTGATTGTA | | R: | TGTTCGCTTCAAATTATCTATCGT |
| SSR11 | F: | CCTTCAATTGACCTCCCTCA | Contig70 | F: | AGATTGACTGTGAAGGCGTCTTTGA |
| | R: | GCATCTGGAAATTAGAGGCG | | R: | ACACCAGCTGGGATTTCATCTTCAT |
| SSR14 | F: | TCTGCATCTGGTGAAGCAAG | CT259 | F: | GGCAACATCAATTGGCGTCTTTC |
| | R: | CTGGATTGCCTGGTTGATTT | | R: | CCTGCTGATATTGGTTTTCCCTCAC |
| SSR22 | F: | GATCGGCAGTAGGTGCTCTC | ID146 | F: | TTGGTGGTTCAAATCCTTATTG |
| | R: | CAAGAAACACCCATATCCGC | | R: | ACACAACTTGTATCCGGAAAACAT |
| SSR27 | F: | CCCAAATCAAGGTTTGTGGT | ID200 | F: | TTGCAAAGAAACAAGTGGACTAC |
| | R: | TCAGATGCCACCACTCTCAG | | R: | ATTGTAATTGCTGGCTGAGTATTC |
| SSR32 | F: | TGGAAAGAAGCAGTAGCATTG | ID222 | F: | TGTTGGAAAGAATTGGCTTTTGAATA |
| | R: | CAACGAACATCCTCCGTTCT | | R: | TCCGGCTATAACTAGGGACATTGAA |
| SSR38 | F: | GTTTCTATAGCTGAAACTCAACCTG | ID250 | F: | GGGGCCACAATCGTAAGAAAT |
| | R: | GGGTTCATCAAATCTACCATCA | | R: | CCGAGCTAACGCATCAAAAAG |
| SSR40 | F: | TGCAGGTATGTCTCACACCA | ID329 | F: | GCTGCAAATGAAGATAAAAGACC |
| | R: | TTGCAAGAACACCTCCCTTT | | R: | GGAGCTTCATTCAATCTATGTTATCT |
| SSR45 | F: | TGTATCCTGGTGGACCAATG | ID352 | F: | GGAGGATGCTGAGGTGTCAAGT |
| | R: | TCCAAGTATCAGGCACACCA | | R: | CTGCGAGGTAGGGGTAAGGAC |
| SSR52 | F: | TGATGGCAGCATCGTAGAAG | PRF1 | F: | ATGGCCATGGAGAAGAGACCTA |
| | R: | GGTGCGAAGGGATTTACAGA | | R: | GGAAATGAGAGTTGGCATAAACAT |
| SSR74 | F: | ACTCACCATGGCTGCTTCTT | RBCS3A | F: | TTGCTAGCAACGGTGGAAGAGTCA |
| | R: | TTTCTTGAAGGGTCTTTCCC | | R: | TTCGGGCTTGTAAGCGATGAAAC |
| SSR86 | F: | AGGGCAACAAATCCCTCTTT | SODCC | F: | GAAGCCAAAATTTATTTCAGAGAGG |
| | R: | GGAGACGAGGCTGCTTACAC | | R: | CAAATCAGCTTGCCAATTAGTTCAG |
| SSR115 | F: | CACCCTTTATTCAGATTCCTCT | | | |
| | R: | ATTGAGGGTATGCAACAGCC | | | |
| SSR135 | F: | TGATCGCTTGTGTCCACCTA | | | |
| | R: | AAAGGAAGTGATGGAAAGCG | | | |
| SSR248 | F: | GCATTCGCTGTAGCTCGTTT | | | |
| | R: | GGGAGCTTCATCATAGTAACG | | | |
| SSR320 | F: | ATGAGGCAATCTTCACCTGG | | | |
| | R: | TTCAGCTGATAGTTCCTGCG | | | |
| SSR356 | F: | ACCATCGAGGCTGCATAAAG | | | |
| | R: | AACCATCCACTGCCTCAATC | | | |

[a]Primers for SSR11–SSR356 were obtained from the Sol Genomics Network at www.sgn.cornell.edu; the other SSR and SNP primers in Table 1 were not published earlier.

Fourteen SNP markers were developed from tomato RFLP probes or gene sequences present in public nucleotide databases (Table 1). SNP polymorphisms were detected using SNaPshot following the protocol of ABI Prism SNaPshot Multiplex Kit Protocol (Applied Biosystems, Foster City, CA, USA). PCR was performed in a 25-ll volume consisting of 10 ng DNA, 0.4 lM each of forward and reverse primer, 2.5 ll of 10· PCR buffer, 0.2 mM each of dNTP, and 0.3 U of HotStarTaq DNA polymerase (Qiagen). Amplification was carried out in a PTC-100 or PTC-200 thermal cycler, programmed for 15 min at 96LC for initial denaturation and 40 cycles consisting of 30 s at 96LC, 45 s at 50LC, and 90 s at 72LC, followed by a final 10-min extension at 72LC. After amplification, PCR products were purified with SAP and ExoI for removal of dNTPs and primers. Up to ten different PCR products were pooled and single base-extended with SNaPshot primers and with fluorescent-labeled ddNTPs on a thermal cycler. Prior to analysis on an ABI 3700 sequencer (Applied Biosystems), samples were purified with SAP and ExoI to remove unincorporated ddNTPs. Data were analyzed using Genotyper 3.6 (PE Biosystems, Foster City, CA, USA).

AFLP analysis was performed by Keygene B.V. as previously described in Vos et al. (1995). The primer combinations used were P11M48, P11M50, P11M51, P11M60, P11M62, P13M47, P13M49, P13M61, P14M50, P14M51, P14M60, and P15M62. AFLP markers were scored codominantly.

### Linkage analysis

The genetic map was constructed using JoinMap 3.0 (Van Ooijen and Voorrips 2001). Grouping of the markers was initially done with a minimum LOD-score of 3.0. The recombination threshold was set at 0.49 and the Kosambi mapping function was used to convert recombination frequencies into map distances.

### QTL mapping

The MapQTL 4.0 software package (Van Ooijen et al. 2002) was used to identify QTL for all traits. First the interval mapping procedure was performed to identify the major QTL. For each trait a 1,000· per-mutation test was performed to identify the LOD threshold corresponding to a genome-wide false discovery rate of 5% ($P < 0.05$). Markers with LOD scores exceeding the threshold were used as cofactors in multiple-QTL-model (MQM) mapping procedures. If new QTL were identified, the linked markers were added to the cofactor list and the analysis was re-peated. If the LOD value of a marker dropped below the threshold in the new model, it was removed from the cofactor list and the MQM was rerun. This proce-dure was repeated until the cofactor list became stable. The final LOD scores and 2-LOD support intervals were determined using Restricted MQM.

### Statistical analysis

All data were analyzed using GenStat 6.0 (Payne et al. 2002). The phenotypic data were transformed if necessary to achieve a normal error distribution.

ANOVA with unbalanced treatment structure and general ANOVA were used to analyze the F2 and F3 phenotypic data, respectively.

Main effects and epistatic interactions between all pairs of markers that were used as cofactors in QTL mapping were analyzed using general linear regression. Regression was performed by first fitting the main additive effect of each locus in the model. Loci with small and non-significant effects were dropped from the model and regressions were repeated, leaving only loci with significant effects at P = 0.05. Next, domi-nance effects were fitted and new regressions were performed by dropping non-significant loci. Interac-tions between loci, starting from the lower to the higher order of interactions, were examined in a similar manner.

## Results

### *Linkage map*

For the construction of a genetic linkage map 176 F2 plants were genotyped with SSR and AFLP markers, whereas up to 171 plants were genotyped with SNP markers. Of 406 polymorphic markers, 389 (31 SSR, 14 SNP, and 344 AFLP) could be mapped on the 12 tomato chromosomes, resulting in a linkage map span-ning 1,176 cM (average density 1 marker per 3 cM), which is similar to the *S. lycopersicum* · *S. pennellii* (syn. L. pennellii) high-density map (1,276 cM; Tanksley et al. 1992). Eighteen markers, which showed linkage to chromosomes 1, 2, and 7 could not be placed in best positions with a 'jump threshold' of 5. Two markers were completely unlinked to all others. The number of markers mapped per chromosome ranged from 18 (chromosome 5) to 53 (chromosome 1). Linkage group length ranged from 71 (chromosome 9) to 143 cM (chromosome 1). A high-marker density was observed in regions where centromeres have been mapped (Tanksley et al. 1992). The maps of chromosomes 5, 6, and 12 contained gaps longer than 20 cM. The order and placement of SSR and SNP markers were generally in good agreement with the S. lyco-persicum × S. pennellii reference map (Tanksley et al. 1992, Sol Genomics Network http://www.sgn.cor-nell.edu). The exceptions were CT259, SSR86, and ASR1, which according to the tomato reference map are on chromosomes 4, 4, and 1, respectively, but were mapped on chromosomes 1, 3, 4 in our population. The orientation of linkage group 4 is unknown, since two SSR reference markers (TMS22 and EST259379) were originally co-mapped on S. lycopersicum × S. pennellii map (Areshchenkova and Ganal 2002). These two markers were separated at 5.5 cM distance in our population. The complete map can be obtained from the corresponding author.

## Distorted segregation

A high proportion of the mapped markers (51%) deviated significantly from the expected 1:2:1 segregation ratio for F2 generation at $P < 0.05$. Distorted segregation was observed on all chromosomes. On chromosomes 1, 2, 4, and 7–9 more than 45% markers were skewed; this usually occurred only in part of the chromosome. The distortion on chromosome 1 was caused by a surplus of heterozygotes and S. arcanum homozygotes on the short arm of the chromosome. Markers on chromosome 9 displayed a higher frequency of heterozygotes, while distortions on chromosomes 2, 4, 7, and 8 were caused by an excess of S. arcanum homozygotes.

## Phenotypic evaluation

In order to achieve approximately normal error distributions of the traits scored in the F2 glasshouse tests, a log transformation was required for LS and RAU-LEC, whereas an arcsine transformation was applied to the PSmL data. The ANOVA analyses revealed sig-nificant block effects. For the F3 field data, EB assessment at 48 DAT for PEBI and at 75 DAT for RAUDPC were used, since the parents and control genotypes were most clearly distinguished at these dates. No transformation was required for PEBI and RAUDPC data, whereas an arcsine transformation was applied to the PStLI data.

All the resistance traits measured showed a contin-uous distribution with the population mean skewed toward resistance (Fig. 1). The phenotypic distributions of LS, RAULEC, PSmL, and PStLI showed a bimodal frequency distribution (Fig. 1). In the F2 data transgressive segregation occurred in both directions, whereas in the F3 data transgression was observed toward resistance only.

## QTL analysis

### *F2 glasshouse test*

Four QTL were identified from the glasshouse data on chromosomes 2, 5, 7, and 9 (Table 2; Fig. 2). The QTL for the three traits overlapped in all cases except that no significant QTL was found for PSmL on chromo-some 5. This co-location is consistent with a higher correlation coefficient between LS and RAULEC ($r^2 = 0.95$) than between PSmL and LS ($r^2 = 0.82$) or between PSmL and RAULEC ($r^2 = 0.86$).

For LS, the four QTL explained in total 40% of the phenotypic variance and individual QTL accounted for 8.1–13.3% of the phenotypic variance. For RAULEC each QTL explained 6.9–15.2% of the phenotypic variance, whereas each QTL for PSmL accounted for 8.6–16.0% of the phenotypic variance. The QTL on chromosome 7 was the most important in explaining the phenotypic variation, regardless the type of traits measured. Beneficial alleles were contributed by the susceptible parent at the QTL on chromosomes 2 and 7.

All QTL exhibited significant additive gene action ($P < 0.05$ or $<0.001$), but dominant effects were also displayed by the QTL on chromosome 2 for PSmL and PStLI ($P < 0.05$), the QTL on chromosome 7 for LS ($P < 0.001$) and PSmL ($P < 0.05$), and the QTL on chromosome 9 for LS and RAULEC ($P < 0.001$). No between-locus interactions were found for the QTL detected in the glasshouse.

### *F3 field test*

One main QTL on chromosome 9 and two QTL with smaller effects on chromosomes 2 and 6 were identified for PEBI (Table 2; Fig. 2). The LOD value

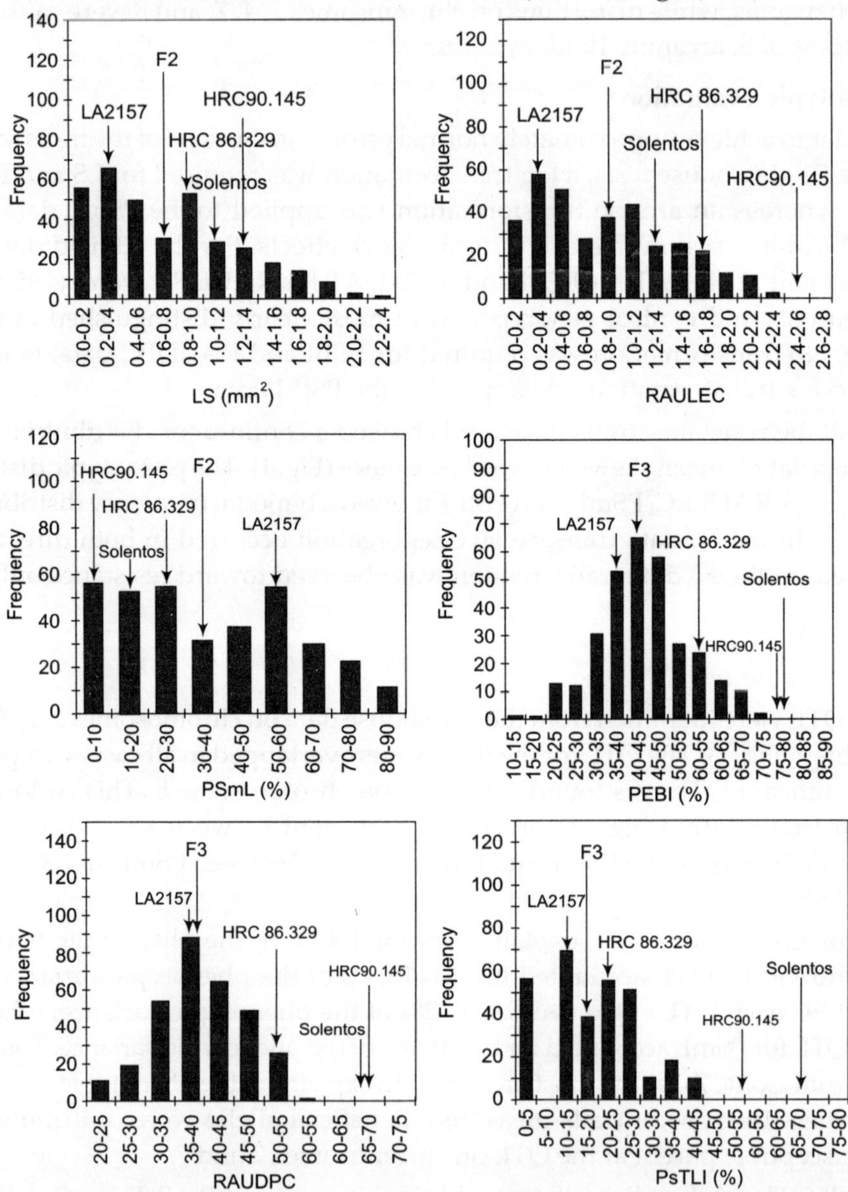


**Fig. 17.1 Frequency distribution for lesion size (LS), percentage of small lesions (PSmL), and relative area under the lesion expansion curve (RAULEC) in an F2 population of the cross of the QTL on chromosome 6 was below the threshold value (3.67), but it was included in the analyses as it was also associated with RAUDPC (see below). When used as co-factor, the marker at this QTL increased the LOD value of the main QTL from 5.91 to 6.57 and the LOD of the other minor QTL from 3.32 to 3.68.**

Five QTL for RAUDPC were identified on chromosomes 1, 2, 5, 6, and 9. Collectively these QTL explained 49% of the phenotypic variance and they all showed additive gene action (P < 0.001). A proportion of more than 10% of the phenotypic variances was explained by the QTL on chromosomes 2, 5, 6, and 9. Except for the QTL on chromosome 2, all QTL inherited the allele for resistance from the resistant parent. The QTL on chromosomes 2, 6, and 9 were also associated with PEBI. This is in agreement with a high correlation between the phenotypic values of the two disease traits ($r^2 = 0.80$).

Resistance to stem lesions was associated with three QTL on chromosomes 2, 5, and 9. The QTL on chromosome 9 was the most important for resistance to stem lesions since by itself it explained 35% of the phenotypic variance. The 2-LOD support intervals of the stem lesion QTL partly or completely overlapped those of three QTL for RAUDPC or PEBI.

Solanum lycopersicum 'Solentos' × Solanum arcanum LA2157, and for percentage of early blight index (PEBI), relative area under the disease progress curve (RAUDPC), and percentage of stem lesion index (PstLI) in a population of F3 lines derived from that F2. The F2 population was tested in a glasshouse in The Netherlands with a single Alternaria solani isolate; the F3 population in a field in Indonesia with mixed field isolates. The means of the parents and the F2 or F3 are indicated, as well as those of two reference tomato lines HRC86.329 (moderately resistant) and HRC90.145 (susceptible)

Irrespective of the type of disease syndrome and the trait measured, the QTL on chromosome 9 was the most important in the field. For each trait measured, it explained the largest proportion of the phenotypic variance.

Additive genetic effects were prevalent for the QTL detected in the field, while the QTL on chromosome 9 also displayed a dominant genetic effect (P < 0.001) on stem lesion resistance. Digenic epistatic interactions of the type additive × additive (P < 0.05) were found for RAUDPC between the QTL on chromosomes 2 and 9.

## Discussion

### *Linkage analysis*

Deviation from the expected segregation ratio is a common feature of tomato interspecific crosses, often with the extent of skewness being higher on wider crosses. A skewness rate of 50% was reported in a S. lycopersicum × S. cheesmaniae (syn. L. cheesmanii) F2 population (Paterson et al. 1991), and up to 80% in a S. lycopersicum × S. pennellii F2 population (De Vi-cente and Tanksley 1993). Less skewed segregation (8– 10%) was exhibited in crosses with S. pimpinellifolium (syn. L. pimpinellifolium), a species closely related with the cultivated tomato (Grandillo and Tanksley 1996; Chen and Foolad 1999). A distortion rate (55%) similar to our result was previously reported by Van Heusden et al. (1999) using a different subset of F2 progeny from the same cross with S. arcanum LA2157. The aberrant segregation on chromosomes 2, 4, 7, and 8 toward S. arcanum alleles was also previously reported by Van Heusden et al. (1999). Additionally, an excess in heterozygotes was observed on chromosome 9, as was also observed by Fulton et al. (1997) in a cross with S. arcanum LA1708 (syn. L. peruvianum LA1708). In our population, QTL for EB resistance were observed both in regions with skewed segregations (chromosomes 2, 6, 7, and 9) and in regions without skewed segregation (chromosomes 1 and 5).

**Table 17.2 Quantitative trait loci for early blight and stem lesion resistance identified by multiple-QTL-models mapping (MQM) method**

| Chr | Trait | Test | Cofactor | Position (cM) | Coverage (cM)[a] | LOD score[b] | %expl | Add | Dom |
|---|---|---|---|---|---|---|---|---|---|
| 1 | RAUDPC | F3, field | P14M60-276P | 138 | 31 | 4.07 | 6.8 | 2.26*** | –0.50 |
| 2 | LS | F2, glasshouse | P11M48-082E | 34 | 42 | 5.58 | 9.5 | –0.19*** | 0.09 |
| 2 | RAULEC | F2, glasshouse | P15M62-073P | 42 | 42 | 4.19 | 7.2 | –0.24*** | 0.12 |
| 2 | PSmL[c] | F2, glasshouse | P13M49-435E | 36 | 42 | 5.42 | 10.3 | 9.45*** | –8.08* |
| 2 | PEBI | F3, field | P11M60-276E | 86 | 18 | 3.36 | 7.6 | –3.64*** | –0.69 |
| 2 | RAUDPC | F3, field | P14M51-146E | 78 | 18 | 8.99 | 16.2 | –4.23*** | 1.00 |
| 2 | PStLI | F3, field | P13M49-352P | 61 | 35 | 4.00 | 4.8 | –3.52** | 1.99* |
| 5 | LS | F2, glasshouse | P14M51-055P | 58 | 36 | 4.75 | 8.1 | 0.15*** | –0.01 |
| 5 | RAULEC | F2, glasshouse | P14M51-055P | 58 | 41 | 3.95 | 6.9 | 0.21*** | –0.03 |
| 5 | RAUDPC | F3, field | P14M51-055P | 58 | 39 | 6.14 | 10.5 | 2.92*** | 0.34 |
| 5 | PStLI | F3, field | P14M50-537P | 55 | 75 | 4.63 | 7.5 | 3.21*** | –1.01 |
| 6 | PEBI | F3, field | P13M49-231E | 51 | 36 | 3.68 | 8.2 | 3.76** | –2.03 |
| 6 | RAUDPC | F3, field | P11M48-266E | 29 | 21 | 6.26 | 10.8 | 3.42*** | 0.23 |
| 7 | LS | F2, glasshouse | P15M62-349P | 36 | 33 | 7.54 | 13.3 | –0.22*** | 0.08*** |
| 7 | RAULEC | F2, glasshouse | P15M62-349P | 36 | 33 | 8.26 | 15.2 | –0.35*** | 0.16 |
| 7 | PSmL[c] | F2, glasshouse | P15M62-349P | 36 | 30 | 8.09 | 16.0 | 11.32*** | –5.03* |
| 9 | LS | F2, glasshouse | P14M50-081E | 53 | 31 | 4.87 | 8.2 | 0.17*** | –0.14*** |
| 9 | RAULEC | F2, glasshouse | P14M50-081E | 53 | 31 | 5.23 | 9.2 | 0.27*** | –0.18*** |
| 9 | PSmL[c] | F2, glasshouse | P11M48-065E | 41 | 22 | 4.61 | 8.6 | –8.56*** | 0.92 |
| 9 | PEBI | F3, field | P11M60-109P | 25 | 23 | 6.57 | 15.4 | 5.32*** | –0.41 |
| 9 | RAUDPC | F3, field | P11M60-109P | 25 | 23 | 8.70 | 15.5 | 3.50*** | 1.35 |
| 9 | PStLI | F3, field | P14M50-072P | 33 | 14 | 17.48 | 34.5 | 7.01*** | –3.93** |

*Chr* chromosome number, *%expl*. explained part of the phenotypic variance, *Add* additive effect, *Dom* dominance effect, *LS* lesion size (mm$^2$), *PSmL* percentage of small lesions, *PEBI* percentage of early blight index, *RAUDPC* relative area under the disease progress curve, *RAULEC* relative area under the lesion expansion curve, *PstLI* percentage of stem lesion index

[a] Based on 2-LOD support interval obtained from restricted MQM mapping; distance between flanking markers

[b] The LOD thresholds obtained from 1,000· permutation tests for a genome wide significance ($P < 0.05$) were 3.70, 3.54, 3.51, 3.67, 3.67, and 3.69 for LS, PSmL, RAULEC, PEBI, RAUDPC, and PStLI, respectively

[c] The QTL effects of PSmL are opposite to those for all other traits, as a high value for PSmL indicates resistance while a high value of the other traits indicates susceptibility

*$P < 0.05$, according to t-test

**$P < 0.01$, according to t-test

***$P < 0.001$, according to t-test

## QTL analysis

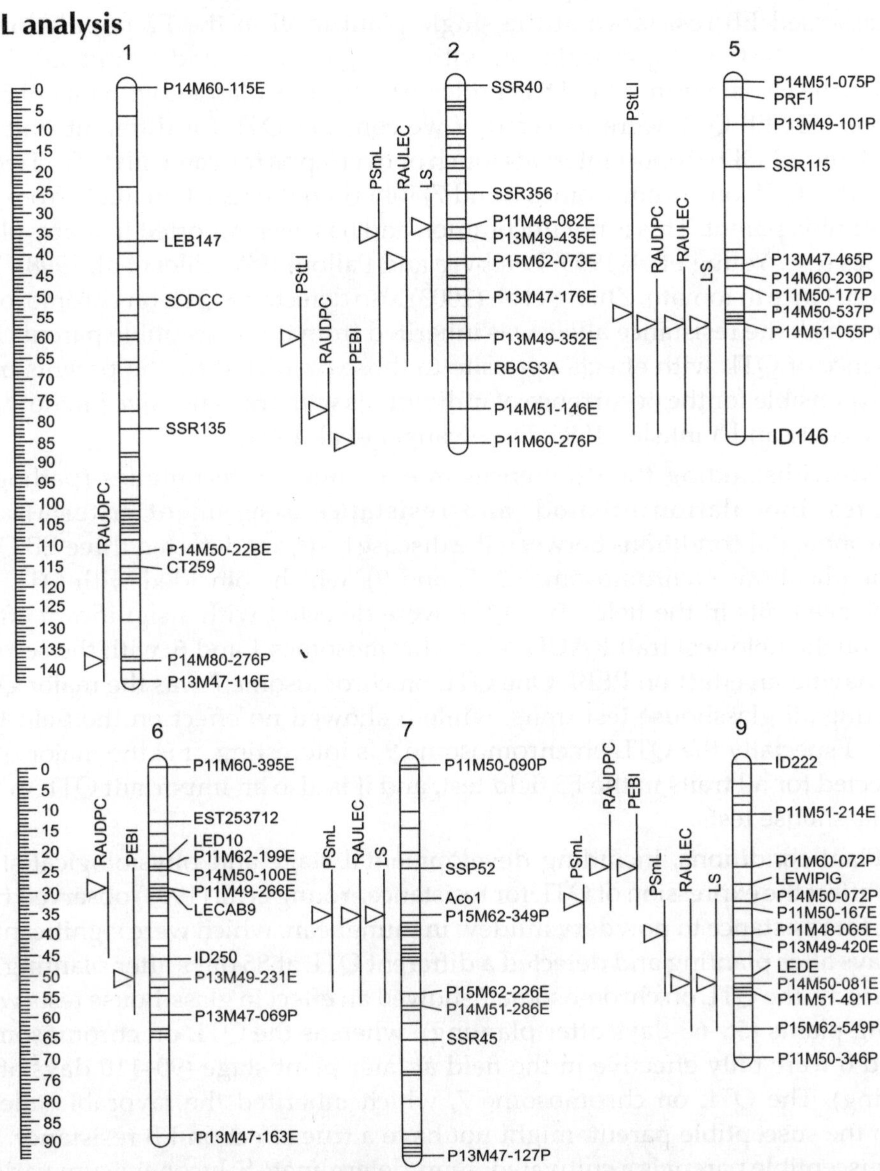


**Fig. 17.2 Map positions of QTL for resistance to leaf and stem lesion of EB disease depicted on a skeletal map based on an F2 population of the cross Solanum lycopersicum cv. 'Solentos' · Solanum arcanum LA2157. QTL are represented by bars covering 2-LOD support intervals obtained by restricted multiple-QTL-method (RMQM) mapping. Triangles indicate the position of the markers used as co-factor; solid triangles indicate that the resistant alleles were contributed by the susceptible parent ('Solentos'). Lesion size (LS), the relative area under the lesion expansion curve (RAULEC), and percentage of small lesions (PSmL) were assessed in the F2 population inoculated with a single Alternaria solani isolate in a glasshouse in The Netherlands; percentage of EB index (PEBI), the relative area under the disease progress curve (RAUDPC), and percentage of stem lesion index (PStLI) were assessed in the F3 population inoculated with mixed field isolates in a field in Indonesia**

We assessed EB resistance at the single plant level in the F2 population in glasshouse tests using inoculation with a single isolate and compared these data to the F3 data from a field test under artificial inoculations with mixed field isolates. Six EB QTL were detected, if we consider QTL for different traits of which the 2-LOD support intervals touch or overlap as the same EB QTL. Two of these (the QTL on chromosomes 2 and 7) inherited the resistant allele from the susceptible parent. This is not uncommon and has been reported in many plant species (*e.g.*, Young et al. 1993; Lefebvre and Palloix 1996; Pilet et al. 1998). For EB resistance in tomato, Zhang et al. (2003) also detected a QTL on chromosome 3 for which the resistance allele was inherited from the susceptible parent. The presence of QTL with effects opposite to those predicted by the parents may be responsible for the occurrence of individuals with transgressive phenotypes (De Vicente and Tanksley 1993; Dirlewanger et al. 1994).

Notwithstanding the differences in experimental techniques (pathogen isolates, inoculation method, and resistance assessment criteria) and environmental conditions between the disease tests, we detected three EB QTL in the glasshouse (chromosomes 2, 5, and 9), which coincided with QTL for resistance traits in the field. Two QTL were detected with a significant effect only on the field-test trait RAUDPC on chromosomes 1 and 6, with the second also having an effect on PEBI. One QTL on chromosome 7 was the major QTL affecting all glasshouse test traits, while it showed no effect on the field test traits. Especially the QTL on chromosome 9 is interesting: it is the major QTL de-tected for all traits in the F3 field test, and it is also an important QTL in the F2 glasshouse tests.

Plant conditions, including developmental stage and physiological state may affect the expression of QTL for resistance. Young et al. (1993) observed two QTL for resistance to powdery mildew in mungbean, which were significant at 65 days after planting and detected a different QTL at 85 days after planting. In our study, the QTL on chromosome 7 showed an effect in glass-house tests with young plants (56–63 days after planting), whereas the QTL on chromosomes 1 and 6 were only effective in the field at later plant stage (90–110 days after sowing). The QTL on chromosome 7, which inherited the favorable alleles from the susceptible parent, might not have a true effect on EB resistance. As the susceptible parent is a cultivated, semi-determinate S. lycopersicum variety and much better adapted to the glasshouse test environment than the resistant, indeterminate S. arcanum parent, this suggests that the QTL on chromosome 7 may affect the condition of the plants in the glasshouse rather than the resistance itself. Thus, plants carrying the S. lycopersicum allele would in general be more vigorous and therefore better able to withstand infection, which overshadows the effect of their genotype at the 'true' resistance QTL. The fact that well-fertilized plants are more resistant than plants starved for nutrients and that young plant generally show more apparent resistance to EB than older plant (Rotem 1994) support the notion that plant condition can affect EB resistance. Whether this speculation is true or not, the QTL on chromosome 7 is not an interesting target for breeders, as it does not show an effect on EB severity in the field.

The detection of common QTL at different experimental locations may be hampered by geno-type × environment or genotype · isolate interactions as was observed in some studies, e.g., by Lu¨bberstedt et al. (1999). We do not preclude the presence of such interactions in EB resistance that might further explain the discrepancy between the F2 glasshouse and F3 field tests; however, such interactions could not be deter-mined in this study. In the two environments different isolates were used, so that the effects of the isolates and experimental conditions were confounded.

### Comparison with classical genetic and molecular mapping studies of EB resistance

The current research is the first genetic study of EB resistance using S. arcanum LA2157 as a donor parent. In a glasshouse experiment where LA2157 was tested together with several well-known resistant accessions, using the same Indonesian A. solani isolate and the same experimental conditions as used in the F2 glass-house test, LA2157 formed lesions of similar size as S. peruvianum PE44 and significantly smaller lesions than all other accessions including S. lycopersicum NC-EBR1 to NC-EBR6, S. peruvianum PE33, and S. habrochaites PE36 (Chaerani et al. 2006). Our results concur with previous classical genetic and molecular mapping studies using S. habrochaites (syn. L. hirsu-tum) or derived materials and S. pimpinellifolium, which indicate that EB resistance is under polygenic control. Additive genetic effects were predominant (Nash and Gardner 1988; Maiero et al. 1990; Thirth-amalappa and Lohithaswa 2000; Foolad et al. 2002; Zhang et al. 2003); in some cases also dominant effects (Nash and Gardner 1988; Thirthamalappa and Lohithaswa 2000) as well as epistatic interactions (Nash and Gardner 1988; Maiero et al. 1990; Thirthamalappa and Lohithaswa 2000) were observed.

It has been observed that EB resistance tends to be associated with indeterminate growth habit, self-incompatibility, low yield and lateness (Nash and Gardner 1988; Foolad et al. 2002). However it is not clear whether this association is due to a direct effect of these traits on EB development, to (other) pleiotropic effects of resistance genes or to linkage drag, In our study, the F2 plants were tested at a juvenile stage where direct effects of these traits on resistance are unlikely. The F3 plants were tested between 10 and 16 weeks after sowing, during which period fruit production started but the plants did not completely mature. Even with this difference in development we observed sub-stantial overlap between the QTL identified in the F2 and the F3 generation, which suggests that the effects of the mentioned plant traits, if present, were not so large as to obscure the segregation of true resistance.

**Table 17.3 Mean values for resistance parameters of F2 plants and the derived F3 lines based on the QTL genotypes on chromosomes 2 and 9**

| | | QTL on chromosome 9 | | | Mean | QTL on chromosome 9 | | | Mean | QTL on chromosome 9 | | | Mean |
|---|---|---|---|---|---|---|---|---|---|---|---|---|---|
| | | LS (mm²) | | | | RAULEC | | | | PSmL | | | |
| | | aa[a] | ab | bb | | aa | ab | bb | | aa | ab | bb | |
| QTL on chromo-some 2 | aa | 0.96[b] (1)[c] | 0.43 (11) | 0.45 (5) | 0.44 (23) | 0.99 (2) | 0.65 (13) | 0.75 (10) | 0.72 (26) | 41.20 (1) | 48.10 (11) | 48.84 (5) | 47.91 (17) |
| | ab | 1.05 (11) | 0.63 (43) | 0.70 (21) | 0.71 (89) | 1.32 (12) | 0.90 (45) | 1.01 (17) | 0.99 (76) | 24.97 (14) | 38.07 (38) | 40.39 (21) | 35.59 (80) |
| | bb | 1.10 (12) | 0.81 (32) | 0.71 (10) | 0.85 (62) | 1.25 (4) | 1.10 (31) | 0.97 (12) | 1.09 (48) | 29.47 (10) | 30.70 (37) | 38.05 (14) | 31.91 (63) |
| Mean | | 1.04 (26) | 0.68 (99) | 0.66 (44) | | 1.35 (26) | 0.95 (99) | 0.90 (44) | | 27.65 (26) | 35.82 (98) | 41.50 (45) | |

| | | QTL on chromosome 9 | | | Mean | QTL on chromosome 9 | | | Mean | QTL on chromosome 9 | | | Mean |
|---|---|---|---|---|---|---|---|---|---|---|---|---|---|
| | | LS (mm²) | | | | RAULEC | | | | PSmL | | | |
| | | aa[a] | ab | bb | | aa | ab | bb | | aa | ab | bb | |
| QTL on chromo-some | aa | 45.94 (5) | 40.60 (24) | 37.75 (11) | 40.48 (40) | 39.34 (2) | 35.11 (12) | 32.71 (8) | 35.27 (25) | 19.32 (2) | 7.68 (7) | 7.57 (5) | 9.76 (15) |
| | ab | 51.64 (18) | 44.49 (39) | 38.52 (17) | 44.76 (76) | 45.04 (19) | 39.70 (46) | 36.43 (18) | 39.98 (89) | 32.16 (15) | 17.43 (49) | 11.25 (22) | 18.26 (89) |
| | bb | 51.98 (4) | 48.61 (13) | 44.81 (11) | 47.60 (28) | 41.69 (5) | 42.30 (19) | 39.00 (11) | 41.38 (38) | 33.23 (7) | 18.71 (11) | 15.53 (11) | 21.01 (29) |
| Mean | | 50.01 (30) | 44.17 (81) | 40.08 (40) | 43.31 (30) | 39.63 (81) | 36.11 (40) | 30.38 (30) | 17.05 (76) | 12.35 (44) | 35.82 (98) | 41.50 (45) | |

The QTL on chromosome 2 inherited the resistant alleles from the susceptible parent 'Solentos'

[a] aa = homozygous 'Solentos', ab = heterozygous 'Solentos'/LA2157, bb = homozygous LA2157

[b] Values are log(x + 1) transformation for lesion size (LS) and relative area under the lesion expansion curve (RAULEC) and arcsine (x/100) transformation for percentage of small lesions (PSmL), and percentage of stem lesion index (PStLI)

[c] Figures in parentheses are the number of F2 plants or F3 lines

Although we used a different resistance source, the 2-LOD support intervals of our QTL overlapped with the QTL regions detected by Foolad et al. (2002) and Zhang et al. (2003), except for the QTL on chromo-some 7 which was not detected in their studies. The smaller number of QTL detected in our study may be due to a higher LOD threshold employed (3.5–3.7 depending on the trait) compared to the previous mapping study using an S. habrochaites source which used a LOD threshold of 2.4 (Foolad et al. 2002). Both studies revealed no major QTL for EB resistance, but rather showed that resistance is controlled by several QTL with small effects: 7–16% explained variance in our study, and 4–22% in Foolad et al. (2002). The number of QTL (7) detected by Zhang et al. (2003) using selective genotyping on a backcross population with S. habrochaites as donor was similar to the num-ber of QTL (6) we identified. A larger mapping pop-ulation and more replications could possibly uncover more QTL for EB resistance, but probably no major QTL will be found.

Previous studies showed that stem lesion resistance was found in the same sources as EB resistance but the genetic relationship was not investigated (Barksdale and Stoner 1973, 1977; Stancheva et al. 1991a, b). In the present study, three EB resistance QTL coincided with stem lesion resistance QTL; one QTL on chromosome 9 even had a major effect on the stem lesion resistance (35%).

**Breeding implications**

For breeding purposes QTL with large additive effects, which are stable across environments and which do not depend on epistatic interactions, are most desirable. QTL, which meet these criteria perfectly were not found in the current study. Nevertheless, it would be useful for breeders to make use of the QTL on chro-mosomes 2 and 9 as they are effective in both envi-ronments and are the most important according to the field test results. Genotypes homozygous for the 'Solentos' allele at the favorable QTL allele on chro-mosome 2 or for the LA2157 allele at the QTL on chromosome 9 showed enhanced resistance as mea-sured by different parameters (Table 3). A further increase in resistance was generally observed in the double homozygotes. It is possible that the QTL on chromosome 2 is already present in most tomato material; in that case only the QTL on chromosome 9 would have to be introgressed. For introgression pur-poses a more precise determination of the QTL positions will be needed. This could be achieved through the development of a population of plants or lines, each containing parts of the S. arcanum QTL regions in a cultivated tomato background.

## Acknowledgments

We thank Gerda Uenk, Hanneke van der Schoot and Wendy van 't Westende for help and advice in the marker analyses; Paul Arens for developing SSR primers; Dirk Budding and Remmelt Groenwold for assistance with in vitro plant culture; Daan Jaspers and Geurt Versteeg for plant care in the glasshouse. Nurul Hidayati, Vita Anggraini and Sularno of East-West Seed Indonesia are gratefully acknowledged for con-ducting the field trial, and the companies Enza Zaden, Syngenta Seeds and Nunhems Zaden for co-funding part of the SNP development and for permission to publish. R.C. was supported by the Royal Netherlands Academy of Arts and Sciences in the framework of the Scientific Programme Indonesia—The Neth-erlands.

## REFERENCES

Areshchenkova T, Ganal MW (1999) Long tomato microsatel-lites are predominantly associated with centromeric regions. Genome 42:536–544

Areshchenkova T, Ganal MW (2002) Comparative analysis of polymorphisms and chromosomal location of tomato microsatellite markers isolated from different sources. Theor Appl Genet 104:229–235

Barksdale TH, Stoner AK (1973) Segregation for horizontal resistance to tomato early blight. Plant Dis Rep 57:964–965 Barksdale TH, Stoner AK (1977) A study of the inheritance of tomato early blight resistance. Plant Dis Rep 61:63–65 Bos G, Kartapradja R (1977) Tomato variety trials on Java with emphasis on yield potential, adaptability to environment and tolerance to pests and diseases. Bull Penelitian Horti-kultura 5:93–113

Bredemeijer GMM, Arens P, Wouters D, Visser D, Vosman B (1998) The use of semi-automated fluorescent microsatellite analysis for tomato cultivar identification. Theor Appl Genet 97:584–590

Bru¨ggemann W, Linger P, Wenner A, Koornneef M (1996) Improvement of post-chilling photosynthesis in tomato by sexual hybridization with a Lycopersicon peruvianum line from elevated altitude. Adv Hort Sci 10:215–218

Chaerani R, Groenwold R, Stam P, Voorrips RE (2006) Assessment of early blight (Alternaria solani) resistance in tomato using a droplet inoculation method. J Gen Plant Pathol (in press)

Chen FQ, Foolad MR (1999) A molecular linkage map of tomato based on a cross between Lycopersicon esculentum and L. pimpinellifolium and its comparison with other molecular maps of tomato. Genome 42:94–103

Christ BJ (1991) Effect of disease assessment method on ranking potato cultivars for resistance to early blight. Plant Dis 75:353–356

De Vicente MC, Tanksley SD (1993) QTL analysis of transgres-sive segregation in an interspecific tomato cross. Genetics 134:585–596

Dirlewanger E, Isaac PG, Ranades S, Belajouza M, Cousin R, de Vienne D (1994) Restriction fragment length polymorphism analysis of loci associated with disease resistance genes and developmental traits in Pisum sativum L. Theor Appl Genet 88:17–27

Foolad MR, Zhang LP, Khan AA, Nin˜o-Liu D, Lin GY (2002) Identification of QTLs for early blight (Alternaria solani) resistance in tomato using backcross populations of a Lycopersicon esculentum · Lycopersion hirsutum cross. Theor Appl Genet 104:945–958

Fulton TM, Chunwongse J, Tanksley SD (1995) Microprep protocol for extraction of DNA from tomato and other herbaceous plants. Plant Mol Biol Rep 13:207–209

Fulton TM, Nelson JC, Tanksley SD (1997) Introgression and DNA marker analysis of Lycopersicon peruvianum, a wild relative of the cultivated tomato, into Lycopersicon escu-lentum, followed through three successive backcross gener-ations. Theor Appl Genet 95:895–902

Grandillo S, Tanksley SD (1996) Genetic analysis of RFLPs, GATA microsatellites and RAPDs in a cross between L. esculentum and L. pimpinellifolium. Theor Appl Genet 92:957–965

Lefebvre V, Palloix A (1996) Both epistatic and additive effects of QTL are involved in polygenic induced resistance to disease: a case study, the interaction pepper-Phytophthora capsici Leonian. Theor Appl Genet 93:503–511

Lu¨bberstedt T, Xia XC, Tan G, Liu X, Melchinger AE (1999) QTL mapping of resistance to Sporisorium reiliana in maize. Theor Appl Genet 99:593–598

Maiero M, Ng TJ, Barksdale TH (1990) Genetic resistance to early blight in tomato breeding lines. HortScience 25:344– 346

Manohara D (1971) Penyakit-penyakit pada tanaman famili Solanaceae di Lembang dan Pacet. Fakultas Pertanian Institut Pertanian Bogor, Bogor, p.33

Murashige T, Skoog F (1962) A revised medium for rapid growth and bioassays with tobacco tissue cultures. Physiol Plant 15:473–497

Nash AF, Gardner RG (1988) Heritability of tomato early blight resistance derived from Lycopersicon hirsutum PI 126445. J Am Soc Hort Sci 113:264–268

Paterson AH, Damon S, Hewitt JD, Zamir D, Rabinowitch HD, Lincoln SE, Tanksley SD (1991) Mendelian factors under-lying quantitative traits in tomato: comparison across species, generations, and environments. Genetics 127:181– 197

Payne RW, Harding SA, Murray DA, Soutar DM, Baird DB, Welham SJ, Kane AF, Gilmour AR, Thompson R, Webster R, Wilson GT (2002) GenStat for Windows™, 6th edn. VSN International, Oxford

Pilet ML, Delourme R, Foisset N, Renard M (1998) Identifica-tion of loci contributing to quantitative field resistance to blackleg disease, causal agent Leptosphaeria maculans (Desm.) Ces. Et de Not., in winter rapeseed (Brassica napus L). Theor Appl Genet 96:23–30

Poysa V, Tu JC (1996) Response of cultivars and breeding lines of Lycopersicon spp. to Alternaria solani. Can Plant Dis Surv 76:5–8

Rotem J (1994) The genus Alternaria biology, epidemiology, and pathogenicity, 1st edn. The American Phtyopathological Society, St. Paul, MN, pp 48, 203

Sandbrink JM, Colon LT, Wolters PJCC, Stiekema WJ (2000) Two related genotypes of Solanum microdontum carry different segregating alleles for field resistance to Phytoph-thora infestans. Mol Breed 6:215–225

Sandbrink JM, Van Ooijen JW, Purimahua C, Vrielink R, Verkerk M, Zabel P, Lindhout P (1995) Localization of genes for bacterial canker resistance in Lycopersicon escu-lentum using RFLPs. Theor Appl Genet 90:444–450

Sherf AF, MacNab AA (1986) Vegetable diseases and their control. Wiley, New York, pp634–640

Smulders MJM, Bredemeijer G, Rus-Kortekaas W, Arens P, Vosman B (1997) Use of short microsatellites from database sequences to generate polymorphisms among Lycopersicon esculentum cultivars and accessions of other Lycopersicon species. Theor Appl Genet 94:264–272

Stancheva I (1991) Inheritance of the resistance to injuries on the growth mass caused by Alternaria solani in the tomato. Genetika-i-Selektsiya 24:232–236

Stancheva I, Lozanov I, Achkova Z (1991a) Sources of resistance to Alternaria solani in the tomato in wild growing species of the genus Lycopersicon. Genetika-i-Selektsiya 24:126–130

Stancheva I, Lozanov I, Stamova L (1991b) Correlations between the resistance to different injuries from Alternaria solani in the tomatoes. Genetika-i-Selektsiya 24:51–55

Tanksley SD, Ganal MW, Prince JP, de Vicente MC, Bonierbale MW, Broun P, Fulton TM, Giovannoni JJ, Grandillo S, Martin GB, Messegeur R, Miller JC, Miller L, Paterson AH, Pineda O, Roder MS, Wing RA, Wu W, Young ND (1992) High density molecular linkage maps of the tomato and potato genome. Genetics 132:1141–1160

Thirthamalappa, Lohithaswa HC (2000) Genetics of resistance to early blight (Alternaria solani Sorauer) in tomato (Lyco-persicum esculentum L.) Euphytica 113:187–193

Van Heusden AW, Koornneef M, Voorrips RE, Bruggemann W, Pet G, Vrielink-van Ginkel R, Chen X, Lindhout P (1999) Three QTLs from Lycopersicon peruvianum confer a high level of resistance to Clavibacter michiganensis ssp. michi-ganensis. Theor Appl Genet 99:1068–1074

Van Ooijen JW, Boer MP, Jansen RC, Maliepaard C (2002) MapQTL 4.0, Software for the calculation of QTL positions on genetic maps. Plant Research International, Wageningen, The Netherlands

Van Ooijen JW, Voorrips RE (2001) JoinMap 3.0, Software for the calculation of genetic linkage maps. Plant Research International, Wageningen, The Netherlands

Veremis JC, van Heusden AW, Roberts PA (1999) Mapping a novel heat-stable resistance to Meloidogyne in Lycopersicon peruvianum. Theor Appl Genet 98:274–280

Vos P, Hogers R, Bleeker M, Reijans M, Van der Lee T, Hornes M, Frijters A, Pot J, Peleman J, Kuiper M, Zabeau M (1995) AFLP: a new technique for DNA fingerprinting. Nucl Acids Res 23:4407–4414

Young ND, Danesh D, Menancio-Hautea, Kumar L (1993) Mapping oligogenic resistance to powdery mildew in mungbean with RFLPs. Theor Appl Genet 87:243–249

Zhang LP, Lin GY, Nin˜o-Liu, Foolad MR (2003) Mapping QTLs conferring early blight (Alternaria solani) resistance in a Lycopersicon esculentum × L. hirsutum cross by selective genotyping. Mol Breed 12:3–19

**Early Blight Disease of Tomato**
***Edited by:*** **Virendra Kumar**
**ISBN: 978-93-5056-879-8**
***Edition:*** **2017**
***Published by:*** **Discovery Publishing House Pvt. Ltd., New Delhi (India)**

# In vitro Control of *Alternaria solani*, the Cause of Early Blight of Tomato

[1]Ashraf Saber Hawamdeh and Shabeer Ahmad

**ABSTRACT**

In vitro control of Alternaria so/an/was studied with different fungicides. Using Poison Food Technique (PFT), seven fungicides, Antracol, Benlate, Copper oxychloride, Dithane M-46, Ridomil, Topas, and Topsin were evaluated at four different concentrations (260, 500, 760, and 1000 ppm) to control colony growth of fungi. The lowest colony growth was recorded in Dithane M-46 treatment at 1000 ppm, and the highest in treatment where no fungicide was used, indicating the significance of using fungicides in controlling early blight disease in tomato.

**Keywords:** Tomato, early blight, Alternaria solani fungicides, in vitro control, Pakistan.

## Introduction

In Pakistan per hectare yield of tomato (10.84 t) is very low due to several production constraints including diseases. One such disease is the early blight cau sed by the fungus *Alternaria solani.* (Ell), Martin. Common names used for the disease at various stages of plant and fruit development include seedling blight and danping off on seedlings, foot rot and collar rot on young plant stem, stem blight and canker on stems and branches, early blight and leaf spot on leaves, blossom blight on the calyx, black rot and hard rot on fruit and fruit drop on fruit and petioles. Leaf spot symptoms are characteristic for early blight. They are circular up to % inch in diameter, brown and contain dark concentric ring. The spots occur singly or in large number on each leaf, yellowish areas may develop on effected leaves and eventually they turn brown and usually drop from the plant.

In the absence of fungicide treatment, maximum fruit Infection for susceptible varieties was about 30%. Potential yield h processing tomato and fruit size are reduced on an average of 30% and 10%, respectively (Sherf & Macnab, 1986). Choulwar and Datar (1989) assessed the efficacy of eight fungicides

[1] Department of Plant Production and Protection, Faculty of Agriculture, Jerash University, Jerash, Jordan

(copper oxychloride, zineb, mancozeb, carbendazim, dithianon, iprodione, thiophanate-methyl and captafol) to reduce mycelial growth of *A. solani in vitro*. Mancozeb (1000 ppm) was the most effective (77% growth inhibition) followed by captafol. Carbendazim and thiophanate-methyl were not effective. Increasing concentration of fungicide generally decreased mycelial growth. Fadl *et al.* (1985) in laboratory tests with 3 fungicides observed that Ridomil MZ (metalaxyl) was most inhibitory to linear growth at low concentration followed by Trimiltox Fort and Bravo 600 (chlorothalonil) whereas at higher concentrations Trimiltox Fort performed best. Sinha and Prasad (1991) tested sevei fungicides in the field over 3 seasons against *A. solani* Dithane M-45 (Mancozeb) @ 0.2% was the best and cost effective treatment with the highest yield. Khade and Joi (1980) reported that all nine fungicides reduced incidence, but the highest yield increases were obtained with Dithane M-46 (Mancozeb), blue Cu 60, Cuman L, Dithane Z-78 (Zineb) and Difolatan (Captafol). Choulwar and Datar (1 988) reported that in tests, 12 treatments of 1-6 sprays of 0.2% mancozeb applied at different times after transplanting significantly reduced the intensity of early blight caused by *A. solani*. The lowest disease intensity and highest yield was obtained with 6 early sprays followed by 6 late and 6 early sprays. Early sprays were generally more effective than equal numbers of late sprays. The yields were negatively correlated with disease intensity. Vidhyasekaran (1983) reported that both mancozeb and Captafol effectively controlled *A. solani* and *Saptoria lycopersici*. These treatments reduced defoliation and increased fruit production. Fruits from sprayed plots had significantly more sugars and vitamin and less phenolics. The attack of early blight has been observed on tomato crop in several parts of the NWFP. It is feared that losses from this disease may increase year after year if no protective measures are-adopted well ahead of time. However, very little work has been done in this province on control of this disease. As a first step towards achieving this goal, this project was conducted to study its in-vitro control.

## Materials and Methods

Diseased specimens of early blight were collected from tomato growing areas of the NWFP. The infected leaves and sterns were cut into small pieces, surface sterilized with mercurb chloride (0.1%) for 30 seconds, rinsed thrice with sterile distilled water, blotted dry and incubated at 25°C on Potato Dextrose Agar (PDA) medium for 7 days. Pure culture of the fungus was maintained at 4°C for further studies. Poison Food Technique (PFT) was used to test different concentrations (260, 600, 760, 1000 ppm) of the fungicides Antracol, Benlate, Copper oxychloride, Dithane M-46, Ridomil, Topas, Topsin, Dithane M-46 + Ridomil, Dithane M-46 + Topas, and Dithane M-45 + Benlate against *A. solani*. Different quantities of the fungicides were mixed with the PDA medium at 50°C before pouring. Each treatment was replicated five times. One treatment was maintained as control where no fungicide was added to the PDA medium. After mixing the fungicides and solidification of the medium, the fungus *A. so/an/*

was seeded in the centre of each petri plate using 5mm ag ar disc having active mycelial growth of the fungus. The plates were incubated at 25°C for seven days. At the end of incubation period, radial colony growth was measured (cm) in each treatment. The data were analyzed statistically ty analysis of variance and the means were compared ty Duncan's Multiple Range Test (Steel & Torrie, 1980).

**Results and Discussion**

The different treatments showed significant differences ($P < 0.05$) among themselves (Table 1). At 250 ppm concentration, the lowest growth (2.02 cm) was observed in the treatment Dithane M-45 and the highest (7.4 cm) h control. At this concentration, treatment Dithane M-45 was significantly different from all other treatments except treatment Dithane M-46 + Benlate. The control was only non-sigmficafitly different from treatment Antracol. Combination of Dithane M-46 with other fungicides such as Ridomil and Topas was not as good as with Benlate (Dithane M-45 + Benlate) which caused the second lowest growth. At 500 ppm, the lowest growth was observed again Dithane M-46, followed by

**Table 18.1: Effect of different concentrations of fungicides on mycelial growth of *A. solani in vitro***

| Fungicides | Mycelial growth (cm) Fungicide concentrations | | | | Mean |
|---|---|---|---|---|---|
| | 260 ppm | 500 ppm | 750 ppm | 1000 ppm | |
| Antracol | 6.49 abc | 4.59 f-l | 2.60 p-t | 3. 76 l-p | 4.35 cd |
| Benlate | 6.06 d-j | 6. 63 c-f | 3.66 l-p | 6.28 c-l | 4.90 be |
| Copper Oxychloride | 5.8 c-f | 5.55 c-g | 1.43 tuv | 3.45 l-q | 4.06 de |
| Dithane M-45 | 2.02 rst | 1.81 stu | 0.67 uv | 0.22 v | 1.18g |
| Dithane M-46 4- Benlate | 2.21 q-t | 4.27 h-n | 1.55 tu | 3. 1 2 m-r | 2.78 f |
| Dithane M-45 + Ridomil | 4.12 l-n | 4.57 f-l | 3.57 l-p | 3.77 k-p | 4.01 de |
| Oithane M-46 + Topas | 4.08 l-n | 6.30 a-d | 3.42 l-q | 3.91 j-o | 4.43 bed |
| Ridomil | 4.36 g-m | 4.92 e-k | 2.20 q-t | 3.36 l-q | 3.78 e |
| Topas | 5.18d-l | 3.02 n-s | 2.68 o-t | 3.66 l-p | 3.61 e |
| Topsin | 4.93 e-k | 5.39 c-h | 3.66 l-p | 6.06 b-e | 5.00 b |
| Control | 7.4 a | 7.20 ab | 5.68 c-f | 7.30 ab | 6.90 a |
| Mean | 4.70 a | 4.84 a | 2.83 c | 3.98 b | ......... |

Figures in the same column followed by different letters are significantly different from one another at 0.05 level of significance.

that in treatment Topas. Both these treatments were non-significantly different from one another. The highest growth was recorded in the control treatment. The latter differed significantly from other treatments with the exception of Dithane M-45 + Topas. In control treatment, the growth was higher by 7.20% and 6.30% than treatments Dithane M-45 and Topas, respectively. It was also higher by

7.40% than the overall mean of the fungiddes at this concentration, indicating that fungicide application has after all decreased the growth of the fungus.

Fungicide treatments at 750 ppm differed significantly from one another (P<0.05). The lowest growth was in treatment Dithane M-45 (0.67 cml, followed by Copper oxychloride and then Dithane M-45 + Benlate. The three treatments did riot differ significantly from one another. The highest growth was recorded in control. The higher growth in this than the other treatments indicated that fungicide treatment depressed the mycelial growth significantly. Growth of *A. solani* varied significantly at 1000 ppm level of different fungicides. The lowest and the highest growth were recorded in treatment Dithane M-45 and in treatment where no fungicide was applied, respectively. These two treatments showed significant differences from one another and from other treatments. None of the combinations including Dithane M-45 and the systemic fungicides were better than treatment Dithane M-45 alone in reducing colony growth of fungi. The overall mean calculated for each fungicide showed th£t the lowest valued. 18 cm) was in case of fungicide Dithane M-45. This was followed by treatment Dithane M-45 + Benlate (2.78 cm) and then Topas (3.61 cm). The highest value was for control. Among the different concentrations being used, the overall lowest growth was calculated for 750 ppm (2.83 cm) and the highest for 500 ppm (4.84 cm). In case of the best fungicide (Dithane M-45), the growth of the fungus was the lowest at 1000 ppm and the highest at 260 ppm. This was the reverse in other treatments where the lowest growth was observed at 750 ppm. The latter concentration can also be recommended for Dithane M-45 as the two treatments (1000 rrnm and 75° ppm) of the fungicide were non-significantly different from one another.

In treatment where fungbides were used, the mycelial growth of *A. so/an/* was depressed substantially as compared to the treatment where no fungicide was used. This indicated the importance of fungicide used in controlling disease. However, these fungicides were variable in their effect which depended on their type and concentration being used. Dithane M-4E caused maximum reduction in mycelial growth at higher concentrations. This broad-spectrum fungicide is used for the control of a number of fungal diseases. The availability of this fungicide at reasonable price in the market is an additional advantage of Dithane M-45 over other fungicides for the effective control of early blight in tomato.

## REFERENCES

Choulwar, A.B. and U.V. Datar, 1988. Cost linked spray scheduling for the management of tomato early blight. Indian Phytopathol., 41: 603-606.

Choulwar, A.B. and U.V. Datar, 1989. Efficacy of fungi toxicants on the mycelial growth of Alternaria solani. Pestology India, 13:17-19.

Fadl, F.A., N. George and I. M. EL-Fangary, 1985. Chemical control of tomato early blight disease in Egypt. Agric. Res. Rev., 63:121-126.

Khade, B.M. and M.B Joi, 1980. Fungicidal control of earl/ blight (A solani ELL Munt) Jones and Gront) of tomato. Maharashtra Agric. Univ. India, 5:176-176.

Sherf, A.T. and A. Macnab, 1986. Vegetable diseases and their control, John Wiley and Sons, New York, pp: 728.

Sinha, P.P. and R.K. Prasad, 1991. Evaluation of fungicides for control of early blight of tomato. Madras Agric. J., 78:141-143.

Steel, R. G. D. and J. H. Torrie, 1980. Principles and procedures of statisics. McGraw-Hill Publ.Co., New York.

Vidhyasekaran, L. 1 983. Efficacy of fungicides on the control of Alternaria leaf spot of tomato. Madras Agric. J., 86:122-123.

# INDEX


**A**

*A. gilliesii*, 75
*A. porri*, 2
*A. purpurea*, 73
*A. solani*, 5, 80
*A. tagetica*, 6
Ahmad, Shabeer, 178
*Allium sativum*, 84
*Alternana* leaf, 149
*Alternaria alternate*, 32
*Alternaria solani*, 2, 1-11, 14, 71-82, 115-121, 178-182
  in India, 1-11
    electrophoresis, 4
    fungal DNA extraction, 3
    introduction, 2
    materials and methods, 2-3
    molecular characterization, 3
    molecular variability, 8-10
    mycelia growth pattern, 5-7
    pathogenic variability, 4
    pathogenicity, 7-8
    PCR amplification, 4
    results and discussion, 5
    sporulation, 5
    statistical analysis,. 4
  isolated from tomato in Jordan valley, 115-121
    discussion, 119
    materials and methods, 116
    physiological studies, 116-117
    physiological studies, 117-118
    results, 117
Althussaen, Khalaf M., 115
ANOVA, 17, 117, 166
Aqueous plant extracts, 83-91
Ashrafuzzaman, M., 97
ASM, 55
AUDPC, 48, 129
*Azadirachta indica*, 84

**B**

Bangladesh, 97
BOD, 3, 55, 57

**C**

*C. senna*, 73
Cardoso, Carine Rezende, 104
*Cassia fistula*, 72
Chaerani, Reni, 12, 122, 159
Characterization of tomato accessions for resistance to early blight, 104-114
  introduction, 104-105
  material and methods, 106-110
  results and discussion, 110-112
Control of *Alternaria solani*, 178-182
  introduction, 178-179
  materials and methods, 179-180
  results and discussion, 180-181
Control of tomato early blight disease by certain aqueous plant extracts, 83-91
  introduction, 83-84
  materials and methods, 84-86
  results, 86-89
    identification of the casual pathogen, 86
    pathogenicity test, 86
    effect of treatments on fruit yield, 89
  discussion, 89-90

**D**

*Datura stramonium*, 84, 90

Derbalah, A.S., 71

DNA, 3, 126

Doplet inoculation method, 12-25

conditions during infection, 14

discussion, 21-24

effect of spore concentration on early blight severity with two inoculation methods, 14-16

experimental design and statistical analyses, 17-18

fungal culture and inoculum preparation, 14

glasshouse screening of tomato accessions, 16-17

glasshouse screenings, 20-21

introduction, 13-14

lesion size distribution, 20

materials and methods, 14

plant material and culture conditions, 14

resistance reaction of selected accessions with two inoculation methods in glasshouse tests, 18-20

results, 18

Dubey, Siddarth, 42

Duncan Multiple Range Test, 180

**E**

*E. chamadulonsis*, 86, 90

*E. japonicus*, 75

Early Blight (EB), 159

Early blight resistance in a *Solanum lycopersicum* × *S. arcanum*, 159-177

breeding implications, 175

comparison with classical genetic and molecular mapping studies of EB resistance, 173-175

DNA isolation and marker analysis, 163-165

distorted segregation, 166-167

discussion, 169-170

linkage analysis, 169-170

early blight resistance evaluation, 161-162

F3 field test, 162-163

introduction, 159-161

linkage analysis, 165

materials and methods, 161

phenotypic evaluation, 167

QTL mapping, 165

QTL analysis, 167-169, 171-173

QTL analysis: F2 glasshouse test, 167

QTL analysis: F3 field test, 168-169

results, 166

statistical analysis, 165-166

Early blight resistance in tomato, 12-25, 97-103, 104-114

EC 520061, 69, 70

Efficacy and safety of some plant extracts against tomato early blight disease caused by *Alternaria solani*, 71-82

introduction, 71-72

materials and methods, 72-75

results, 75-79

toxicity evaluation, 79

discussion, 80

El-Mahrouk, 71

El-Sayed, A.B., 71

Eucalyptus chamadulonsis, 84

Evaluation of different germplasms/cultivars of tomato against early blight in field conditions and by artificial inoculation method, 32-41

discussion, 38-40

introduction, 32-33

materials and methods, 33-34

reaction of cultivars to leaf blight in polyhouse conditions, 37-38

reactions of cultivars to leaf blight in field screening, 37

results, 36-37
screening of germplasms/cultivars in polyhouse condition, 34-36

G

General Linear Model (GLM), 116, 117
Grigolli, Jose Fernando Jurca, 104
Groenworld, Remmelt, 12
Gupta, R.C., 26, 148
Gupta, Sachin, 42

H

Haldar, Sanchita, 1
Hawamdeh, Ashraf Saber, 178

I

Identification of resistant sources against early blight disease of tomato, 151-158
introduction, 151-152
materials and methods, 152-154
results and discussion, 154-157
Identification of resistant sources and epidemiology of early blight of tomato, 42-52
correlation of disease intensity with weather parameters, 49-50
materials and methods, 43
disease assessments and data anlaysis, 44-45
screening of germplasm, 44
results and discussion, 45
occurrence of disease, 45
screening of germplasm, 45-48
Indian Institute of Vegetable Research (IIVR), 68
Islam, Nazrul, 97
Isolates of Alternaria solani of Lycopersicon esculentum, 53-67
comparative study between conidial morphology of *A. solani* from host decoction media and infected host tissues, 56-57
discussion, 63-65
introduction, 53-54
materials and methods, 54-56
results, 57
variability of *A. solani* on
different nutrient media, 59-60
different pH, 61-63
different temperatures, 61
PDA, 57-59

J

Jammu and Kashmir, 42-52
Jordan valley, 115-121

K

*Kashi Amrit*, 148
Khan, Ali Ayaz, 92
Khokon, Atiqur Rahman, 97
Kumar, Ajay, 32
Kumar, Rajesh, 68, 148, 151
Kumar, V., 26
Kumar, Virendra, 32, 53, 1, 148

L

Late blight and early blight under natural eiphytotics, 97-103
introduction, 97-98
materials and methods, 98
results and discussion, 98-102
Late blight, 97-103
Linden, C.G. van der, 159
LSD, 17
*Lycopersicon esculentum*, 13, 14
*Lycopersicon hirsutum*, 152

M

Management of early blight disease of tomato cv *Kashi Amrit* through fungicides, bioagents and cultural practices in India, 148-150
Mishtra, Kaushlesh Kumar, 53

N

Naeem, Faiza, 32
Nerium oleander, 84
NWFP, 179

**O**

*O. basilicum*, 90

**P**

Pandey, Koshlendra Kumar, 1, 53, 68, 148
PCR, 4
PEBI, 172
Phytophthora, 97, 98
Poison Food Technique (PFT), 179
Potato Dextrose Agar (PDA), 2, 3, 7, 54, 55, 64, 84, 179
Pramanik, Bimal Kumar, 97

**Q**

QTLs, 137, 138
Quantitative trait loci (QTLs), 123

**R**

Rai, AB, 148
Rai, Ashutosh, 151
Rai, Mathura, 68, 148, 151
Rani, Sunita, 42
RAPDs, 126
RAUPDC, 172
Razdan, V.K., 42
Resistance of two tomato species to five isolates of *Alternaria solani*, 92-96
  introduction, 92-93
  materials and methods, 93-94
  results and discussion, 94-96
Rockefeller Foundation, 105
RSA, 64

**S**

*S. arcanum*, 159-177
*S. chilense*, 21
*S. habrochaites*, 13, 19
*S. pennellii*, 21
*S. peruvianum*, 14
*S. pimpinellifolium*, 21
Sallam, Nashwa M.A., 83
*Salsola baryosma*, 84
*Saptoria lycopersici*, 179
Screening of tomato genotypes against early blight in natural epiphytotic condition, 26-31
  discussion, 30-31
  materials and methods, 27-29
  results, 29-30
Singh, Achuit K., 1
Singh, J., 26
Singh, M., 68
Singh, M.C., 151
Singh, Major, 151
Singh, P.C., 26, 148
Singh, Prabhash C., 1, 68, 151
Singh, R.P., 26
Singh, Rana P., 1
Singh, Ranbir, 42
Sinha, B., 68
Smulders, M.J.M., 159
*Solanum lycopersicon*, 106
*Solanum lycopersicum* x *S. arcanum*, 159-177
Solentos, 175
Source of resistance against early blight in tomato, 68-70
Stam, P., 159

**T**

*Tamarix aphytta*, 84
*Thespesia populnea*, 72
Tomato (*Lycopersicon esculentum*), 26
Tomato early blight, 122-147
  association of early blight resistance with plant maturity, potential yield, and determinism, 138-140
  characterization of resistance, 140-141
  classical studies of genetics of resistance, 132-137
  disease cycle, 124-125
  disease symptoms, 127-128
  field screening, 128-129